ACA Simplified

Cracking Case™ – How to Pass the ACA Case Study (July 2018)

Note

Although ACA Simplified is a participant in the ICAEW Partner in Learning scheme, all views and opinions expressed in this book are our own and not those of ICAEW, except where explicitly indicated otherwise.

In order to explain the patterns evident in recent Case Study examinations and markschemes, this book contains analysis of Case Study examinations covering the July 2012 to November 2017 sittings inclusive, including related Exam Paper requirements. **If you would prefer to attempt any of these examinations as unseen timed practice papers then please do so *before* reading this book.**

However, rather than sitting past papers, we would strongly recommend that you prepare for your examination by using our own set of mocks based on the live July 2018 Advance Information. Our live mock exams will give you 5 opportunities to practise your examination technique based on a single set of relevant Advance Information: this is a better use of time than reading 5 different sets of irrelevant past paper Advance Information on 5 different Case exams to get the same amount of technique and timing practice. Please see page 6 for further information on our live July 2018 mock exams.

A Reminder About Copyright

Please do not photocopy or otherwise distribute this book. Copyright theft is a clear breach of professional ethics and may therefore be reported to ICAEW. We have put a considerable amount of time and effort into developing innovative materials which we genuinely feel will give you an edge in your examination. We would be grateful if you would respect these efforts by not copying this text.

The terms "*Cracking Case*™" and "40 Task Approach" are trademarks of ACA Simplified and should not be used without our express permission. We reserve all related legal rights in full.

1

Disclaimer

The text in this book does not amount to professional advice on any particular technical matter and should not be taken as such. No reliance should be placed on the content as the basis for any investment or other decision or in connection with any advice given to third parties.

ACA Simplified expressly disclaims all liability for any losses or other claims, whether direct, indirect, incidental, consequential or otherwise arising in relation to the use of these materials.

We have made every effort to ensure that the materials are accurate and free from error. Please inform us immediately if you believe that you have discovered any problems with the text.

Whilst we strongly believe that our learning materials are an effective method of preparing for your examinations, ACA Simplified does not accept any liability whatsoever for your ultimate performance in the examination as a result of using this text.

Abbreviations used to refer to recent ICAEW Case Study examinations

R4	R4 Limited	November 2017
PL	Piccolo Limited	July 2017
TT	True Taste Limited	November 2016
Bux	Bux Limited	July 2016
CC	Cyclone Cycles Limited	November 2015
Bod	Bod Limited	July 2015
RS	Rolling Stores Limited	November 2014
ZM	Zoo-Med Limited	July 2014
LT	Lighter Tread Limited	November 2013
Palate	Palate Limited	July 2013
FS	Fluent Speech Limited	November 2012
LL	LuvLox Limited	July 2012

Acronyms used in this book

This list is purely for ease of reference – extensive further details on each concept are provided in the main text of the book.

AMR   **Appendices and Main Report**

The final 4 Boxes on a Case Study markscheme which assess the quality of the candidate's Appendices and other aspects of their report such as legibility, use of a disclaimer, use of appropriate paragraph length, page numbering, and so on.

CoP   **Context of Performance**

Our recommended title of the first section of Requirement 1 in your report. In editions of this book prior to the July 2018 edition, we suggested that the term "Market Background" should be used as the title of the first section of Requirement 1 in your report but, for the reasons explained elsewhere in this book, we now prefer the term "Context of Performance".

3

ET   **Extra Task**

An additional task in Requirement 1 other than accounts analysis. In editions of this book prior to the July 2018 edition, we used the term "EPIA" (Exam Paper Impact Adjustment) to refer to this concept but, for the reasons explained elsewhere in this book, we now prefer the term "Extra Task".

IIR   **Issue, Impact, Recommendation**

Our suggested framework for developing appropriate points on each ethics issue arising in the examination.

SOC   **Strategic and Operational Context**

Our recommended title of the first section of Requirements 2 and 3 in your report. In editions of this book prior to the July 2018 edition, we suggested that the term "Project Background" should be used as the title of the first section of Requirements 2 and 3 in your report but, for the reasons explained elsewhere in this book, we now prefer the term "Strategic and Operational Context".

Table of Contents

* Note – our reference to the **2017** edition of the ICAEW Study Manual is NOT an error in this July 2018 edition of *Cracking Case™*. The 2017 edition of the ICAEW Study Manual represented a major update to the ICAEW materials, and the most substantial update for several years. We therefore summarised some key points from this edition of the Study Manual in the 2017 editions of *Cracking Case™*. As the 2018 version of the ICAEW Study Manual is almost identical to the 2017 version of the Study Manual, we have simply retained the discussion of the major changes made to the 2017 edition of the Study Manual in Appendix 4 as these remain fully relevant to your preparations and have not been altered by the 2018 edition of the Study Manual. The reference to 2017 in a 2018 edition of this book is therefore intentional and **not** an error.

THIS PAGE IS WORTH £20!

All purchasers of this July 2018 edition of *Cracking Case™ – How to Pass the ACA Case Study* are entitled to a discount of £20 (plus VAT, if applicable) on the pack of 5 mock exams which we will be writing once the July 2018 Advance Information has been released.

Why do we believe that our mocks will be one of the best ways of preparing for the July 2018 exam?

1. Realistic, exam-standard papers including full markschemes

Our pack of mock exams is designed to give you 5 opportunities to test and improve your Case Study technique under full exam conditions. All mock Exam Papers are written to full ICAEW standard, including standard question formats, detailed Exam Paper impact information and press articles.

We will also provide full ICAEW-standard marking "grids" to allow you to mark your own work, self-assess your performance and identify weak areas. Self-assessing your work and looking at 5 sets of marking "grids" will be very valuable in terms of getting you into the mindset of an examiner. The different mocks within the mock pack will provide you with different styles of marking "grid" as examples of the different allocation of Boxes seen in various recent ICAEW past papers so our mock pack provides a full explanation of the nuances in the marking "grid" of each specific mock: you can use this to develop an understanding of the various different recent past paper "styles" of markscheme Box allocation so that you are prepared for all eventualities on exam day. Our mock pack will also contain fully written out and realistically-achievable narrative answers for all 5 mocks to show you how to write succinctly under headings which focus on the right areas: our narrative answers have been carefully written to reflect an achievable number of words in the time available so they will provide you with a realistic standard to aim for in your own work.

2. Time efficient – 5 opportunities to practise technique based on 1 set of Advance Information

When we studied for Case Study, we found it frustrating and time consuming to have to read a full new set of past paper Advance Information on a different company every time that we wanted to sit down and practise our time management and exam technique by doing a full practice exam. Our mocks will avoid this problem by putting all your practice of technique within the context of a **single** set of Advance Information which is **relevant** to all attempts at our mocks and of course your real exam itself. This will make better use of your scarce preparation time.

3. Exposure to possible exam day scenarios

Since every Case Study focuses on a completely different business, practising past papers cannot give you any opportunity to think about possible scenarios relevant to your own exam. Our pack of 5 mock exams gives you exposure to many potential scenarios which could actually be tested in your real examination and as the only ICAEW Partner in Learning to produce 5 full live mocks for every sitting, use of our mocks will give you exposure to more scenarios than the mocks prepared by other providers.

4. Realistic paper format

We provide our mock exams in PDF format. This allows you to print off the papers and sit the mocks under full exam conditions – unlike some providers, we have not restricted our exams to being online-only as we do not believe that this gives you a fully realistic and "hands-on" experience where you can annotate and highlight pages, quickly flick between information sheets and so on.

Release date – 22 June 2018 (or as close as possible to this date)

We are aiming to release the first mocks from our pack of 5 mock exams on **22 June 2018**, giving you 5 full weekends to sit down and practise your technique via question papers relevant to the live Advance Information. (Please note that this release date is subject to change if the Advance Information is released late or if there are other factors outside our control. We also reserve the right to delay publication if this is necessary to preserve the quality of the mock pack. Please check our Case Study-specific website at **www.acasimplifiedcase.com** for the latest updates on our release schedule.)

£20 Mock Exam Pack Discount – Instructions

If you would like to take advantage of our discount, please retain your proof of purchase (Amazon email receipt) of this copy of *Cracking Case*™. Please then forward this to us together with your proof of purchase of our mock exam pack and after the examination session is over we will issue a £20 refund (plus VAT, if applicable) to the credit or debit card used to purchase your mock exam pack.

Please note that refunds will not be processed until August 2018 **after** the July 2018 examination session has finished, due to heavy demands on our administrative staff in the run up to examination day. Thank you for your understanding.

Please forward your discount request **at the time of purchase** rather than waiting until August 2018 – we will then gather and collate all discount claims ready for batch-processing by the end of August 2018.

Offer is limited to one set of mock exams per purchase of a **new** copy of the July 2018 edition of *Cracking Case*™. Offer excludes students on our classroom tuition courses. Proof of purchase must be received by us on or before **15 August 2018** or no refund will be made.

Due to the number of messages we expect to receive in connection with this offer, please note that we will not acknowledge your discount request unless you specifically ask us to do so. We expect to process all refunds by **31 August 2018** so please contact us if you have not received your refund by this date.

If you have any queries on the refund process before purchasing our mock exams, please do not hesitate to contact us at **getqualified@acasimplified.com** for clarification.

Can You Crack It? Code Breaking Challenge

Why is this book called *Cracking Case*™?

It is not just to create a marketable title (although hopefully it does so!). Rather, it reflects our view that the unique and complicated "competency-based framework" which is used to mark the Case Study is like a type of "code" which needs to be "cracked" or "decrypted" in order to understand what to do in your examination script.

Once you understand how to crack a coded message, everything seems simple and straightforward: hopefully after reading this book, you will be left with this understanding. However, if you do not know how the code works, then things can seem a mystery.

We believe that this is an appropriate metaphor for the way in which candidates need to translate the complex, "Box-based" marking approach used in Case Study into specific business points to write into their answer, "decoding" or "cracking" the markscheme into appropriate written work.

To remind you of this philosophy, we have created a code breaking challenge by including our own coded message within the cover image of this book.

The first purchaser to successfully crack this code and send us an email with the decrypted message, together with a full explanation of how the message was encoded, will be entitled to a **£500 cash prize**. Only one prize is available for this edition of the book so get cracking soon (but **do not** let it get in the way of your preparations for the examination!).

Foreword to the July 2018 Edition and Review of R4 (November 2017)

Welcome to this July 2018 edition of *Cracking Case*™ and many thanks for your purchase!

As a result of the change in approach to the marking of "Own Research" points which took effect from the November 2017 examination onwards, as well as some other useful learning points raised by the November 2017 markscheme and the February 2018 ICAEW Tutor Conference, this edition has been heavily updated as compared to the November 2017 edition.

As normal, this Foreword includes a brief review of the most recent Case Study examination (November 2017) which had been taken at the time of writing this latest edition of *Cracking Case*™ (May 2018). This initial brief review simply aims to highlight some of the key learning points from the most recent examination – we have obviously integrated all these ideas where relevant later in the text as well. Please note that the Foreword does require some knowledge of the terminology that we discuss in greater length later in the book so we would recommend that you read the rest of the book first and then return to this Foreword as everything will then make a lot more sense.

We hope you will find this updated edition of *Cracking Case*™ useful to your preparation for your examination. Don't forget that as a purchaser of this book, you are entitled to a discount of £20 plus VAT (if applicable) on our pack of 5 full mock examinations based on the live July 2018 Advance Information – the mock exam pack is due for release on **22 June 2018**, shortly after the release of the Advance Information itself by ICAEW on **12 June 2018**.

We are also very pleased to announce the launch of our companion *Cracking Case On-Demand*™ video course in support of the examination technique set out in this book. Whilst we obviously believe that this book provides an effective way of preparing for the examination, there are certain technique issues that are easier to teach via a video format and our *Cracking Case On-Demand*™ course will also contain various videos recorded after the July 2018 Advance Information has been released (including a very detailed 4 hour review of every page of the Advance Information) to ensure that we provide the latest advice tailored to your own examination. We are very excited about the launch of this new course and hope you will be too! Please refer to Appendix 5 of this book for further details.

Good luck with your examination and please do let us know how you got on.

All the best,

The ACA Simplified Team   **May 2018**

Review of R4 (November 2017)

Overall, in our opinion the R4 Limited Case Study examination was very much in line with the patterns seen in recent examinations. However, the nature of Requirement 3 was slightly different to normal and there was also a major change in the markscheme in relation to the awarding of credit for the candidate's Own Research.

Apart from these changes, the examination should have been well within the capabilities of students who used our standard techniques as outlined in the November 2017 edition of this book. However, as always, we have fully updated this new edition of the book to take into account the latest information available.

Please see our detailed review below to obtain insight into the latest subtle tweaks to the markscheme in the most recent Case Study examination.

Credit for Candidate's Own Research – Change in the Markscheme

Perhaps the most unusual aspect of the markscheme for the R4 Limited Case Study was the fact that there was no separate credit given in Boxes 1.2, 2.2 or 3.2 for the candidate's Own Research point obtained from independent research undertaken before the examination. In all previous Case Study markschemes, there has been an open "free response" mark available as the final diamond in Boxes 1.2, 2.2 and 3.2: in other words, in these previous examinations, a candidate could obtain a free mark for **any** valid own research point, with a source. This was a very rare opportunity to gain a mark without having to match a point specified by the examiners (as is required for almost all other markscheme points). Essentially, this mark was a guaranteed mark in each Requirement, provided that a candidate had included some of their Own Research.

The R4 Limited markscheme was the first ever Case Study markscheme not to award these "free response" marks. It was clarified at the Case Study Workshop at the 2018 ICAEW Tutor Conference that the examiners will no longer be awarding a separate mark for Own Research in future examinations.

At the 2018 Tutor Conference, the examiners explained that under the new approach, candidates will effectively have 2 opportunities to gain each of the marks in Boxes 1.2, 2.2 or 3.2. If the candidate refers to a point within the relevant Box based on information in either the Advance Information or the Exam Paper then a mark can be given. If the candidate introduces some of their Own Research which makes a point within the relevant Box (but without referring to the Advance Information or Exam Paper point) then, again, a mark can be given. However, and unlike in the past, a candidate can no longer obtain credit **both** for marking the point based on information in the Advance Information or Exam Paper **and** for including an Own Research fact that makes the same point.

Additionally, and also unlike in the past, if the Own Research point does not overlap with any of the points in the relevant Box, then it will **not** be given credit.

This means there are really now 2 possibilities regarding Own Research points, neither of which favours actually bothering to include any Own Research and both of which represent a major change from the previous marking approach:

1. the Own Research information makes a similar point to one of the points in the relevant Box, which is in turn connected to information in the Advance Information and/or Exam Paper – in this case, a good student should have made the point without using Own Research and, if so, adding the Own Research does not attract any further credit

2. the Own Research information does not a make a similar point to one of the points in the relevant Box – in this case, no credit can be obtained

Therefore, either the Own Research point is relevant but unnecessary (possibility 1) or it is not relevant (possibility 2).

As an example from the November 2017 markscheme, Box 1.2 contained the following contextual points (we have added the numbering for tutorial purposes: no numbering is contained in the original markscheme):

1. Consumer awareness/recycling rates/government policy

2. National growth rate 4.9%/R4 2016 growth rate 20.9%

3. Gate fees static (at £20)

4. Recycling prices increased £92 versus £86/£6

5. MRF costs static (at £91)

6. Bank loan £3m repayable in 2019

If the Own Research introduced by the candidate related to levels of consumer awareness, declining recycling rates or government policy (point 1 in Box 1.2), growth rates in the industry (point 2), unchanged gate fees in the industry (point 3), recyclate prices in the industry (point 4), MRF costs in the industry (point 5) or R4's bank loan (point 6) then the Own Research point would attract credit but only if the candidate had not already mentioned anything from the Advance Information and/or Exam Paper which made a similar point.

As all points other than points 1 and 2 above relate quite closely to the specific performance of R4 Limited for the year, in our opinion, the most likely Own Research information that a candidate might have gathered before the examination would have had to relate to the broader industry themes of consumer awareness, recycling rates and government policy (point 1) or the growth rate in the industry (point 2). However, in our opinion, a good candidate should really have raised these fundamental points/links anyway **based purely on the Advance Information** so adding their Own Research would not achieve anything beneficial.

On this basis, the approach to Own Research marking has changed dramatically: we have moved from a situation where Own Research was essentially a source of free marks to a situation where Own Research will either result in wasteful duplication that does not attract a mark (possibility 1) or will not attract a mark because it is not closely enough related to any of the points in the relevant Boxes (possibility 2), points which can be fully obtained without doing any Own Research in the first place.

Looking at points 1 and 2 above, reference to consumer awareness and recycling rates and the national industry growth rate of 4.9% should most certainly have been in your answer anyway as these were very heavily flagged in the Advance Information: as explained elsewhere in this book, it is always worth referring to specific percentage growth rates in the Advance Information as these are very often in Box 1.2. Similarly, the points in Boxes 2.2 and 3.2 should already have been made by a good candidate who had picked up important Advance Information points or made appropriate contextual comparisons to stream performance from Requirement 1 so Own Research points would not be of any benefit.

11

Given this significant change in the marking, please ensure that you adapt your approach if you have taken the examination in the past and been advised to always include Own Research points.

Executive Summary

The R4 Limited Executive Summary markscheme was very much in line with previous examinations. As is usual for November examinations, the second Box available for each Requirement (Boxes E.2, E.4 and E.6 in our labelling system) contained some quite specific points which the candidate would have had to match rather than the marks being more "open" (awarded for any point in the approximate area). Also as usual for November examinations, this was particularly the case with respect to Requirement 1 as 3 of the 4 marks available in Box E.2 required a specific point to be matched.

In addition, it was noteworthy that candidates had to refer to both overall company revenue **and** at least 1 revenue sub-stream, with figures in both cases, to obtain just a single mark in relation to revenue discussion in the Executive Summary. Similarly, it was necessary to refer to both overall gross profit (or gross profit margin) **and** the gross profit performance (either in absolute terms or margin terms) for both the business as a whole and at least 1 sub-stream to earn the single mark available for discussion of gross profit in the Executive Summary. As such, please ensure that you do not simply discuss the overall company position nor just the position of individual streams in your Requirement 1 Executive Summary – always look at both perspectives!

Requirement 3 arguably had more specific points than normal for the Requirement 3 Executive Summary Boxes: normally, Requirement 3 is quite open but in the R4 Limited markscheme, 3 of the 8 acceptable points required candidates to make a specific suggestion (the loss of LWC (a key client) would be significant to the business, operational problems should be addressed promptly and there should be a financial review of all contracts).

Overall, these aspects of the R4 Limited markscheme made it relatively difficult to pass the Executive Summary component of the examination. As discussed elsewhere in this book, this is very much in line with the statements by the examiners that they are deliberately making the Executive Summary more difficult to pass in order to penalise students who simply uncritically copy the Conclusions sections to each Requirement.

As explained elsewhere in this book, the Conclusions sections to each Requirement continue to form the "core" of your Executive Summary sections but as we have advised in this book for several sittings now, you must also try to add to this "core" by spending just a couple of minutes thinking about the really fundamental points facing the business (the "Big Picture", as the examiners term it).

As we have noticed an increase in the number of students who come to us to retake the examination (after failing with another provider) having passed all elements of the examination other than the Executive Summary, these examiner statements about increasing the difficulty of the Executive Summary do appear to have played out as intended in practice. As such, as we have advised for several sittings now, please do not disrespect the Executive Summary as it is perfectly possible to fail the examination as a whole, undoing a lot of excellent work in the rest of your report, if your Executive Summary does not respect the specific demands of the markscheme.

Requirement 1

Overall, the markscheme for Requirement 1 was extremely standard in nature with no innovations to consider other than the Own Research issue discussed in more detail above.

It was noticeable that the calculations required for the Extra Task (i.e. additional to the accounts analysis) were extremely basic. After an additional task in the July 2017 examination which did not involve any figures at all, the November 2017 examination did return to the more usual pattern of awarding credit for some calculations but, even so, the calculations required were certainly a lot less complicated than they used to be for this aspect (for example, in examinations set in 2015 and earlier, candidates normally had to put together 5 or 6 lines of calculations based on an unexpected event or problem in order to have a chance of passing the Boxes for the non-accounts analysis task).

Given this sustained move away from fairly challenging calculations in relation to an event or problem in Requirement 1, we have decided to implement a change in our terminology for the July 2018 edition of the book. Previously, we referred to the non-accounts analysis task in Requirement 1 as the "EPIA" or Exam Paper Impact Adjustment. We will now be referring to this task as the "ET" or Extra Task: this is to reflect the fact that candidates no longer seem to need to consider any major calculated adjustment caused by the impact of an unexpected event or problem. Rather, in some examinations there may simply be a narrative-only discussion required (such as in the July 2017 past paper) whilst in others there may be only a simple comparison of the issue with the current level of profitability to assess significance, rather than any detailed calculations involving any kind of "adjustment". The term EPIA therefore seems to be out of date as the reference to an "adjustment" may suggest that the non-accounts analysis task is more complicated than it is likely to be.

We will therefore now be adopting the term ET or "Extra Task" as this will hopefully indicate that you may not necessarily have to perform calculations to determine any financial "adjustment" and, even if you do have to do any calculations, these will not tend lead to any important "adjustment" in the sense of a difficult calculation.

Put another way, the non-accounts analysis task now seems to relate to a less material issue than in the past so we will be adopting terminology which appropriately downplays the significance of this element: the term EPIA, with its reference to "impact" and "adjustment" may again suggest that the matter is more important than it has been in recent examinations.

The move by the examiners from what we used to call an "EPIA" approach to what we now call an "ET" approach is good for candidates because it will make Requirement 1 easier to pass than in the past: you will no longer need to take so long to think through your calculation – once again, in some examinations such as the July 2017 examination, you will not even have to do any calculations at all for the ET.

Given that the accounts analysis in Requirement 1 was already relatively easy to pass (with no changes to note in recent examinations), there really now should not be any excuse at all for failing this element of the examination. Indeed, considering how easy Requirement 1 seems to have become, the main danger may now lie in the candidate overcomplicating Requirement 1, thinking that there must be more to be done in order to pass: this could then lead to the candidate overrunning as a result of "overcooking" the first part of the examination, ultimately resulting in the most common

13

reason to fail the examination as a whole (namely, failure to complete Requirement 3 properly). Consider yourself warned!

Requirement 2

Requirement 2 was very much in line with other recent markschemes but there are still a few points worthy of note.

A different approach was taken regarding Box 2.1 than was taken in either the July 2017 or November 2016 examinations. As discussed in more detail elsewhere in this book, in the July 2017 and November 2016 examinations, Box 2.1 was relatively unusual in that it did not award credit for correctly identifying the inputs needed to build the Requirement 2 financial model: this was a notable contrast to all examinations prior to November 2016 when Box 2.1 was relatively easy to pass simply by building the model using the right inputs (even if the results of the model turned out to be incorrect). Both the July 2017 and November 2016 markschemes moved away from awarding credit simply for identifying inputs and instead required candidates to discuss specific operational and strategic narrative points such as the nature of the potential customer, the length of the contract and other similar basic elements of the opportunity.

The November 2017 Box 2.1 marked a return to the previous approach of awarding credit simply for identifying the inputs. There was no credit at all for narrative operational and strategic points. (However, as mentioned below, discussion of basic contract terms such as an exclusivity clause or the length of the deal would have gained some credit in Box 2.2 in the R4 Limited markscheme.)

Whilst this was good to see in itself (as explained above, gathering the inputs to the model is relatively straightforward and therefore this style of Box 2.1 is much easier to pass than the type seen in July 2017 and November 2016 which require specific narrative points to be matched), as we have only had 1 examination which has returned to this previous approach, it is not yet clear whether this is a permanent change – perhaps the July 2018 examination will have narrative points in Box 2.1 or might have a mixture of input points and narrative points. Therefore, to hedge your bets and play things safely, you may wish to assume that Box 2.1 is narrative in nature – if it turns out that this Box simply requires identification of the inputs to the model then you are likely to pass it simply by attempting the calculation so the worst-case scenario is that you will have lost a bit of time writing narrative points that do not attract credit in this Box: however, if they are the correct type of point then you might attract credit in one of the other operational or strategic Boxes on the Requirement 2 markscheme. On the other hand, if you assume that Box 2.1 only requires the inputs to be gathered but it then turns out that you were wrong and the Box awards credit for narrative points, you may lose out if you did not attempt to make such points (and you also will not have the chance to gain narrative marks elsewhere on the Requirement 2 markscheme).

As there was only 1 financial model to perform and as Box 2.1 related to the model (by giving credit for identification of the correct inputs to the model), there was only one further Box (Box 2.3) in relation to the model calculations. Therefore Box 2.4 (which can sometimes be allocated to numbers marks) was allocated to "operational and strategic issues". This reinforces a point that we make elsewhere in this book – in the grand scheme of things, getting the correct answer to the Requirement 2 model is not really the be all and end all of Requirement 2: you must instead ensure that you have lots of narrative analysis as this will always account for a greater proportion of the Boxes in Requirement 2.

14

As is typical for a November examination, many of the points in the R4 Limited Box 2.2 on the wider context required comparison back to the most recent set of results as analysed in Requirement 1. Specifically, there was credit for discussing the revenue, gross profit and output performance of the revenue stream which formed the subject of the Requirement 2 proposal. As such, and as discussed above, there again does not seem to be much point in including Own Research points since most of the marks in Box 2.2 are specific to the Requirement 1 performance of R4 Limited, something which could not be known before the examination, meaning that it would be unlikely that Own Research points would overlap with that performance.

The only other points in Box 2.2 would again not lend themselves very well to an overlap with an Own Research point since the fourth point related to R4 Limited's own annual capacity (rather than an industry fact) whilst the final point related to the nature of the contract with the new customer mentioned in the Exam Paper: again, since this could be not be known before the examination, it is unlikely that a candidate would have gathered Own Research information which would have made the same point and therefore attracted credit.

As discussed elsewhere in this book, in some examinations the Requirement 2 markscheme will award 2 Boxes in relation to the criticism of the model's assumptions whereas other markschemes will award just a single Box for this skill. The R4 Limited markscheme took the approach of awarding 2 Boxes for the criticism of assumptions and the method was in line with the "assumptions extension" technique that we outline elsewhere in this book: in other words, it may be worth making 2 points in relation to each input which is being criticised – a first or basic point which indicates that the figure could be different or is unpredictable and then a second (more insightful) point which reinforces your concerns by making a comparison with something known from the Advance Information or the figures revealed by the Requirement 1 analysis.

The R4 Limited Requirement 2 required discussion of ethical and business trust issues. In line with most recent examinations, the markscheme awarded 2 Boxes for this discussion so, as advised elsewhere in this book, it is worth ensuring that your ethics discussion is of a reasonable length. As usual, the second Box for ethical and business trust discussion awarded quite a few marks for ethical recommendations so it is worth being thorough in this aspect.

Box 2.9 for Conclusions contained 1 point which had to be matched specifically (discussion of the Local Authority recycling target) so this point departed from the usual rule that Conclusions points are open in nature. However, the other 4 points in Box 2.9 were all open in nature so any conclusion on revenue and gross profit supported by figures (even if the figures were wrong), any point evaluating assumptions, any conclusion on ethics and business trust and any decision on whether or not to proceed with the project would, as is usual for Box 2.9 in other Case Study markschemes, have attracted credit. As candidates only need to achieve 3 matching points in a Box, it would have been easy to pass Box 2.9 in R4 Limited, despite the inclusion of 1 specific point to match.

Box 2.10 for Commercial Recommendations was very standard in nature so hopefully our Planning & Reminder Sheets would have helped readers of the November 2017 edition of this book to generate mark-scoring points. As expected, there was credit for recommending Due Diligence on a new prospective customer (a very common Commercial Recommendation in Case Study). It was also not surprising to see a recommendation to review the cash flow implications of the project as it was made very clear in the Advance Information that R4 Limited had a weak cash position, being heavily overdrawn (close to its overdraft limit, which was mentioned repeatedly in the Advance Information) with a significant loan due for repayment in the short term.

Our final point on R4 Requirement 2 would be to note that the Requirement 2 markscheme had 2 Boxes for Assumptions points and 2 Boxes for ethics. This was the first time that 2 Boxes were given to both skills since the Bux (July 2016) examination: in both TT (November 2016) and PL (July 2017), there was only 1 Box for Assumptions and 2 Boxes for ethics. This may be because both TT (November 2016) and PL (July 2017) had 2 calculations to perform so it was necessary to take a Box away from Assumptions so that it was available to reward the second calculation: in both Bux (July 2016) and R4 (November 2017), there was only 1 calculation to perform so it was possible to allocate 2 Boxes to Assumptions. Therefore, the learning point appears to be that you should assume there will be 2 Boxes for ethics and that the number of Boxes for Assumptions will depend on whether or not there are 2 calculations to perform.

Requirement 3

As indicated above, Requirement 3 in R4 Limited was relatively unusual in nature. Unlike most recent examinations, Requirement 3 did not relate to a future expansion project for the business. Instead, candidates were required to advise R4 Limited on how to deal with an existing problem with a major client.

Prior to results day, we received a very large number of worried emails from Case Study candidates. Based on these emails, students were clearly unsettled by the fact that the R4 Limited Requirement 3 was backwards-looking in nature: this would have prevented students from using their usual standard ideas in relation to future proposed expansion issues.

Without wishing to blow our own trumpet too loudly, we did identify during our taught course sessions that there was a possibility that Requirement 3 would not relate to a strategic development project. Our reason for this was the fact that, unlike other recent sets of Advance Information, the R4 Limited Advance Information contained almost nothing on the Board's views as to how the business could expand: in place of the usual "business plan"-style Exhibit, the R4 Limited Advance Information only contained a review of "risks" facing the business. This emphasis on risks, rather than the more positive expansion opportunities as usually found in a "business plan"-style Exhibit, suggested to us that the examination might be similar in nature to the July 2013 examination (Palate Limited) in which Requirement 3 similarly involved analysis of an existing problem with a client. We therefore explained to our taught course students that they should be prepared for an unusual Requirement 3.

The examiners confirmed the basis of this form of reasoning during the Case Study workshop at the 2018 ICAEW Tutor Conference. The author of the November 2017 Advance Information indicated that he had deliberately left out any mention of strategic development possibilities as a hint to candidates that the examination would be of a more backwards-looking nature. This is a very important learning point to take away from the R4 Limited examination.

Looking at the markscheme for Requirement 3, the allocation of the Boxes was very much in line with a "standard" business development-style Requirement 3. In an entirely normal way, the R4 Limited Requirement 3 markscheme allocates 2 Boxes to the financial model calculation (one for identifying the correct model inputs and one for deriving the correct model results), a Box for discussing the wider context, 2 Boxes for operational and strategic issues (many of which were similar in nature to

16

those within a "standard" business development-style Requirement 3), 2 Boxes for ethics and business trust, a Box for discussion of the impact of the problem on the business as a whole and then the usual Conclusions and Commercial Recommendations Boxes. As such, the learning point is that even if Requirement 3 appears to be unusual on the surface, the underlying nature of the markscheme will have to be as "normal" and therefore there is no reason to fear a "problem-based" Requirement 3.

In a similar manner to Requirement 2, Box 3.1 in the R4 Limited markscheme demonstrated a return to the style of Box 3.1 seen in examinations prior to November 2016 in that it required nothing more than the identification of the correct inputs to the model (rather than specific strategic or operational points). In the July 2017 and November 2016 examinations, Boxes 2.1 and 3.1 were not allocated to inputs but rather required the matching of specific strategic and operational points. However, in R4 Limited, Box 3.1 related purely to inputs and so would, in theory, have been easier to pass.

Also in a similar manner to Requirement 2, Box 3.2 in the R4 Limited markscheme would not have lent itself very well to Own Research points because most of the marks related to issues identified from the Exam Paper information (whether narrative or numerical in nature) and so could not have been known (and therefore researched) in advance: more specifically, some of the points related to the nature of the client involved (not necessarily something relevant to the industry in the real world) whilst others related to numerical issues such as the recycling targets required in the Advance Information or the level of the bank overdraft according to the information given in the Exam Paper. Perhaps the only overlap with an Own Research point would therefore have been the fourth point in Box 3.2 which mentioned the fact that missing recycling targets would lead to an increasing level of penalty (something true of the industry in the real world). Once again, we now doubt the benefit of including Own Research points because all the points in Box 3.2 should have been made by a well-prepared candidate, using both the Exam Paper and Advance Information data alone: no additional credit would therefore be obtained for an Own Research remark on the same underlying point.

As you are hopefully aware, Requirement 3 will now almost certainly include a calculation to perform. Several years ago, Requirement 3 used to be "the narrative one" as no calculations at all were required. The examiners have gradually introduced a calculation element to this part of the examination and, in our view, the amount of credit for the Requirement 3 calculation has been steadily growing from sitting to sitting: when it was first introduced, the credit for the Requirement 3 calculation was restricted to Box 3.1 alone but this has since changed and in the R4 Limited markscheme, Boxes 3.1 (inputs to the calculation), 3.3 (results of the calculation) and 3.6 (comparison of the results of the calculation to the rest of the business to assess impact) were all connected to the financial modelling work (although note that there were some points available in Box 3.6 which were unrelated to the financial model). As such, you should perhaps now respect the Requirement 3 calculation a bit more than in the past ... probably something you do not want to hear, given the Requirement 3 is likely to be relatively rushed if you do not exercise good time management ...

Based on the emails received from students who were worried by the nature of Requirement 3, many candidates were concerned that they had either not written enough points or had not included points which were sufficiently different to (nor more complex than) the usual strategic and operational points which would be discussed in a more "normal" business development-style Requirement 3. However, a review of the R4 Limited markscheme should reveal that the nature of the operational, strategic and wider impact points required in an unusual "backwards-looking" Requirement 3 does not really differ from the "classic" points required in a more "normal" business development-style Requirement 3. For

17

example, the R4 Limited markscheme awarded plenty of credit for "classic" points such as overdependence on a particular client, capacity constraints, contract terms such as the length of the contract, requirements for extra staff and the impact on cash flow and costs. All of these points would probably have scored credit even if the Requirement 3 scenario have been of the more traditional type so this again reinforces the point made above that there is really nothing to worry about if Requirement 3 is more backwards-looking in nature: the nature of the points is not really any different either in style or complexity. The worry of some candidates that they somehow have to do something more complicated than "normal" because of the nature of Requirement 3 was definitely misplaced as the points were no harder than usual.

Similarly, we note that candidates were worried about what to write in their Commercial Recommendations since the scenario did not relate to the development of a future project. It is certainly true that some of the Commercial Recommendations such as the need to address problems promptly and the need to review the performance of other contracts were perhaps not points that would normally be mentioned. However, other Commercial Recommendations such as the suggestion to negotiate the contract terms and investigate the long-term development of related projects, as well as to monitor the performance of the business in the future, were very much of the normal type. So, once again (and with the considerable benefit of hindsight), perhaps students were worrying unnecessarily here.

In a similar manner to Box 2.9 (see above), Box 3.9 on Conclusions included 1 specific point that candidates had to match exactly (that the client in question was too important to lose or that the financial impact of losing the client would be significant). The other 3 marks available in Box 3.9 were all open in nature so even if the candidate did not match the point regarding the importance of the client, any conclusion on the financial model with a figure (even if the figure were wrong), any conclusion on operational or strategic issues and any conclusion on ethics and business trust issues should have secured a pass in Box 3.9. Having said this, it is noteworthy that Box 3.9 only had 4 marks available in contrast to the 5 marks available for Box 2.9 so arguably the Conclusions were harder to pass in Requirement 3 than in Requirement 2.

Overall, as is hopefully clear from the above, we do not believe that there was really anything to fear from the unusual nature of Requirement 3 in R4 Limited. We would not expect there to be 2 examinations in a row which have a backwards-looking Requirement 3 so you would expect the July 2018 examination to return to the more usual analysis of the future development project ... but even if this is not the case then please do not panic! Based on the statements of the November 2017 Case Study examiner reviewed above, you should use the existence (or not) of statements by the Board on how to develop the business as an indicator of the likely nature of Requirement 3 in your examination.

Finally, we would note that, for the second sitting in a row and as a change from examinations prior to PL (July 2017), there was some credit within the ethics Boxes in the R4 Requirement 3 for referring to the fact that an aspect of the ethics issue was in line with the company's highly ethical stance and therefore there was an opportunity for something to happen which would be **positive** from an ethical point of view. Prior to the PL (July 2017) examination, no marks of this kind were ever seen on the markscheme: the marks were always for pointing out ethics problems. However, before you start looking for too many positives, please note that in both the R4 (November 2017) and PL (July 2017) examinations there was only a single mark available in Box 3.5 and a single mark available in Box

18

3.8 for points on potentially positive outcomes. Therefore, your primary task still remains to find the ethical **problems** raised within the Exam Paper information.

Appendices and Main Report (AMR) presentation Boxes

We do not have anything to note in relation to these Boxes on the R4 Limited markscheme because, as usual, the points in the AMR Boxes were exactly the same as in all recent Case Study examinations. Based on the Advance Information, the candidate worked at an external advisory firm (rather than as an employee of R4 Limited) so, as usual, there was a need to include a relevant disclaimer to obtain the first mark in Box AMR.4.

Summary of Key Learning Points from the November 2017 Past Paper

We appreciate that the above discussion is rather long but we always try to be thorough in our analysis, particularly when it relates to the most recent examination.

The key points to take away from our analysis are:

1. It may no longer be worth including any Own Research points since a good candidate should be making the types of point with which Own Research points might overlap simply from using the Exam Paper and Advance Information, meaning that adding Own Research points on top does not actually attract any further credit. You should certainly not assume that your Own Research points are still "freebie" marks: in fact, you will almost certainly not gain anything for your Own Research unless you have not made any other contextual remarks.

2. Boxes 2.1 and 3.1 may not relate to strategic and operational narrative points so you may pick up these Boxes simply by performing the calculations (since this will imply that you have gathered together the inputs required). However, to hedge your bets, and given that strategic and operational narrative points have a chance of scoring elsewhere on the markscheme, we would still recommend that you consider the basics of the contract, suppliers and customers in the same way that would have attracted credit in these Boxes in the July 2017 and November 2016 examinations. See our discussion elsewhere in this book for more advice on this point.

3. The Requirement 3 calculation and its related analysis has taken a steadily increasing share of the marks in Requirement 3 so you should perhaps take a little bit more time than was advisable in the past to attempt this aspect of the final Requirement. This is a contrast with Requirement 2 where the calculation is arguably becoming less important than in the past.

4. In the event that Requirement 3 is not a strategic and operational development project, do not panic! The strategic and operational points required to gain credit, both in general and in the Commercial Recommendations section, are likely to be of the same type as you would make in a more "normal" Requirement 3. The examiners are not trying to catch you out by setting a different style of Requirement 3 – they are simply trying to vary the examination so that it does not become too predictable but this does not mean that you should completely scrap your approach, nor the standard points you perhaps expected to make in a more "normal" Requirement 3. According to the November 2017 Case Study examiner, the "red flag" that Requirement 3 may be different in nature will be the absence of discussion of future strategic development opportunities by the Board in the Advance Information. So always check the "business plan" or "risk review" Exhibit in the Advance Information quite carefully.

19

We hope that this review has been useful. As noted, we have incorporated the relevant points into our advice throughout the remainder of this book to ensure that our technique advice and popular Planning & Reminder Sheets have been fully updated for the latest available information.

Chapter 1   **Why We Have Written This Book**

Learning Points

After reading this chapter, you must be able to:

1. understand the reasons why this book has been written
2. understand the structure of the remainder of the book
3. appreciate that, in Case, **everything** hinges on whether you understand the markscheme

---

1   **Why we have written this book**

Put simply, we have written this book because we believe we have developed a more effective method of planning and writing up your Case Study examination answer.

Over the last few years, we have been struck by the number of technically-competent accountancy students who have struggled to pass Case. This includes students who have previously passed all their other ACA examinations first time with high grades but who then fail Case without understanding why. It also includes students who have taken the Case examination perhaps 5 or 6 times with other tuition providers but who then pass first time after using our different technique.

To appreciate why so many able students struggle with Case, it is important to understand the highly unusual (and somewhat restrictive) way in which the examination is marked. This marking approach is different to all other ACA examinations and, indeed, different to any other examination you will take. Since passing an examination is ultimately all about obtaining sufficient marks, it follows that the methods you have used to pass other examinations may not necessarily work with Case.

Our view is that an effective approach to Case must begin with a recognition of the implications of the unique marking approach applied. Therefore, this book will analyse the Case markscheme in significant detail.

We firmly believe that if students had a better understanding of the patterns in the markscheme, they would have a much better chance of passing the examination.

The aim of this book is therefore to pass on this understanding.

2   **A unique marking method – the importance of "matching" and "distributing"**

As Case involves writing a business report for a client, it is possible that one reason why so many good students struggle with the examination is because they have been assuming that their Case examination script will be marked in the same way as reports or essays that they may have written in their previous examinations (such as at university or in school).

In these other assessments, the marking is often subjective in nature and the marker will perform the assessment process by forming an overall view as to whether the script is good enough or not. As you may have experienced, this could lead to a certain variation in marking, with the same essay or report being given different gradings by different markers. We are perhaps all familiar with teachers or lecturers who marked "generously" compared with teachers or lecturers who were "harsh markers".

In order to eliminate this aspect of subjectivity from the final examination prior to qualification as a Chartered Accountant, ICAEW have adopted a different approach to the marking of Case.

Rather than forming an overall, subjective opinion, a Case marker will read through every sentence in your report and check whether the point that you have made is contained within the list of approximately 240 approved points which are stated on the official ICAEW markscheme[1]. The marker is not trying to form an overall "view" on your report – they are simply performing a "**matching**" exercise, on a sentence by sentence basis, checking whether what you have said matches the list of approved points.

There are 2 important implications of this "matching" approach:

1. Even if your point is a very good practical business idea, if the point is not on the approved list then you will not obtain credit for the point – more than this, you will, in a sense, actually be **penalised** for the idea because you will have wasted precious time to write something which does not get any credit.

2. Each acceptable point on the list has equal credit – you do not score any additional or bonus marks for making points that were hard to spot compared to points that were obvious: all that matters is whether or not the point is on the approved list. This means that you cannot compensate for the fact that you have may have missed 3 or 4 basic points by spotting 1 or 2 brilliant points.

For these 2 reasons, passing Case is all about achieving a good coverage of basic, predictable points rather than trying to do anything too unusual or creative.

As well as "matching" points which are on the approved markscheme, it is also important to understand that your points must be **distributed** in an appropriate way.

The approved markscheme will contain 40 markscheme "Boxes", with each of these Boxes containing between 4 and 7 acceptable points. Regardless of the number of points available in a Box, if you "match" at least **3** of the points in that Box, then you are considered to have passed that Box.

Provided that you pass half of the available Boxes in **all** elements of the examination (Executive Summary, Requirement 1, Requirement 2, Requirement 3 and the 4 final Boxes which assess the presentation of your Appendices and Main Report), then you should pass the examination as a whole. You must therefore ensure that your points are **distributed** appropriately, in order to give yourself a good chance of passing at least half of the Boxes available – if you were to achieve full marks with perhaps 7 matching points in 2 or 3 Boxes but performed poorly in other Boxes, then you may not pass the Requirement as a whole and would therefore fail the examination. Another candidate who

---

[1] As explained further below, there are 40 specific "Boxes" of acceptable points on the markscheme and on average each Box will contain 5 or 6 acceptable points. The probable maximum number of "acceptable" points is therefore approximately 240 (40 Boxes x 6 points per Box) but this can vary slightly from examination to examination.

only matches 3 points, but in a larger number of Boxes, will perform better than you and may well pass the examination whilst achieving a lower **total** number of matching points than you.

For example, consider a candidate who scores 6 matching points in 4 Boxes and who then scores 2 matching points in the remaining 6 Boxes in the Requirement. This would be a total of 36 scoring points (calculated as 6 points x 4 Boxes plus 2 points x 6 Boxes). This candidate would not have passed half of the available Boxes in the Requirement because they only gained at least 3 marks in 4 Boxes. Such a candidate is likely to **fail** the examination, despite making a good number of points that **match** the markscheme.

Now consider a candidate who scores 3 matching points in 5 Boxes and who then scores 2 matching points in the remaining 5 Boxes in the Requirement. This would be a total of 25 scoring points (calculated as 3 points x 5 Boxes plus 2 points x 5 Boxes). This candidate would have achieved the passing standard of 3 or more points in at least half of the available Boxes in the Requirement, even though they have only matched 69% (25/36) of the points made by the first candidate.

In other words, by matching only 69% of the points made by the first candidate but by **distributing** these more efficiently, the second candidate will perform better in the examination.

This illustrates that it is the **distribution**, and not just the total **number**, of marks which is critical to your chances of success. The obvious implication is that you need a planning technique which will give you an opportunity to spread or **distribute** your points well across the different Boxes, increasing your chances of success.

As we have indicated, this really is a unique marking method and it can lead to certain perverse results, as demonstrated above. Given that the marking method is so unusual, we think it is important to develop a distinctive approach which respects the importance of **both** "matching" and "distributing" your points, in order to maximise your chances of success.

It is this approach which we will try to teach you in this book.

3   Scepticism of the "4 Column Planning Grid"

When we studied for our own Case examinations, we were not taught to base our planning around the 40 Boxes which constitute the detail of the official markscheme. Instead, we were told to create a planning sheet based on the 4 column headings found at the top of the official markscheme (headings which organise the 40 Boxes into 4 specific columns).

This meant that we were advised to create a blank planning sheet for each element of the examination (Executive Summary, Requirement 1, Requirement 2 and Requirement 3) formatted as follows:

Assimilating & Using Information	Structuring Problems & Solutions	Applying Judgement	Conclusions & Recommendations

While the use of the same headings as the official markscheme will allow this form of planning sheet to give you **some** guidance on the right kinds of point to make, we believe that knowing the detail of the 40 Boxes would provide **more specific** guidance – in particular, it is not clear to us what the terms "Assimilating & Using Information", "Structuring Problems & Solutions" or "Applying Judgement" actually mean in terms of the type of points that you should make: there are many ways in which you could be considered to be "Applying Judgement" in a report but what we want to know is the way that the **Case Study examiners** will reward you for applying judgement – this is particularly important given that only points which "match" the official markscheme will be given any credit: if you apply judgement in the "wrong" way (meaning "wrong" from the point of view of the markscheme, rather than "wrong" in any more absolute sense) then you will end up wasting valuable time and will not obtain credit.

We remain perplexed as to why this form of planning sheet is still provided to students by some other tuition providers. In our view, it does not make sense to plan on the basis of the open and relatively vague column headings – why not base your plan on the specific and concrete detail of the Boxes **within** each column as this will provide you with better guidance as to what to write? Given the "matching" approach of the marking, you simply cannot afford to be unlucky with the points that you are making and therefore you need more **specific** guidance on what is likely to be within the Boxes contained in each column. Reference only to the headings of the columns cannot, by definition, provide you with this guidance: we can only know what the term "Assimilating & Using Information" means by looking at the detail of the Boxes so since we have to look at the Boxes anyway to know what the heading means, why not just use those Boxes to plan around?

We therefore adopt a different approach in this book by ignoring the vague column headings found at the top of each column of the markscheme. We will instead look at the content and concrete detail of the Boxes that you will find within each column. Fortunately, there are very definite patterns across examination sittings in terms of what the Boxes within each column will always require you to do to score well. We adopt the approach that it is better to plan around these predictable and specific Tasks rather than the unhelpful and vague column headings.

This book will therefore spend a considerable amount of time working through the content of the 40 Boxes and you should read our analysis very carefully.

Having read our analysis thoroughly before the examination, you will be in a position to use our popular Planning & Reminder Sheets on exam day to remind you of the lessons contained in the book, allowing you to stay focused on points with a high probability of "**matching**" the approved list of points whilst also "**distributing**" your points effectively.

4   The importance of understanding patterns

We will spend the remainder of the book looking at the Case Study markscheme in great detail. Please try to note all the **patterns** in what we are saying – the key thing to develop is a sense that there are **always** specific things to say/do to get the marks and then, secondly, to understand that you should do **only these things** on exam day, given the significant time pressure involved in the exam.

Case is not an opportunity to get creative – it is, first and foremost, an exam, and one with a highly unusual assessment method so **stick to the patterns** and do not try anything too clever.

5   A note on the terminology used in this book

In the remainder of the book we will refer to the different "Boxes" or "Tasks" on the ICAEW markscheme using our own referencing system explained in more detail in chapter 4. When we refer to "Task 2.3" or "Box 2.3", we are referring to the ICAEW **markscheme**. Our references to the ICAEW **markscheme** therefore include **only numbers** (no letters) in the reference.

However, the markscheme is used for **marking** rather than **writing** your report. It follows that the order in which these Tasks or Boxes are included on the markscheme is not necessarily the order in which you should write up your points in your own report. Therefore, our Planning & Reminder Sheets (chapter 6) will also provide you with a clear set of skeleton headings for use in your report to give you good coverage of the Boxes but without having an unwieldy and unnecessary 10 sub-sections per Requirement.

When we refer to our suggested **report section headings** in our Planning & Reminder Sheets (as opposed to the ICAEW markscheme) we will use a reference including a number plus a **letter** such as "report section 2.C". Our **report section** heading references therefore include **both numbers and letters** in the reference.

We strongly recommend that you stick to the specific "number plus letter" headings which we include in our Planning & Reminder Sheets as these headings have been very carefully chosen to give you appropriate coverage of a sufficient number of relevant areas in each Requirement.

It is important to be clear about this distinction because the references used are similar and can potentially be confused. In summary, the terms we use function as follows:

Reference to "Task" or "Box" with a reference such as "2.5"

As there are no letters in the reference "2.5", this means a reference to the ICAEW **markscheme** Boxes. Our Planning & Reminder Sheets **do not** use this kind of reference.

Reference to "report section" with a reference such as "2.E"

As there is a letter in the reference "2.E", this means a reference to the **report section headings** in your own report. Our Planning & Reminder Sheets **do** use this kind of reference.

We also recommend that you familiarise yourself with the abbreviated names of recent Case Study examinations so that you can quickly refer to the relevant underlying material if needed. We provide a full list of our abbreviated references on page 3 of this book.

6   Comments from students

> ***Student 1 says:*** *"First time around, I was overconfident – I know I can write, I know I can research and I know I can come up with original ideas in relation to business. I thought that Case would test these skills and I was actually looking forward to a chance to show some creativity and practical business thinking. Yet in the end my points were way off the mark and I almost cried when I saw the simplistic nature of the points which were rewarded in LL (July 2012). I wished I had put more time into learning the patterns in past exams rather than just assuming "I'll be fine". Second time around I kept this point in mind throughout – don't try to be creative, don't try to show off, just keep things nice and simple."*

> ***Student 2 says:*** *"There are essentially 2 ways to pass Case. One is to not really understand what the markscheme entails, write a half decent report on the day and strike upon the right answer. The second is to really get to grips with the markscheme. When you are familiar with what is repeated time after time you can go in with confidence knowing that you can achieve a good proportion of the marks with very little thought on the day."*

Chapter 2   Case Study: Some Common Fallacies

Learning Points

After reading this chapter, you must be able to:

1. understand some common misconceptions about Case Study
2. appreciate the dangers involved in these fallacies and how to avoid them in your own work

---

In this chapter, we show you why it is dangerous to believe certain incorrect statements that we continue to hear, from both students and tutors at other tuition providers. Although the statements may appear to be plausible on the surface, following the implications of these statements is likely to harm your grade significantly and could even result in you failing the examination through an incorrect method of preparation. This chapter explains why the statements are wrong and what you should be doing instead.

Fallacy 1   "You cannot prepare for Case"

This is one of the most frequent statements made. Presumably it is based on the contrast between the Advance Information, which is released 6 weeks before the examination (presenting an opportunity to prepare before exam day), and the unpredictable requirements of the Exam Paper, which you have to react to on the day (potentially frustrating your attempts to prepare prior to the examination if the examination scenarios are not as you expected).

Whilst it is certainly true that you will have to do some thinking on your feet on the day and therefore cannot fully prepare your answers in advance, how is this any different to other exams? When do you ever NOT need to think on your feet or respond to new information in an exam? Does the fact that there will be an unpredictable **part** in an exam mean that you do not prepare for it at all? On the contrary – you work hard in preparing and revising to ensure that you have different possibilities covered and can react well on the day, making things as comfortable as possible.

Case is in fact a golden opportunity to prepare – how often are you given a huge proportion of the subject matter of the exam and 6 weeks of notice, allowing you to prepare a significant amount of at least one third of your answer (Requirement 1) in advance (see chapters 8 and 17)? The answer is never, apart from in Case, so why ignore this excellent opportunity to prepare? Similarly, you will rarely have an opportunity to use such a predictable report structure in an essay-based answer as you will in Case so make the most of knowing in advance what Tasks (and hence section headings: see our Planning & Reminder Sheets in chapter 6) will be required.

As one example of what can be done in advance, you should prepare by thoroughly drilling the Requirement 1 calculations. You know that you will be asked about changes in revenue, changes in gross profit and, in most cases, changes in operating profit. You have your baseline figures already given to you in the Advance Information, meaning that you can be certain of having the right figures for half of your calculations (the "prior year" from the point of view of the figures given in the Exam Paper). The Advance Information will also hint at some of the potential reasons for changes: these

27

will often be amongst the "correct" explanations once the Exam Paper figures are known because many trends will continue to be as expected in the examination information[2]. Therefore, if you use some example Exam Paper figures or our mock exams, you can drill both the calculations **AND** explanations many times beforehand.

Drilling the calculations serves both to ensure that you get the figures correct under exam pressure and also ensures you know exactly where to look in the financial statements for the information. If you have a good memory, drilling will mean that you just know that the prior year gross profit margin was, for example, 43.2% and that operating profit margin was 9.0%. Then you do not have to waste any time checking or calculating these elements.

If you drill the calculations well, you should be able to complete your Appendix 1 in 20 minutes or less. This will save you a very valuable 10 minutes (relative to the standard 30 minutes which your Appendix 1 is supposed to take, according to some other tuition providers): your efforts to prepare will allow you to invest more time in writing your report, giving you more opportunity to score marks.

You can also drill your Requirement 1 explanations. Revenue can either increase or decrease. We do not know if it will increase or decrease in the Exam Paper, but we can prepare some possible narrative explanations either way. You can also pre-prepare some ideas regarding particular patterns or high and low points in terms of revenue streams and so on: these will be rewarded within the Requirement 1 markscheme. A mixture of these ideas from the Advance Information and points taken from the information in the Exam Paper should see you through.

These are just **some** examples of how preparation can benefit you on exam day, looking only at Requirement 1 as an illustration. The remainder of this book will explain many other methods to you. Believing Fallacy 1 (that preparation is of no benefit because it is impossible to predict what would be on the Exam Paper) would prevent you from capitalising upon these opportunities.

---

[2] You should, however, always prioritise the Exam Paper over the Advance Information as your initial source of reasons for changes: the Exam Paper is significantly shorter than the Advance Information so there is much less chance that you will be unlucky with the reason selected if you use the Exam Paper – the range of possible points is much narrower than the Advance Information.

> ***Student 1 says:*** *"The advice to drill Requirement 1 is really good advice. By drilling, I mean not just the numbers but the explanations, based on the Advance Information. Get those explanations in on the day, even if they seem boring or obvious. Then make sure you look for any further explanations regarding Requirement 1 in the Exam Paper – there will definitely be marks for anything on the Exam Paper. You don't know what the Exam Paper will say but rarely will the events/changes in the Exam Paper information contradict or radically change the potential explanations you will have practised in the Advance Information – these are often long term trends. You are not trying to make definite claims about what has caused revenue to increase, just give reasonable explanations – that is enough and the Exam Paper information is unlikely to overrule all of your pre-prepared explanations. You can also usually drill ethics as the ethical issues in the exam will always link back to ethical issues hinted at in the Advance Information.*

> ***Student 2 says:*** *"Take a look through the markschemes for some of the past papers and the ACA Simplified mocks. Look at how frequently the same or similar answers crop up. Then compare with the number of marks that are available for the unpredictable elements of the exam. The point I am making is you can build yourself a healthy number of marks before you even start tackling the new or 'unpredictable' elements.*
>
> *It takes me 3 hours to write the recommended number of words. I drilled myself down so that Requirement 1 Appendix took only 15 minutes – this saved me from failing on insufficient content alone."*

Fallacy 2   "Case is an open-ended examination – there is no right answer so don't worry"

This statement is entirely wrong – of course there is a right answer: the answer that will get you the marks! Case in fact has the **most restrictive** marking scheme of any ACA exam – if you have a good idea which is not on the markscheme, you get no credit at all. This is a very tough and rigid approach which you may not have experienced in other exams, whether ACA or otherwise. The marking is very definitely **not** open-ended at all.

Therefore, it is **very** dangerous to think that as long as your points are reasonable and practical, you will be fine. It is still more dangerous to assume that a really outstanding point will compensate for the fact that you have not mentioned more basic points elsewhere – the markscheme does not work on the basis of an overall, subjective appraisal but instead requires **all** points to be explicitly and individually stated, so you will drop marks if you forget to mention the basics.

Whilst this may appear frustrating, think of a silver lining to this cloud – by trying to individually **match** each of your points against the approximately 240 permitted points[3], the examiners are assessing each individual paragraph and sentence in a completely **self-contained way**. The benefit of this is that if you do not finish off a section or you say something which is completely wrong or stupid, then the marker cannot take this into account when evaluating any other elements nor in providing your

---

[3] See page 22 for an explanation of this calculation.

final grade. Contrast this with standard essay marking where different examiners could easily give a grade ranging from A to C (or 100% to 70%, say) depending on their personal reaction to, for example, an incomplete section or incorrect remark.

A second reason to feel hopeful is that many of the approximately 240 acceptable points[4] can be predicted through careful analysis of recent markschemes, as undertaken in this book. After reading this book, you will have a very good idea of what the marker will be rewarding. Again, this contrasts with subjective essay marking where there is no real way of knowing what the marker's view will be.

So although the restrictive nature of the Case marking scheme can be very frustrating (particularly if you are an unusual or creative thinker), for the 2 reasons outlined immediately above, there are some benefits in this unusual Box-based marking approach.

> **Student 1 says:** *"This is very important advice and a good point. Saying that "there is no right answer" could lead you into thinking that "a range of possible, plausible answers will be rewarded" but nothing could be further from the truth – there is NO discretion for the marker in this exam. Hence it means you have to know how the markscheme works inside out and much more than other exams where you can get away with basically doing "a good job". This is why it is so wrong to say that you cannot prepare for Case."*

> **Student 2 says:** *"The markscheme doesn't say "Is this a good point? Is this a good report? Pass/Fail" – it says "Has the candidate made points which fit onto this markscheme?" You need to take this difference into account, both in your preparation and on the day."*

Fallacy 3   "I'm pretty good at analysing businesses and writing reports. I'll be fine."

You may well be an excellent business analyst but business analysis is not quite the same thing as scoring points in 40 Boxes. There is no reason to think that a good, realistic client report will necessarily make the same points that are contained in the approximately 240 acceptable points on the markscheme[5] and there have been many, many instances of student scripts which would be more than acceptable as real world business reports but which fail the exam.

In any case, is the Case Study really a realistic test of report writing? How often do you handwrite a report in 4 hours, having done all your calculations by hand? How often do you write at length on the ethical implications of what a client is doing when reporting to that client? How often do you tell a Financial Director that his or her assumptions and calculation methodology are seriously flawed? Not very often, again suggesting a need to be cautious in assuming your practical skills are a relevant predictor of your potential to pass the exam.

---

[4] See page 22 for an explanation of this calculation.
[5] See page 22 for an explanation of this calculation.

Student 2 says: *"I missed many points on my mocks because I skipped past points that were totally obvious. Don't fall into the trap of thinking "that's too easy" or "too obvious". As an example, you will gain marks for telling the client that revenue and profit have increased – in the real world, the client would know this very well! That kind of comment is probably too easy or obvious for a business report in real life but not in Case."*

Chapter 3   The Correct Case Study Writing Style

Learning Points

After reading this chapter, you must be able to:

1. understand the importance of writing concisely in "almost bullet-like" style
2. understand how to remove irrelevant, time-wasting material from your own writing
3. understand the significant time savings which are possible with the correct style

---

1   The easiest way to fail Case – poor time management

According to the examiners, the most likely cause of a failure of the Case exam is that a candidate simply runs out of time and does not complete their script properly (usually Requirement 3 is extremely short in this situation). Although 4 hours sounds like a lot, given the availability of 40 different Tasks, a large amount of Exam Paper information to absorb and the fact that you need to allow time to physically write over 3,000 words of text, it is unfortunately very easy to fail due to poor time management alone.

We see a large number of retake students on our tuition courses (retaking after failing with another provider, rather than with us) who are making their effective timeframe even shorter by writing in too elegant or wordy a style. It is very important to understand that the examiners cannot award any marks at all for the literary style or elegance of what you are writing: all the examiners care about is checking if the **content** of what you have written "matches" anything within the list of acceptable points on the markscheme.

Therefore you need to forget about niceties of style such as introductory paragraphs, elegantly-written linkages between paragraphs or long explanations of your point: instead, you need to develop an "almost bullet-like" style of writing in which you just make the basic point and then move on, thus making as many **different** points as you can in the time available.

This clearly does not suit some students, particularly if they have a background in a report- or essay-writing subject or degree. Certainly in the UK, school and university students are told to "expand" their points to ensure that they fully explain each idea to the reader. In Case, on the other hand, it is enough just to **touch** on a point and then move on – that will be enough to gain the mark, given the **binary** or **yes/no** marking approach used: either you have referred to an issue or you have not – the "stylish" nature of your writing or quality of your justification is not relevant.

We provide below a real example of a first attempt at a Case Study answer taken from a student's script written as their first mock submission on our classroom tuition course. We then transform the student's writing into the "almost bullet-like" style which is needed to succeed in Case. We will show you that it is possible to make the same number of points in **half the time** if you follow our approach: as we are sure you can calculate yourself, this would effectively give you twice as much writing time. In many instances, it is this alone which means that we can turn a failing candidate (and even a candidate who has failed the exam several times) into a candidate who passes well.

It is up to you to develop the writing discipline needed to preserve your precious time in the exam. Given that the number one cause of failure is to run out of time, it should be a **priority** for you to critically evaluate your own writing in all attempts at mock exams – critically re-read your work and ask yourself whether you really have said something in the minimum number of words: if not, try to rework your writing and then retain the more efficient sentence structure and style for next time[6].

We know you will be keen to get into the technical content and analysis of the Case markscheme in the remainder of this book but our advice here on writing style is arguably even more important than those other areas – **if you do not have the time to write, there is no point studying what to write**. This is why we have provided a chapter on writing style right at the start of the book. Please do not gloss over this chapter simply because it is provided early on – this could be the chapter that saves your life!

2   How to write efficiently: an example from a student script

---

Example 1 – Student's original text (213 words or 8.5 minutes of writing time[7])

1.A Background

In the current economic climate, the recession may have affected the demand for FS's products. However, the regulatory environment is likely to have had a stronger impact. Student visa restrictions imposed by the UKBA are likely to have reduced the demand for English Language tuition programmes. Exhibit 14a indicates that such changes in regulation can result in a large decrease in students on English Language courses. The regulation that prevents students from working full time while they study caused one college's students to drop by 70% in one year.

Another factor which may be affecting the market for English Language courses in the UK is increased competition from other countries. According to the British Council, the average annual growth rate in international student enrolments in the UK over the period 1998-2004 was 6.4%, compared with 14.9% and 29.0% in Australia and New Zealand, respectively.

1.B Revenue

Revenue from English Language tuition programmes has decreased from £2,475k to £1,818k, which is a decrease of £657k or 26.5%. The reason for this decrease is likely to be the fact that UKBA regulations have made it harder for overseas students to study in the UK. This shows that FS will need to continue to diversify and shift its resources into the other two revenue streams.

We will now rewrite the student's text in a more economical style, whilst retaining all the points made.

---

[6] In a relatively predictable Requirement such as Requirement 1 it may even be possible to recycle your phraseology as you work through revenue, gross profit and so on, once you have determined the most efficient way of writing particular points such as the description of movements in the management accounts figures from year to year, together with reasons. In other words, you might develop a set sentence structure which is used each time – there are no marks for style in Case so there is no point mixing up the phraseology simply for variety, particularly if this ends up meaning that you are simply writing more than you need to. Please see chapter 8 for further details on how to develop a "standardised" sentence structure.

[7] Assuming a typical handwriting speed of 25 words per minute.

Example 1 – Our re-written text (105 words or 4 minutes of writing time[8])

1.A Context of Performance

The recession may have affected demand for FS and student visa restrictions imposed by UKBA are likely to have reduced demand for English Language teaching (EL): restrictions on working caused a 70% reduction in demand at one language college in a year.

Other countries are also increasingly offering EL, competing with FS. The British Council found that between 1998-2007 market growth in the UK was 6.4% compared to 14.9% in Australia and 29.0% in New Zealand.

1.B Revenue

Revenue from EL decreased substantially by £657k (-26.5%), probably as a result of UKBA rules, and this justifies FS' plan to diversify revenues.

For Example 1, the time saved by writing more economically is 4.5 minutes or 53%.

Example 2 – Student's original text (175 words or 7 minutes of writing time[9])

1.F Commercial Recommendations

I would recommend that FS changes its staffing and capacity in order to not have to repeat the problem with the Olympics work. This problem was caused by not having enough translators from the right countries.

I recommend that FS examines its costs for translation and interpretation services in order to determine why the gross profit margin is relatively poor.

I suggest that FS reviews its pricing policies with regard to English Language tuition programmes – perhaps a discount could boost demand and revenue.

I also suggest that FS undertakes some market research into an alternative industry to obtain clients from, thereby reducing its dependence on the motor industry.

I would encourage FS to discuss and negotiate with LOCOG to see if the penalty can be reduced in any way (e.g. through future discounts) or FS could consider taking legal advice. Perhaps the penalty could be reduced.

I also recommend that FS undertakes some research into an entirely new primary revenue stream that is completely independent of changes in UKBA laws and regulations.

We will now rewrite the student's text in a more economical style, whilst retaining all the points made.

---

[8] Assuming an average writing speed of 25 words per minute.
[9] Assuming an average writing speed of 25 words per minute.

Example 2 – Our re-written text (56 words or 2 minutes of writing time[10])

1.F Commercial Recommendations

FS should:

-ensure that it has sufficient translators to prevent a repeat of the Olympics issue

-investigate poor gross profit margin in T&I

-review pricing of EL and consider discounts

-perform market research to diversify away from the motor industry

-negotiate with LOCOG to reduce the penalty

-investigate a new primary revenue stream

For Example 2, the time saved by writing more economically is 5 minutes or 71%.

Considering just the above 2 examples (which are only a couple of selected examples from the student's script) we have saved a total of almost 10 minutes **without any loss of marks**.

We trust that this makes clear to you the significant benefits of writing concisely: in many instances, students who complain that there is not enough time to complete their report are making things very difficult for themselves by writing in an inefficient style.

3 Writing efficiently in Case: some phrases to avoid

Based on the above advice and our review of a sample student script, here are some suggested phrases and points that are best avoided for the purposes of the Case exam:

Introductory sentences

It is completely unnecessary to introduce your Requirement answer: just get on with the analysis. Therefore sentences such as "In this part of the report, we will analyse the performance of ZM over the past 12 months" are completely pointless as there will be no marks on the markscheme for this kind of language.

Link sentences

There is no need to write beautiful linkages between paragraphs as this again will not be rewarded. Therefore phrases such as "Following on from the above analysis of profit per year ..." or "In contrast

---

[10] Assuming an average writing speed of 25 words per minute.

to the improvement in gross margin …" are a waste of time. The marker cannot award any marks for these linkages between points: marks can only be awarded for the points themselves.

Enumerative sentences

There is no need to say "Another factor which may be affecting the market for English Language courses is …" – just state the factor itself!

Section sentences

There is no need to say "In conclusion …" or "As a recommendation we would advise": if you follow our suggested section headings per our Planning & Reminder Sheets (see chapter 6) then the marker will know which section you are writing: once again, just get on with the analysis rather than introducing it.

Although these section sentences may not individually appear to use up many words, if you are writing in too wordy a style throughout the exam then the cumulative effect can be surprisingly large, easily amounting to at least 100-200 words or 5-10 minutes of writing time (and often more) – if we offered you another 5-10 minutes at the end of the exam, would you take it? You would, in which case it makes sense to pay attention to your writing style during your preparation – any time that you can gain in the exam will be extremely valuable.

4   How much should I write? How much time should I spend on each section?

To some extent, these questions are personal matters which will vary by student. However, assuming first that you have fixed your writing style and are therefore writing very efficiently, we would recommend that you aim to write at least 400-500 words for the Executive Summary and 900 words for each Requirement. This gives a total wordcount of 3,200 words for your report as a whole.

On the standard 2+2 timetable (i.e. 2 hours for planning and 2 hours for writing up) which is advocated by some tuition providers, writing 3,200 words is only achievable within 2 hours if you have a **very** quick writing style (27 words per minute, or 1 word every 2 seconds, assuming that you do not stop writing for the whole 2 hours). We do not think that this is really possible so we suggest much less time for planning, as described below.

We strongly recommend that you plan a Requirement, write the Requirement up, write the Executive Summary section for that Requirement, and then plan the next Requirement and write it up and write the related Executive Summary section, and so on, rather than writing all 3 Requirements in one go (and only then turning your attention to the Executive Summary, also writing this in one go right at the end of your examination time). Our method will allow you to plan and then immediately write up each Requirement, reducing the cognitive overload from planning 3 different sections at once. It also means that you will not have to remember a plan that you prepared as much as 2 hours earlier e.g. if you planned everything at the start

then it may well be at least 2 hours before you actually write up that plan for the last Requirement[11].

Using the strategies suggested in this book, and particularly our advice to drill and pre-prepare your Requirement 1 Appendix before the exam (see chapter 17), you should be able to make some significant time savings.

We suggest that through rehearsal of predictable elements and a clear focus on the 40 Task Approach™, you should be able to significantly reduce the traditionally recommended 2 hour planning period so that you can fit with our general timings as below:

Read Exam Paper questions carefully	10 mins
Read Requirement 1 Exam Paper information	5 mins
Draft Appendix 1	15 mins
Write up Requirement 1 including Executive Summary	50 mins
Read Requirement 2 Exam Paper information	5 mins
Draft Appendix 2	15 mins
Write up Requirement 2 including Executive Summary	50 mins
Read Requirement 3 Exam Paper information	5 mins
Write up Requirement 3 including Executive Summary	50 mins
Total planned time allocation	**3 hours 25 mins**
Spare time to allow for overruns/problems on exam day	35 mins
Total exam time	**4 hours**

Obviously, we do realise that the examination is 4 hours in length but we do not think it is a good idea to create a plan based on a very precise minute by minute allocation right through to the maximum time available because this allows no time at all for any overruns or problems on the day, potentially causing you to panic if you end up being even a few minutes behind your carefully created minute by minute schedule[12]. We therefore build in some time (35 minutes) which is not allocated to anything specific because we know that things often do not go as intended on exam day.

Allocating a lot more time to writing up will give you a significant advantage over other candidates. As you read the above allocation for the first time, we appreciate that you may be sceptical but we can

---

[11] It is interesting to note that the examiners themselves also do not recommend doing all planning at once but rather on a Requirement by Requirement basis (see chapter 14).

[12] On our taught courses, we sometimes start to work with retake students who previously used time plans (created by other tuition providers) specified to the nearest 15 seconds of time for the completion of various stages throughout the examination. In our opinion, such time plans create unrealistic expectations for an examination. Attempting to plan in such precise detail is very likely to cause you to waste so much time checking the clock and worrying about meeting the next target that you are likely to lose more marks than you gain. Rather than plan in such detail right through to the 4 hour mark, we strongly advise you to take a more prudent approach and build in some "emergency" spare time by default.

assure you that the above time allocations **are** possible if you practise and rehearse as much as you can, as explained throughout this book.

> **Student 1 says:** *"Other tuition providers tell you to allow 2 hours in total for writing up. I am really not sure about this. It implies that you have to write 3,200/120 = 27 words per minute and I just cannot physically do that, even if I am literally just writing (remember that you will still have to do **some** thinking in your 2 hours of writing time). If you leave all the writing to the end, you have to do a lot of flicking back between sections/plans to look at what you planned some time earlier and I just don't think this is a good idea. I know 2 colleagues who got ridiculously high grades and they told me they simply ignored the idea of 2 hours planning and just wrote for the whole 4 hours. Maybe they are exaggerating a little there, I think I need **some** time to plan, but I agree with the principle. In my first attempt at the examination with another tuition provider, I followed the standard advice to undertake very extensive planning but for my re-take I realised I needed to carve out another 15-20 minutes just for writing, and I think this extra time really helped. If you drill and drill Requirement 1 until you know where the figures are in your sleep, it becomes mechanical and you can do it at a machine speed. I think you can save 10-15 minutes just from that tip. Also don't spend too long on the ET."*

> **Student 2 says:** *"Some practical advice: write out some sentences in exam format and time yourself. The 3,200 word target is a good one, it leaves enough space to write in sufficient detail without being too wordy. Work out how long it actually takes you, personally, to write the 3,200 words and work backwards from your writing speed (bearing in mind that you won't be able to sustain that speed all the time) to plan your tactics accordingly. If you write quickly then you have the luxury of refining your technique. If you write slowly (like me), start developing ways of buying yourself time. Finally, take in a stopwatch. If you are drifting over time, move on. Time management is absolutely crucial in this exam. You have to be disciplined and move on at the appropriate times. Don't aim for perfection. You won't lose marks just for leaving a section unfinished – you will, however, gain no marks for sections which never get started."*

Chapter 4   The Case Markscheme

Learning Points

After reading this chapter, you must be able to:

1. understand the unique way in which Case Study is marked
2. understand how many Boxes you need to pass in order to pass each element of the examination
3. appreciate that it is the **distribution** of your points, not the **total** number of points, which matters
4. understand the generic requirements ("Tasks") of each of the 40 markscheme Boxes
5. visualise a generic Case Study markscheme in your "mind's eye"

---

1   The unique Case Study marking approach

Unlike all other ACA examinations, a marker in Case Study has no discretion at all to award marks: instead, a Case Study marker must simply check whether each of your points **matches** any of the points on the finalised ICAEW markscheme. If your point is a good one but is not on the approved list then you **will not score any credit**.

In light of this potentially harsh approach, we think it is imperative that all preparation for Case Study focuses on the markscheme – after all, if you do not know what is likely to be on the markscheme then you will be relying on luck to pass the examination. We remain surprised just how little time appears to be spent looking at past paper markschemes by students on the tuition courses provided by some competitors – it is all very well spending time analysing the Case Study business and doing group exercises but if you do not know what kinds of point are going to score then you may end up heading off in the wrong direction entirely.

We will therefore review the Case Study marking approach in detail in this chapter. Hopefully by the end of the chapter you will have a much better idea of what tends to be found in each of the 40 markscheme "Boxes" (groups of acceptable points on a particular theme/skill) and so you will be able to concentrate on "**matching**" points with a greater chance of being given credit.

The other point that we want to make completely clear in this chapter is the importance of **distributing** your points correctly in order to have a good chance of achieving the **3** scoring points needed to pass a Box. The Case Study marking approach is not based on the total number of **acceptable points** made but rather on the total number of **Boxes passed**. It therefore follows that you need to understand how to score "batches" of at least 3 points in each Box to pass that Box. We recommend that you re-read the section in chapter 1 on the importance of "distribution" before proceeding with the remainder of this chapter.

2 Tasks, Boxes and the passing standard for each element of the examination

In each of the 3 main Requirements, the ICAEW marking grid will assess your performance within 10 specific competencies or "Tasks" (and within a further 6 "Tasks" for the Executive Summary). Each of these "Tasks" is assessed by a Box on the markscheme: we will use the terms "Task" and "Box" fairly interchangeably but it is important to conceptualise the writing of your report as an attempt to complete these various "Tasks", which are common to every exam: in this sense, you should think of the examination as one big "To Do" list, with the items on that list always being of the same general type regardless of what the specific examination Requirements turn out to be on the day.

In order to ensure that you pass an individual Task you must achieve 3 scoring points or more from a specified list of between 4 and 7 points. If you score more than 3 points then this will not compensate for the fact that you scored less than 3 points in another Task: each Task is assessed completely separately and your performance is assessed based on the number of Tasks passed, rather than the **number of acceptable points** made. Therefore, your points must be **distributed** correctly across the various Tasks in batches of at least 3 points per Task/Box: we will return to this point later.

In order to pass a Requirement (Requirement 1, Requirement 2 or Requirement 3, the 3 main elements of your report) you must achieve **5 passing Tasks** which means that you must have made a minimum of 15 acceptable points (3 acceptable points in 5 different Tasks or Boxes), but subject to these being distributed in such a way as to achieve 3 points in 5 Boxes (i.e. 15 points in **total** is not the criterion to aim for).

As the marker reads your answer, he or she will compare your sentences with the specified list of acceptable points: if your point matches one of the points on the list then you score a mark or "diamond"[13]; if your point is not on the list, you get no mark (and in a sense you are actually penalised through a wasting of precious time on writing for no reward).

It is therefore essential to (1) have a good idea of what the Tasks will be and (2) to achieve a good **distribution** of points across the Boxes, rather than doing really well in just a few Tasks: it is better to get 3 diamonds in 5 Boxes (15 acceptable points **evenly** distributed) than to get 6 diamonds in 4 Boxes and 1 diamond in 1 Box (25 acceptable points **unevenly** distributed), for example.

As the Tasks within each Requirement are relatively predictable, we will spend a **lot** of time analysing these Tasks in the remainder of this book. We believe that this will give you better guidance than the open 4 Column Planning Grid used by some other tuition providers.

In addition, we will show that certain Tasks are much easier than others (yet each individual Task has the same reward, in the sense of taking you closer to the 5 passing Boxes you need). It is essential for you to understand the best ways to achieve those 5 passing Boxes by targeting Tasks which are predictable and/or easier as this will give you the very best chance of passing the examination.

Before we begin our review of the Boxes, a word of caution (or rather a word to reassure you). Do not be intimidated by the existence of **40** different Boxes – you only need to score your 3 points ("diamonds") in 5 of the Boxes in each Requirement (and in 3 of the Boxes in the Executive Summary)

---

[13] We use the term "diamond" because this is the symbol (♦) used on the markscheme. It is also a more exciting way of referring to a "mark".

so you certainly do not need to pass all 40 Boxes, nor even 30. In the interests of giving you as many opportunities as possible to pick up marks, our 40 Task Approach™ sets out **all** 40 Boxes in full but as we will try to show, there will always be certain Tasks which are easier to complete than others. **In fact, we will show that within each Requirement, there will always be the same 4 or 5 key Boxes which are the easiest ways of achieving the Boxes you need to pass that Requirement.** You should concentrate on ensuring that you get these Boxes and then add the others as a margin of safety but remember that you do not need to do all 40 Tasks perfectly to pass the exam easily.

3   The predictable nature of the Boxes

We will now start to work through a generic, blank 40 Box markscheme to give you an opportunity to understand and visualise the general, basic patterns. As this generic markscheme is just an example derived from our observation of patterns in the last 12 past paper markschemes, it does not relate to any specific real or mock Case Study. The content of each Box has therefore been left blank in our overview but we do include the correct number of marks or "diamonds" which generally tend to be available within each Box[14]. Our aim here is just to give you a simplified and generic idea of the markscheme: we will spend plenty of time looking at concrete points in later chapters.

The point we are trying to illustrate via the overview below is that the generic Task of each Box is **always the same**. Hence even without knowing anything at all about the content of a particular Case Study, we can tell you with confidence what almost all of your 40 Tasks will be. This specific guidance is completely unavailable using a 4 Column Planning Grid where the only guidance is the **column headings**, which are in themselves rather vague.

It is very important that you spend some time trying to learn this generic outline, fixing it in your "mind's eye" so that you will automatically stay focused on relevant points rather than wandering off into other ideas (no matter how interesting or innovative) which will gain no marks and merely waste precious time. If you can commit the 40 Boxes to memory then you should find that you instinctively focus on the correct areas without having to think about this too hard: you should find that you just naturally focus on the appropriate areas.

Although a real ICAEW markscheme is not numbered, we have added our own quick cross-referencing number to each of the Boxes, starting with the Executive Summary. We will use this cross-referencing to the 40 Tasks elsewhere in this book so please put some time into understanding how the referencing works.

In the generic markscheme overleaf, we indicate the general requirement of each Box by use of square brackets and italicised text. This is our 4-5 word summary of the relevant Task – **learn these summaries very well!**

---

[14] An exception is with respect to the 4 Boxes on presentation, spelling and Appendices (we term these the "Appendices and Main Report" or AMR Boxes): since these Boxes do not depend on making specific technical points, the composition of the marks in these Boxes is precisely known in advance and hence these Boxes are not analysed in detail in this book. See later in this chapter for the content of these Boxes (which does not vary at all from sitting to sitting).

Although you are able to take your own notes and reminders into the examination with you, we strongly believe that you should attempt to memorise the 40 generic **Tasks** as this will ensure that you instinctively focus on the correct areas: this will be quicker than having to use notes as reminders.

We will now provide you with a generic Case Study markscheme and basic explanation of what each Box/Task requires you to do. Please just try to gain an overview for now – we will spend a lot of time filling in the details in the remainder of this book.

4 Executive Summary Markscheme: a generic example[15]

Financial Analysis (Req 1)		Numerical Analysis of Project(s) (Req 2)	
E.1a	**Description**	**E.2a**	**Figures**
♦		♦	
♦	Task E.1a	♦	Task E.2a
♦	*[Review Requirement 1 Appendix figures]*	♦	*[Results of Requirement 2*
♦		♦	*calculations and assumptions]*
E.1b	**Evaluation/Conclusions/Recommendations**	**E.2b**	**Evaluation/Conclusions/Recommendations**
♦		♦	
♦	Task E.1b	♦	Task E.2b
♦	*[Evaluation and recommendations on*	♦	*[Other Issues, scepticism,*
♦	*financial performance and ET]*	♦	*proceed or not, recommendations]*

Strategic Evaluation of Project(s) (Req 3)	
E.3a	**Discussion**
♦	
♦	Task E.3a
♦	*[Results of Requirement 3 calculation*
♦	*and 2 main Issues]*
E.3b	**Evaluation/Conclusions/Recommendations**
♦	
♦	Task E.3b
♦	*[Proceed or not, ethics, scepticism, Other*
♦	*Issues, recommendations]*

Notice how the 4 Column Planning Grid is especially irrelevant to the Executive Summary: the 4 skills areas (A&UI, SP&S, AJ and C&R) are not used as column headings to this part of the markscheme so do not even form part of the marking as there are instead 2 very specific Tasks per Requirement. It would therefore be an especially bad idea to use the 4 Column Planning Grid in the Executive Summary.

---

[15] In real ICAEW markschemes, the 3 parts of the Executive Summary markscheme are presented across 2 different A4 pages (Requirement 1 and Requirement 2 on the first page and Requirement 3 on the second page) but we have condensed the 3 columns onto one page purely for ease of presentation here.

5 Requirement 1 Markscheme: a generic example

Requirement 1 markscheme (page 1 of 2)

Assimilating & Using Information	Structuring Problems & Solutions
1.1 Uses AI / EP information (report / appendix) ♦ ♦ Task 1.1 ♦ *[Results of Appendix 1 calculations* ♦ *for overall company headlines]* ♦	**1.3 Analysis of financial figure 1** ♦ ♦ Task 1.3 ♦ *[Basics for financial figure 1 – F skill]* ♦ ♦
1.2 Identifies business issues and wider context ♦ ♦ Task 1.2 ♦ *[Discuss wider context of performance]* ♦ ♦ ♦	**1.4 Analysis of financial figures 2 & 3** ♦ ♦ Task 1.4 ♦ *[Basics for financial figures 2 & 3 – F skill]* ♦ ♦
	1.5 Analysis of ET calculations[16] ♦ ♦ Task 1.5 ♦ *[Calculations for ET]* ♦ ♦

---

[16] Extra Task (ACA Simplified terminology). Do not use this term on your exam script – we use it only for teaching purposes. The ET concept will be explained in detail in chapter 8.

Requirement 1 markscheme (page 2 of 2)

Applying Judgement	Conclusions & Recommendations
1.6[17] **Evaluate financial figure 1**	**1.9** **Draws conclusions (under a heading)**
◆	◆
◆ Task 1.6	◆ Task 1.9
◆ *[Reasons and pattern spotting for*	◆ *[Conclusions **with figures**]*
◆ *financial figure 1 – RP skills]*	◆
◆	◆
◆	
1.7 **Evaluate financial figures 2 and 3**	**1.10** **Makes recommendations**
◆	◆
◆ Task 1.7	◆ Task 1.10
◆ *[Reasons and pattern spotting for*	◆ *[Commercial Recommendations]*
◆ *financial figures 2 & 3 – RP skills]*	◆
◆	◆
◆	◆
1.8 **Evaluation of ET**	
◆	
◆ Task 1.8	
◆ *[Narrative on ET]*	
◆	
◆	
◆	

---

[17] Tasks X.6 and X.7 are the least predictable of all Tasks in every Requirement and often cause excessive concern for students (given the fact that there are 8 other easier Tasks in each Requirement: you only need to pass 5 of these Tasks, by scoring 3 or more diamonds in any 5 Tasks/Boxes). We analyse Tasks X.6 and X.7 in our detailed chapters on Requirements 1, 2 and 3: see chapters 8, 9 and 10, respectively. Always check the question wording for insight into what may be required.

6   Requirement 2 Markscheme: a generic example

Requirement 2 markscheme (page 1 of 2)

Assimilating & Using Information	Structuring Problems & Solutions
2.1 Uses AI / EP information (report) ♦ ♦ Task 2.1 ♦ *[Outline contract terms & strategic and* ♦ *operational context OR model inputs]* ♦	**2.3 Calculation 1** ♦ ♦ Task 2.3 ♦ *[Correct results for calculation 1* ♦ *with brief discussion]*
2.2 Describes business issues and wider context ♦ ♦ Task 2.2 ♦ *[Discuss wider context and R1 linkages* ♦ *regarding relevant revenue stream]* ♦ ♦	**2.4 Calculation 2 or an extra narrative task** ♦ ♦ Task 2.4 ♦ *[Correct results for calculation 2 with* ♦ *brief discussion OR Other Issue]* **2.5 Assumptions 1 (basics)** ♦ ♦ Task 2.5 ♦ *[Query and evaluate assumptions]* ♦ ♦ ♦

Box 2.1 has been slightly variable in recent examinations. It may require narrative points on the proposed project terms and how these connect to the "Strategic and Operational Context" (SOC) of the company or, alternatively, the marks may simply be for identifying the correct inputs to the financial model. In the latter case, the marks in Box 2.1 will be awarded based on your Appendix 2 and so you do not require any specific narrative in your Requirement 2 report section to obtain credit. However, if Box 2.1 is not allocated to inputs, you will have to do some writing on the alternative areas mentioned here (project terms and strategic and operational context) within Requirement 2 to obtain the marks. In this book, we therefore prudently assume that Box 2.1 is not allocated to inputs (since if it is then you will obtain the marks anyway provided that the marker can determine your use of inputs in Appendix 2 and your SOC points may well attract credit in other Boxes instead).

You will note that Box 2.4 can be either a second calculation or an additional narrative task: in recent examinations from 2014 onwards, only TT (November 2016) and PL (July 2017) involved a second calculation so it is more likely that you will be asked to perform some narrative analysis for this Box.

Please ensure that you read the client/partner request on the first page of the Exam Paper very carefully **to identify the additional narrative Tasks required**. Many students appear to miss such requests, perhaps on the basis that they think of Requirement 2 as a "numerical one" – this is not really true.

Take your time and read the question wording carefully, perhaps drawing lines or using numbers to split the question wording out into the various different narrative things that you need to do in order to ensure that nothing is missed.

Requirement 2 markscheme (page 2 of 2)

Applying Judgement		Conclusions & Recommendations	
2.6[18] **Financial analysis or narrative issue**		**2.9** **Draws conclusions (under a heading)**	
♦		♦	
♦	Task 2.6	♦	Task 2.9
♦	*[Discussion of calculation*	♦	*[Conclusions **with figures**]*
♦	*results or Other Issue]*	♦	
♦		♦	
♦			
2.7 **Narrative task**		**2.10** **Makes recommendations**	
♦		♦	
♦	Task 2.7	♦	Task 2.10
♦	*[Other Issue (may be ethics)]*	♦	*[Commercial Recommendations]*
♦		♦	
♦		♦	
♦		♦	
2.8 **Assumptions 2 (extension) or ethics**			
♦			
♦	Task 2.8		
♦	*[Assumptions extension point OR*		
♦	*ethics recommendations]*		
♦			
♦			

In recent examinations such as TT (November 2016) and PL (July 2017), there have been 2 Boxes for ethics in Requirement 2, meaning that there was only 1 Box for Assumptions. Our generic markscheme above is therefore based on an examination **without an ethics element in Requirement 2**. However, if ethics is tested then Box 2.4 and Box 2.8 are likely to be allocated to ethics. As such, you may wish to prioritise ethics (2 Boxes) over Assumptions (1 Box) in such an examination. In Bux (July 2016) and R4 (November 2017), there were 2 Boxes for Assumptions and 2 Boxes for Ethics so it is also possible for there to be an equal balance between Assumptions and Ethics.

---

[18] Tasks X.6 and X.7 are the least predictable of all Tasks in every Requirement and often cause excessive concern for students (given the fact that there are 8 other easier Tasks in each Requirement: you only need to pass 5 of these Tasks, by scoring 3 or more diamonds in any 5 Tasks/Boxes). We analyse Tasks X.6 and X.7 in our detailed chapters on Requirements 1, 2 and 3: see chapters 8, 9 and 10, respectively. Always check the question wording for insight into what may be required.

7 Requirement 3 Markscheme: a generic example

Requirement 3 markscheme (page 1 of 2)

Assimilating & Using Information		Structuring Problems & Solutions	
3.1	**Uses AI / EP information** ♦ ♦ Task 3.1 ♦ *[Outline contract terms & strategic and* ♦ *operational context OR calculations]* ♦ ♦	**3.3**	**Discussion/explanation – Issue 1** ♦ ♦ Task 3.3 ♦ *[Discussion of Issue 1]* ♦ ♦ ♦
3.2	**Describes business issues and wider context** ♦ ♦ Task 3.2 ♦ *[Discuss wider context and R1 linkages* ♦ *regarding relevant revenue stream]* ♦ ♦	**3.4**	**Discussion/explanation – Issue 2** ♦ ♦ Task 3.4 ♦ *[Discussion of Issue 2]* ♦ ♦
		3.5	**Ethics – Issue and Impact** ♦ ♦ Task 3.5 ♦ *[Ethics – Issue and Impact]* ♦ ♦

In a similar manner to Requirement 2 (see above), Box 3.1 has been slightly variable in recent examinations. In most examinations, the marks are awarded for calculations but in PL (July 2017), the marks were narrative in nature and required a discussion of the customer, contract terms and other "Strategic and Operational Context" factors. On the assumption that most candidates will attempt and discuss the calculations in Requirement 3 anyway, in this book we will prudently assume that Box 3.1 is not allocated to calculations so that you spend a bit of time hedging your bets in case Box 3.1 is for narrative points – this will be less obvious from the question wording than the necessity of performing calculations in Requirement 3 and hence we apply our prudent approach to ensure that you at least try to obtain this type of Box 3.1 mark. If it then turns out that Box 3.1 is for calculations, you will have focused on the correct alternative area anyway from the more obviously needed numerical work that you will perform based on what is explicitly requested by the question wording: your SOC points should then hopefully score elsewhere in the markscheme in later Boxes.

Requirement 3 markscheme (page 2 of 2)

	Applying Judgement		Conclusions & Recommendations
3.6[19]	**Evaluation 1**	**3.9**	**Draws conclusions under a heading**
♦		♦	
♦	Task 3.6	♦	Task 3.9
♦	[Further Issue 1 points	♦	[Conclusions **with figures**]
♦	or Other Issue]*	♦	
♦		♦	
♦			
3.7	**Evaluation 2**	**3.10**	**Makes recommendations**
♦		♦	
♦	Task 3.7	♦	Task 3.10
♦	[Further Issue 2 points	♦	[Commercial Recommendations]
♦	or Other Issue]*	♦	
♦		♦	
♦		♦	
3.8	**Ethics – Recommendations**		
♦			
♦	Task 3.8		
♦	[Ethics – Recommendations]		
♦			
♦			
♦			

* As explained in more detail in chapter 10, you must read the Requirement 3 question wording very carefully to determine whether there are any additional specific issues to look at ("Other Issues"): if not, then Box 3.6 and 3.7 are likely to contain further points on the same topics as Issue 1 and Issue 2 which are rewarded in Boxes 3.3 and 3.4.

8   Appendices and Main Report (AMR) Markscheme: a generic example

	Appendices		Main Report
AMR.1	**Appendices R1: Content and style**	**AMR.3**	**Report: Structure**
♦	Tabulated and mix of £ and %	♦	Sufficient appropriate headings
♦	Figures as required by question – figure 1	♦	Appropriate use of paragraphs/sentences
♦	Figures as required by question – figure 2	♦	Legible
♦	Figures as required by question – figure 3 & ET	♦	Correctly numbered pages
AMR.2	**Appendices R2: Content and style**	**AMR.4**	**Report: Style and language**
♦	Well-presented and numbers clearly derived	♦	Appropriate disclaimer (if an external report)
♦	Attempts aspect 1 of model	♦	Suitable formal language
♦	Attempts aspect 2 of model	♦	Tactful/ethical comments
♦	Attempts aspect 3 of model	♦	Reasonable spelling/grammar

---

[19] Tasks X.6 and X.7 are the least predictable of all Tasks in every Requirement and often cause excessive concern for students (given the fact that there are 8 other easier Tasks in each Requirement: you only need to pass 5 of these Tasks, by scoring 3 or more diamonds in any 5 Tasks/Boxes). We analyse Tasks X.6 and X.7 in our detailed chapters on Requirements 1, 2 and 3: see chapters 8, 9 and 10, respectively. Always check the question wording for insight into what may be required.

Please note that here we can be very confident indeed on the text contained in the AMR Boxes – the text for Boxes AMR.3 and AMR.4 is literally identical from sitting to sitting (with the exception of a possible adjustment to the first mark in Box AMR.4 if the report is an internal report – see below) whilst the text in Boxes AMR.1 and AMR.2 is extremely similar each time.

Regarding the first mark in Box AMR.4, most of the time, you will work on behalf of an external advisory firm which assists the Case Study business as a client. This will require you to write a brief disclaimer to protect your firm and you must also ensure that the report is in the name of your instructing partner. However, if (and this is quite rare) the report is an **internal** report (i.e. your character is a member of the company's staff or an accountant on secondment from a practice firm) then no disclaimer is required but the report should be stated to be written by the individual instructing you on the first page of the Exam Paper (probably your manager as referred to in the Advance Information). See the Bux (July 2016) markscheme for an example of this.

It will be very clear from the Advance Information what type of report is needed because the Advance Information will explain your character's role in detail. You will therefore know how to deal with this matter well in advance of examination day.

9 A reminder to finish with

You are strongly advised to spend some time learning the 40 Tasks outlined in the above generic overview: the time spent on this will be some of the most efficient preparation time that you can spend ahead of the exam because it will ensure that you stay focused on the correct areas in your report.

Although it may look like a lot of information to comprehend at this stage, our taught course students usually have no problems in **learning and committing to memory the 10 Tasks per Requirement**: as an exercise, in our final classroom session we often ask students to write down or state all 40 Tasks from memory. The fact that many of our course students have correctly internalised all 40 Tasks means that they leave the course with an "instinctive" knowledge of what to write about so they automatically focus on the right areas and can reduce their planning/note-checking time accordingly.

We stress the value of instinct because instinct works quickly and is reliable under pressure: these are both useful qualities in a time-pressured exam such as Case.

> **Student 1 says:** *"This is a really fundamental chapter, which gives you a good overview of what you are trying to do. Along with chapters 7 to 10, I would regard this as a key chapter – do not just gloss over it because it is near the start and relatively easy."*

> **Student 2 says:** *"Read this chapter, then come back to it often when you've finished the book because it is important to keep an overall idea in your head about what the skills areas being tested are. To pass Case you need to address the various typical skills areas and your preparation needs to involve developing your understanding of how these will always be tested."*

Chapter 5   Our 40 Task Method™

Learning Points

After reading this chapter, you must be able to:

1. understand the probable content of each of the 40 Boxes/Tasks
2. appreciate the patterns in terms of the mark-scoring points in the post-2011 exams
3. develop a "mind's eye" view of the Boxes so that you have an "instinctive" notion of what to do

---

1   A simpler version of the markscheme

In the previous chapter, we outlined a generic Case Study markscheme in full detail, including the correct number of marks or "diamonds" per Box and showing you how to summarise each Box as it is presented spatially on the page. We provided this presentation to introduce you to the 40 Tasks and also to help you analyse the patterns in past paper markschemes more effectively.

In this chapter, we will revisit the markscheme (sorry but we have to: you cannot prepare for Case without constantly referring to the markscheme!) through a condensed version which hopefully will give you another way to try to commit the skills/Tasks to memory.

2   No need to be a hero/heroine

In any Case Study examination, the marker will be attempting to "**match**" the points that you have made against the approved points in the 40 Boxes or Tasks on the markscheme.

Some Boxes are easy, some Boxes are hard and some Boxes are very hard. Whichever way, every Box/Task represents a single and independent opportunity to pass one of the 5 Boxes that you need to pass each Requirement and therefore to pass the exam as a whole. (Remember that you also need to pass 3 of the 6 available Boxes in the Executive Summary.)[20]

Regardless of the number of potential answers allowed in a Box (i.e. between 4 and 7 possible points) and regardless of the intrinsic difficulty of the skill being tested, your aim is always to score **3** points or diamonds – this gets you a passing grade for that Box.

---

[20] ICAEW applies a complex algorithm to your raw score to determine your final grade, once the performance of all candidates at a particular sitting of the examination has been determined. This can have the effect of boosting your raw score so a script which does not have 3 passing Boxes in the Executive Summary plus 5 passing Boxes in each of the 3 Requirements **can** be sufficient to pass in hard exam sittings. However, as this aspect is entirely outside your control, we think that it is advisable for you to "play it safe" and ensure that you achieve passing grades in at least half of the Boxes available in each Requirement (i.e. 3 Boxes in the Executive Summary and 5 Boxes in each of the 3 Requirements): this will guarantee that you pass the exam, regardless of the performance of other students.

Passing a Box which is difficult does not gain any more credit than passing a Box which is easy: either way, you have 1 of the 5 passing Boxes that you need. This is why we say there is no need to be a hero/heroine by trying to pass everything (or spending too long on harder Boxes).

Since the number of diamonds required to pass a Box is fixed but the number of permissible points within a Box is variable, you should try to develop a sense of which Boxes require a lower "strike rate" in terms of the number of points you should write to stand a good chance of scoring the 3 points that you need – for example, a Box with 6 possibilities (as is common in Requirement 3) would appear to be an easier opportunity than a Box with only 4 possibilities (as is now the rule in the Executive Summary: see chapter 7).

Boxes with higher percentage "strike rates" such as in the Executive Summary (where you need to score 3 diamonds out of the 4 available) will require you to have a **very** clear idea of what you need to be doing because there are fewer acceptable ways of gaining the marks.

It is therefore very helpful to analyse the patterns within the Boxes/Tasks in the markschemes from July 2012 onwards. You are advised to look into these patterns in your own time but this chapter will get you started and provide some initial guidance: later chapters will then provide further details.

3   The 40 Task Method™ – Executive Summary Tasks

Task	Nature of Task	Advice	Difficulty
Executive Summary			
Task E.1a	Review Requirement 1 Appendix figures	Be methodical but stick to key figures. Refer to Exam Paper question to focus on the right areas	Easy
Task E.1b	Evaluation and recommendations on financial performance and ET	Evaluate R1 performance and comment and recommend on the ET	Medium
Task E.2a	Results of Requirement 2 calculations and assumptions	State the results (but not the workings) of all calculations. Query assumptions	Easy
Task E.2b	Other Issues, scepticism, proceed or not, recommendations	Review other issues. Apply scepticism. Decide whether or not to proceed.	Easy
Task E.3a	Results of Requirement 3 calculation and 2 main issues	No specific advice other than previous column	Easy
Task E.3b	Proceed or not, ethics, scepticism, Other Issues, recommendations	No specific advice other than previous column	Easy

4   The 40 Task Method™ – Requirement 1 Tasks

Task	Nature of Task	Advice	Difficulty
Requirement 1			
Task 1.1	Results of Appendix 1 calculations for overall company headlines		Easy
Task 1.2	Discuss wider context of performance	Connect the performance of the Case Study company to industry benchmarks and trends	Medium
Task 1.3	Basics for financial figure 1 – F skill	State your numerical findings regarding figure 1 (probably revenue – check Exam Paper)	Easy
Task 1.4	Basics for financial figures 2 & 3 – F skill	State your numerical findings regarding figures 2 & 3 (check Exam Paper)	Easy
Task 1.5	Calculations for ET	State your numerical findings regarding the ET	Hard
Task 1.6	Reasons and pattern spotting for financial figure 1 – RP skills	Briefly explain reasons for changes. Do some pattern spotting – compare to PY revenue growth	Medium
Task 1.7	Reasons and pattern spotting for financial figures 2 & 3 – RP skills	Briefly explain reasons for changes. Do some pattern spotting – Δ revenue v Δ GP, Δ GP v Δ OP	Medium
Task 1.8	Narrative on ET	Impact, mitigation, ethics, causes, other issues	Easy
Task 1.9	Conclusions **with figures**	Easy to pass: refer back to Exam Paper question and offer conclusion on each key aspect	Easy
Task 1.10	Commercial Recommendations	Hard to pass: many plausible Recommendations but only some will be on the markscheme	Hard

5 The 40 Task Method™ – Requirement 2 Tasks

Task	Nature of Task	Advice	Difficulty
Requirement 2			
Task 2.1	Outline contract terms & strategic and operational context OR model inputs	Review terms such as fees, costs, duration. Refer to named companies and individuals. OR inputs*	Easy
Task 2.2	Discuss wider context and R1 linkages regarding relevant revenue stream	Link to any industry benchmarks and trends. Review R1 performance of revenue stream involved in the project	Medium
Task 2.3	Correct results for calculation 1 with brief discussion	State and briefly comment on results for first calculation	Hard
Task 2.4**	Correct results for calculation 2 with brief discussion OR Other Issue	You will need to judge whether there is a second calculation and whether sensitivity is needed and also whether this is a narrative Box instead	Hard
Task 2.5	Query and evaluate assumptions	Work through each input and criticise it by referring to Advance Information or Exam Paper. Add a second evaluative point per assumption	Easy
Task 2.6	Discussion of calculation results or Other Issue	Discuss significance of calculation results or follow our Task 2.7 advice if clearly a further narrative Task to consider	Hard
Task 2.7	Other Issue (may be ethics)	Use 8 core practical areas to generate ideas – see chapter 11 on the 8 core areas. Read Exam Paper to identify issue	Hard
Task 2.8	Assumptions extension point OR ethics recommendations	Look for a second point to extend the criticism of the input and consider practical impact. Alternatively, Box may relate to ethics.	Easy
Task 2.9	Conclusions **with figures**	Easy to pass: refer back to Exam Paper question and offer conclusion on each key aspect	Easy
Task 2.10	Commercial Recommendations	More patterns are evident in past papers than Requirement 1 Recommendations so not as hard to pass	Medium

* See previous chapter – Task 2.1 can sometimes be awarded simply for identifying the correct inputs to your Requirement 2 calculation but in other examinations it requires some narrative discussion of the contractual terms and other Strategic and Operational Context (SOC) points.

** See page 45 – Task 2.4 may become a narrative Task if there is a specific request in the Requirement 2 wording.

6   The 40 Task Method™ – Requirement 3 Tasks

Task	Nature of Task	Advice	Difficulty
Requirement 3			
Task 3.1	Outline contract terms & strategic and operational context OR calculations	Same advice as Task 2.1	Medium
Task 3.2	Discuss wider context and R1 linkages regarding relevant revenue stream	Same advice as Task 2.2	Medium
Task 3.3	Discussion of Issue 1	Check Exam Paper carefully to identify issue	Easy
Task 3.4	Discussion of Issue 2	Check Exam Paper carefully to identify issue	Easy
Task 3.5	Ethics – Issue and Impact	Identify at least 2 ethical problems and their impact	Easy
Task 3.6	Further Issue 1 points or Other Issue	May involve more points on Issue 1, or alternatively a different Task – check Exam Paper	Hard
Task 3.7	Further Issue 2 points or Other Issue	May involve more points on Issue 2, or alternatively a different Task – check Exam Paper	Hard
Task 3.8	Ethics – Recommendations	Explain how the client should deal with the ethics issues	Easy
Task 3.9	Conclusions **with figures**	Easy to pass: refer back to Exam Paper question and offer conclusion on each key aspect	Easy
Task 3.10	Commercial Recommendations	More patterns are evident in past papers than Requirement 1 Recommendations so not as hard to pass	Medium

* See previous chapter – Task 3.1 can sometimes be awarded simply for elements of your Requirement 3 calculations but in other examinations it requires some narrative discussion of the contractual terms and other strategic and operational context points.

7   Learn your Tasks!

We strongly recommend that you put some time into studying our Task summary in this chapter. Try to learn both the **generic** nature of each Task and also our more **specific** advice on how to create points that will fulfil these Tasks[21].

There is plenty more exciting material to come but this chapter really is key.

We cannot really emphasise this enough – put simply, understanding the above tables really is **the key** to **decoding** the markscheme and "Cracking Case".

---

[21] We provide much more information on how to address each Task in the remainder of this book – here our aim is merely to give you an overview.

8   **Comments from students**

> ***Student 1 says:*** *"It really is worth putting some time into studying the generic content of the 40 Tasks and then into understanding how to fulfil these Tasks with specific comments which are likely to be on the markscheme. In my resit, I messed up my timing on Requirement 1 and overran (very bad strategy). I was seriously short of time by the time I got to Requirement 3 and had to completely scrap any planning at all. However, due to all my practice, I had a sort of mental image in my mind of the 10 Tasks relating to Requirement 3, so I "instinctively" knew what areas to cover and wrote these straight into my Exam Paper without any planning (although, again, I do not recommend this). If you end up in this kind of emergency situation, knowledge of the **Tasks**, rather than the **4 Columns**, is what you really need to be able to work very quickly and get the marks.*
>
> *Obviously I don't advocate messing up your timing, but what I am saying is that if you learn the Tasks well then you will instinctively know what you are supposed to be doing. I'm pretty sure I got a really good spread over the Boxes for Requirement 3 after all, even without planning. If you mess up your timing, you need to "just know" what to do for the Boxes. Overall, I think that investing time in looking at the 40 Tasks saved me in the resit."*

> ***Student 2 says:*** *"In my resit, I took in the markscheme to the previous exam from which I had deleted the specific elements to the markscheme and had left on the generics. I essentially had a quick-and-dirty 40 Tasks approach. This I found invaluable to trigger the "put the obvious basic answer down" reflex in my brain. With enough practice you can start to "feel" how the Case moulds to the markscheme (and not vice versa). You get a sense of what you always need to do and it becomes a much less open exam. That's good, considering that the markscheme is not open – overall, neither you nor the marker have much scope to wander off track. Knowing the 40 Task method will keep you on the right lines and you are then guaranteed to pick up the marks."*

Chapter 6   Planning & Reminder Sheets

Learning Points

After reading this chapter, you must be able to:

1. understand the format and presentation of our Planning & Reminder Sheets
2. understand the importance of personalising the Sheets to your own requirements
3. understand the benefits (and risks) of adding annotations to the Sheets, based on the live Advance Information
4. appreciate why we have not simply used the term "Planning Sheets" to refer to this resource

In this chapter, we present our popular Planning & Reminder Sheets. This resource has been gradually developed and refined based on our classroom tuition courses for the last 12 sittings of the Case Study examination in order to provide you with very quick reference reminders of what to do in every section of your report.

We recommend that you create your own version of our Planning & Reminder Sheets, personalising our general approach to your own specific requirements. Please then practise all of your mock exam attempts using your own personalised Planning & Reminder Sheets. You should then of course take your personalised sheets into your real examination so that you do not forget to do something when under time pressure.

Please note that, for copyright reasons, we are not able to provide you with an electronic version of the Planning & Reminder Sheets so we kindly ask not to be emailed with any such request. It really will not take long at all for you to create your own personalised version and the design and creation process will help you to remember the points involved.

As we have not yet reviewed in detail how to tackle each Requirement (see chapters 7 to 10 for our advice here), some of the points in the Planning & Reminder Sheets will not make sense to you at this stage. However, we wanted to introduce the Planning & Reminder Sheets fairly early on in the book so that you have something to refer back to throughout your study of the remainder of the book – this will allow you to flick back and immediately check how you are going to be reminded in the examination to do the things that we will suggest in chapters 7 to 10.

1   Format

We include in bold in the lefthand column of our Planning & Reminder Sheets our recommended report section headings. The righthand column then includes reminders of what to do in the corresponding report section.

We do not have 10 report section headings for each Requirement: although there are 10 Boxes per Requirement on the markscheme, some of your report sections will deal with more than 1 Box at once.

Please do use the precise report section headings that we have specified. They have been carefully developed to ensure that you stay focused on the right areas. We always have students on our tuition courses who decide to go their own way and use different section headings (or none at all) but they almost always end up missing key points if they do so.

We have had to compress our sheets to fit the margins of this book, which has a smaller printable area than A4 paper. **We therefore recommend that you use these pages as a model for the creation of your own Planning & Reminder Sheets** (preferably on a computer as this will allow you to create clear sheets and will make it easier to make changes for your own personal needs: it will also allow you to add key points from the live Advance Information when this has been released – see below on how to do so).

Please note that we provide 2 versions of the Planning & Reminder Sheets for Requirement 2: 1 version if ethics **is** tested and 1 version if ethics **is not** tested. Although ethics has been tested in Requirement 2 in every examination from July 2016 onwards, if ethics were for some reason not tested in Requirement 2 then we would suggest a slightly different approach to your answer and so we have provided a set of Planning & Reminder Sheets to deal with this unlikely possibility. We only provide a single version of our Requirement 2 Executive Summary Planning & Reminder Sheets (which assume that ethics **is** tested in Requirement 2 as this seems likely) but obviously if ethics is not tested in Requirement 2 then you do not need any Recommendations on ethics in your Requirement 2 Executive Summary section.

We only provide a single version of the Planning & Reminder Sheets for Requirement 3 because ethics has been tested in every Requirement 3 markscheme since 2012 and we do not think there is any real possibility of ethics not being tested in Requirement 3. However, should this happen, then simply drop section 3.D on ethics as described in our Planning & Reminder Sheets.

2 Personalisation and addition of July 2018 Advance Information points

We do strongly recommend that you personalise our planning sheets so that you have reminders of things which you personally struggle to do well. However, please ensure that you finalise your sheets at least a week before the exam so that you can apply your sheets in a few mock exam attempts and therefore become familiar with how the sheets work via practical work – try to avoid tweaking and adjusting all the way through to exam day because if you do so then you will not be familiar with the sheets in the real exam and this could lead to a loss of time and/or confidence.

Once the July 2018 Advance Information has been released and you have had time to read and understand the business (perhaps after sitting our mock exams), we recommend that you try to add reminders into the right hand column of your sheets so that you do not forget to include these useful exam-specific points (whilst remembering never to force in Advance Information points just for the sake of mentioning the point: always apply your judgement to determine whether the point is actually relevant to the specific question set by the examination wording). We encourage you to add these

57

points to the Planning & Reminder Sheets (or even better to your own customised versions of the sheets), rather than keeping a separate set of notes, so that you have everything in an easily accessible place on exam day.

Having advised you to add these reminders, please do not go to the opposite extreme and have too many Advance Information points to squeeze in – your first source of information must always be the **Exam Paper** as it is highly unlikely that something stated in the Exam Paper will not figure on the markscheme whereas with the Advance Information there is always the possibility that you could be unlucky and include a valid point that is not on the markscheme in the end. Therefore, play the percentages game and always **fully utilise the Exam Paper first**.

Our live mock exams provide an ideal way to get used to your planning approach, within the context of 5 full exam-standard papers which focus on the live Advance Information. See our website at **www.acasimplifiedcase.com** and page 6 of this book for further details on our popular live mock exam pack.

3   Annotation of "Key" sections

We have placed a * mark next to the report sections which we believe are relatively easier and therefore sections which you must do well to have a good chance of passing the exam.

Doing a good job of these sections every time will give you a great foundation to pass the exam because it will give you a very good shot at passing 4 or 5 markscheme Boxes: remember that you must pass at least 5 Boxes to be able to pass a Requirement (you must pass at least 3 Boxes in the Executive Summary).

We encourage you to attempt all Tasks/Boxes but without a decent attempt at the key or * sections it will be much harder to pass.

4   Mainly reminders

Naming our sheets as "Planning & **Reminder** Sheets" is a conscious decision – we have not simply named them "Planning Sheets" for a very specific reason: we want you to reduce your planning time to the minimum possible. We have therefore not left you huge amounts of space for your own planning notes in the lefthand column. With sufficient practice, you should be able to rely mainly on the righthand column for reminders of what to do and some report sections (particularly your Conclusions and Recommendations sections, but others as well) can be written directly into your answer sheets without doing any planning at all (see chapter 15 for further details on this point): just use the reminders to help you generate ideas and write your ideas straight into your answer sheets. This will save a huge amount of time.

For this reason, we do not want you to think of these sheets as just "Planning" sheets – they are actually intended to be mainly "**Reminder**" sheets.

58

We will now present the July 2018 version of our Planning & Reminder Sheets. As mentioned, many aspects of the sheets will become much clearer once you have read chapters 7 to 10 so do not worry for now – just try to get a general feel for how the sheets work. Once again, due to formatting limitations, our sheets are somewhat compressed so **please create your own personalised sheets** (perhaps in a landscape format) to ensure that you have sufficient working space available.

Remember that if a section is marked with an asterisk (*) then this is a section which is relatively easier and therefore a section which must be done well if you are to have a good chance of passing the examination.

Executive Summary Planning & Reminder Sheet (Page 1 of 1)

Section 1 – Review of performance to XX XXX 2018

-Comments **AND** figures for key figures requested
-Overall **AND** stream comments/figures each time
-Revenue mix comment **AND** figures
-GP £k **AND** GPM%
-Comment **AND** figure for cash
-Key drivers of performance
-ET comments **AND** figures
-Fundamental points facing the business: loss-making (or close to)? overdraft?
-Specific Recommendations may be needed: consider the "Big Picture", take a **prudent** and **transparent** approach

Commercial Recommendations
[Company name] should:
-
-
-
-
-
-

-Aim for "Big Picture" points
-**Recommendations on ET x4**
-Other Recommendations x2

Section 2 – [add SHORT title]

-Comments **AND** figures for each calculation result (quote each year)
-Evaluate result – **significant** revenue/GP/GPM%?
-Query 2 inputs
-2 points on each Other Issue(s)
-Comment on each ethics issue (if ethics tested)
-State whether to **proceed or not**
-What is the right thing to do?

Commercial Recommendations
[Company name] should:
-
-

Ethics Recommendations [if required]
[Company name] should:
-
-

-Aim for "Big Picture" points

-Check facts, discuss, consider response, legal advice, not be associated, brief points on any possible positive outcomes e.g. opportunity in line with company ethos

Section 3 – [add SHORT title]

-Refer to results of calculation and **significance**
-Query data for calculation: source, evidence
-2 balanced comments on Issue 1 (e.g. one benefit, one risk)
-2 balanced comments on Issue 2 (e.g. one benefit, one risk)
-2 points on each Other Issue(s) if needed
-Comment on each ethics issue
-State whether to **proceed or not**
-Link to business plan/risk review or similar from AI?
-What is the right thing to do?

Commercial Recommendations
[Company name] should:
-
-

Ethics Recommendations [if required]
[Company name] should:
-
-

-Aim for "Big Picture" points

-Check facts, discuss, consider response, legal advice, not be associated, brief points on any possible positive outcomes e.g. opportunity in line with company ethos

60

Requirement 1 Planning & Reminder Sheets (Page 1 of 2)

Section 1   **Review of performance to XX XXX 2018**

1.A Context of Performance (5 ideas)
Show the **impact** of your points on Appendix 1 results

Do not **repeat** any points that you make later in your answer

-Use AI but **also use Exam Paper**
-Mention key industry £ or % figures from the AI (e.g. market growth forecasts)
-Consider industry trends and consumer preferences
-Level of competition in the market per AI
-Mention Brexit but with client-specific explanation of **impact**
-Only use **broader context points that relate to the performance of the company**

CONSIDER LEAVING SPACE AND WRITING THIS SECTION LAST SO THAT YOU GET A CHANCE TO BE REMINDED OF USEFUL POINTS FROM DOING THE OTHER PARTS OF THE REQUIREMENT – THIS WILL ALSO PREVENT YOU REPEATING POINTS THAT MAY BE NEEDED ELSEWHERE

*1.B [Financial figure 1] (6+ ideas with a number, reason and pattern-spotting point for each idea)

Consider discussing revenue mix in section 1.C to force you to connect movements in the revenue mix with changes in GPM%

-Quote App 1 numbers **thoroughly**
-Check question paper to determine the figure needed
-Use **Exam Paper** and AI to explain
-Comment and figures on **overall** and **stream** revenue performance
-Compare to **PY** revenue growth
-**Pattern spotting**: highest, lowest, all up, all down
-**Brief** suggestions on **reasons**
-Descriptive words: marginally, significantly, impressively with **every** movement figure

*1.C [Financial figures 2 & 3] (4+ ideas for each figure with a number, reason and pattern-spotting point for each idea)

Discuss revenue mix in this section to connect it to changes in GPM%

Quote margins such as GPM%/OPM%

-Quote App 1 numbers **thoroughly**
-Check question paper to determine the figures needed
-Use **Exam Paper** and AI to explain
-**Pattern spotting**: highest, lowest, all up, all down,
-**Brief** suggestions on **reasons**
-Descriptive words: marginally, significantly, impressively with **every** movement figure
-Comment on impact of changes **in revenue mix** on GPM%
-Comment on change in GP v change in revenue **and** change in GP v change in OP
-Comment on quality of cost control implied by relative move in revenue v GP (direct cost control) and GP v OP (overhead cost control)

Note – our references to revenue, GP, GPM%, OP and OPM% are for illustrative purposes only – always check the precise question wording of your own exam to determine which areas to discuss.

Requirement 1 Planning & Reminder Sheets (Page 2 of 2)

1.D [ET] (6 ideas)

-Results of calcs but also **narrative**
-**Significance** of figures – high amount of profit? Turn profit to loss? Close to break even?
-Apply **PSS** framework– practical, strategic, scepticism points
-Consider impact: reputation, **cashflows, financial impact**
-Stop and think: is it actually a big problem? Does it have to happen?*

[ET] Recommendations (4 bullet points)
-check information, discuss/negotiate

DO NOT LOSE TIME ON THE ET
If the ET appears not to involve any calculations at all, add more points to your accounts analysis in 1.B & 1.C as ET may be worth only 1 Box

[* assuming that the ET relates to a problem facing the business]

*1.E Conclusions (6 ideas)

-**Always include supporting figures**
-Comment on financial figure 1
-Comment on financial figures 2 and 3
-Refer to **size/significance** of changes
-2 comments (not Recommendations) on significance of ET **with figures**
-Cash position **with figure**

Ensure you cover all the above points – this section lays the foundation for the Executive Summary

1.F Commercial Recommendations (7+ bullet points)
[COMPANY NAME] should:
-
-
-
-
-
-
-

•Review costs
•Investigate/assess reasons for problems
•Diversify
•Further analysis of key figures/streams
•Continue to promote strong stream
•Improve performance of weak stream
•Consider cash position

Remember to include ET Recommendations in 1.D and state non-ethics Recommendations in 1.F

62

Requirement 2 Planning & Reminder Sheets (Page 1 of 2) assuming ethics NOT tested

Section 2   **[Add a BRIEF title]**

2.A Strategic and Operational Context (5 ideas)
Points must be relevant to the specific project – show the **impact** of the background points – section may be worth 2 Boxes

Do not **repeat** any points that you make later in your answer

-R1 linkages: cash, stream margin, stream growth rate, capacity
-Use AI but **also use Exam Paper**
-Outline contract terms and what we know about people, companies, competitors involved
-**Consider** industry trends but only use relevant **project-specific** points

CONSIDER LEAVING SPACE AND WRITING THIS SECTION LAST SO THAT YOU GET A CHANCE TO BE REMINDED OF USEFUL POINTS FROM DOING THE OTHER PARTS OF THE REQUIREMENT – THIS WILL ALSO PREVENT YOU REPEATING POINTS THAT MAY BE NEEDED ELSEWHERE

-AI points:-

2.B Results of financial model (3 ideas)
Ensure you compare the result to the existing company or stream revenue/GP and comment on relative **significance**

Should be a **short** section: figures, significance, move on!

-Clearly present numerical **results** of calculations
-Do **NOT** discuss inputs or workings (not needed) – marker will look at Appendix 2
-Brief narrative on **significance**: % of current revenue or GP, years with losses or profits, accounting profit v cash flows, sensitivity
-Re-read Exam Paper to identify figures requested: **present all of these**
-Present results **by year and** in **total**
-R1 linkages if not done in 2.A: cash, stream margin, stream growth rate, capacity

*2.C Evaluation of assumptions (6 assumptions with extensions, 3-4 scepticism points)

Assumptions   Scepticism

Query assumptions
-Query each **given** input, **comparing to the AI** wherever possible
-Give **reasons** why a figure appears high/low, using AI if possible
-Think how to get the second Assumptions point – practical points?

Scepticism
-Always say "Changes in assumptions will affect the estimated revenue/profit"
-Forecast too short/too long
-Look for bias in the source(s)
-Query the **methodology**
-Look for unknowns
-Is this right for the business?
-Project start date: too soon/too late
-Capacity and cashflow concerns

If no ethics, almost certainly 2 Boxes for assumptions …

THE BEST ASSUMPTIONS POINTS WILL ALLOW YOU TO MAKE **COMPARISONS** TO FIGURES IN THE ADVANCE INFORMATION OR EXAM PAPER – MAKE SURE YOU **COMMENT** ON THE COMPARISON

Requirement 2 Planning & Reminder Sheets (Page 2 of 2) assuming ethics NOT tested

2.D [Other Issues[1]] (5+ ideas per issue)

-This section covers 2 or 3 Boxes
-**Read exam question carefully** to understand requirements
-May be practical, strategic or further detail on the calculations
-Use Exam Paper as much as possible
-Consider following points if relevant:
●Management time
●Costs
●Timing
●Staffing
●Capacity
●Operational disruption

*2.E Conclusions (6 ideas)

-Comments **AND** figures for each calculation result (quote each year)
-Evaluate result – **significant** revenue/GP/GPM%?
-Query 2 inputs
-2 points on each Other Issue(s)
-State whether to **proceed or not**

Ensure you cover all the above points – this section lays the foundation for the Executive Summary

2.F Commercial Recommendations (7+ <u>bullet points</u>)
[COMPANY NAME] should:
●
●
●
●
●
●
●

●Check inputs
●Market research
●Staffing
●Capacity
●Due diligence on new partners
●Discuss/Negotiate T&Cs
●Consider alternatives

---

[1] Try to avoid using the heading "Other Issues" – replace this generic label with something more specific once the subject matter is known from your specific Exam Paper. **Always read the Exam Paper question wording very carefully to identify the narrative Tasks required.**

64

Requirement 2 Planning & Reminder Sheets (Page 1 of 2) assuming ethics IS tested

Section 2   **[Add a BRIEF title]**

2.A Strategic and Operational Context (5 ideas)
Points must be relevant to the specific project – show the **impact** of the background points – section may be worth 2 Boxes

Do not **repeat** any points that you make later in your answer

-R1 linkages: cash, stream margin, stream growth rate, capacity
-Use AI but **also use Exam Paper**
-Outline contract terms and what we know about people, companies, competitors involved
-**Consider** industry trends but only use relevant **project-specific** points

CONSIDER LEAVING SPACE AND WRITING THIS SECTION LAST SO THAT YOU GET A CHANCE TO BE REMINDED OF USEFUL POINTS FROM DOING THE OTHER PARTS OF THE REQUIREMENT – THIS WILL ALSO PREVENT YOU REPEATING POINTS THAT MAY BE NEEDED ELSEWHERE

-AI points:-

2.B Results of financial model (3 ideas)
Ensure you compare the result to the existing company or stream revenue/GP and comment on relative **significance**

Should be a **short** section: figures, significance, move on!

-Clearly present numerical **results** of calculations
-Do **NOT** discuss inputs or workings (not needed) – marker will look at Appendix 2
-Brief narrative on **significance**: % of current revenue or GP, years with losses or profits, accounting profit v cash flows, sensitivity
-Re-read Exam Paper to identify figures requested: **present all of these**
-Present results **by year and** in **total**
-R1 linkages if not done in 2.A: cash, stream margin, stream growth rate, capacity

*2.C Evaluation of assumptions (5 assumptions with extensions, 3-4 scepticism points)

Assumptions   Scepticism

Query assumptions
-Query each **given** input, **comparing to the AI** wherever possible
-Give **reasons** why a figure appears high/low, using AI if possible
-Think how to get the second Assumptions point – practical points?

Scepticism
-Always say "Changes in assumptions will affect the estimated revenue/profit"
-Forecast too short/too long
-Look for bias in the source(s)
-Query the **methodology**
-Look for unknowns
-Is this right for the business?
-Project start date: too soon/too late
-Capacity and cashflow concerns

THE BEST ASSUMPTIONS POINTS WILL ALLOW YOU TO MAKE **COMPARISONS** TO FIGURES IN THE ADVANCE INFORMATION OR EXAM PAPER – MAKE SURE YOU **COMMENT** ON THE COMPARISON

65

Requirement 2 Planning & Reminder Sheets (Page 2 of 2) assuming ethics IS tested

*2.D Ethics and Ethics Recommendations

-Issue: why is the issue unethical? What principles have been broken?
-Impact on business
-Mention **reputation**
-Brief points on any possible positive outcomes e.g. opportunity in line with company ethos

Ethics Recommendations (use **bullet points**)
6-7 points

-**Check facts**, **discuss**, consider **response** (legal advice, social media)
-Not become involved/find alternative

2.E [Other Issues[1]] (5+ ideas per issue)

-This section covers 2 or 3 Boxes
-**Read exam question carefully** to understand requirements
-May be practical, strategic or further detail on the calculations
-Use Exam Paper as much as possible
-Consider following points if relevant:
•Management time
•Costs
•Timing
•Staffing
•Capacity
•Operational disruption

*2.F Conclusions (6 ideas)

-Comments **AND** figures for each calculation result (quote each year)
-Evaluate result – **significant** revenue/GP/GPM%?
-Query 2 inputs
-2 points on each Other Issue(s)
-Comment on each ethics issue
-State whether to **proceed or not**

Ensure you cover all the above points – this section lays the foundation for the Executive Summary

2.G Commercial Recommendations (7+ bullet points)
[COMPANY NAME] should:
•
•
•
•
•
•
•

•Check inputs
•Market research
•Staffing
•Capacity
•Due diligence on new partners
•Discuss/Negotiate T&Cs
•Consider alternatives

[1] Try to avoid using the heading "Other Issues" – replace this generic label with something more specific once the subject matter is known from your specific Exam Paper. **Always read the Exam Paper question wording very carefully to identify the narrative Tasks required.**

66

Requirement 3 Planning & Reminder Sheets (Page 1 of 2)

Section 3   [Add a BRIEF title]

3.A Strategic and Operational Context (5 ideas)
Points must be relevant to the specific project – show the
impact of the background points

This section may be worth 2 Boxes

-R1 linkages: cash, stream margin, stream growth rate, capacity
-Use AI but **also use Exam Paper**
-Outline contract terms and what we know about people, companies, competitors involved
-**Consider** industry trends but only use relevant **project-specific** points
-Link to business plan/risk review or similar from AI?

CONSIDER LEAVING SPACE AND WRITING THIS SECTION
LAST SO THAT YOU GET A CHANCE TO BE REMINDED OF
USEFUL POINTS FROM DOING THE OTHER PARTS OF THE
REQUIREMENT – THIS WILL ALSO PREVENT YOU
REPEATING POINTS THAT MAY BE NEEDED ELSEWHERE

-AI points:-

*3.B [Issue 1] (6+ ideas (add more if no 3.E needed)

Note – recent exams have allocated 2 Boxes **solely** to
discussion of financial issues so make sure you have
plenty of points on financial issues, including the calculation

-Keep it brief and simple
-Aim for range, not depth
-Prioritise **Exam Paper** over AI
- … but think if there is a specific AI Exhibit to refer back to (business plan/risk review?)
-Comment on **significance** of calc result (or put in 3.C)
-Brief scepticism: e.g. source, missing info

*3.C [Issue 2] (6+ ideas (add more if no 3.E needed)

-Keep it brief and simple
-Aim for range, not depth
-Prioritise **Exam Paper** over AI
- … but think if there is a specific AI Exhibit to refer back to (business plan/risk review?)
-Comment on **significance** of calc result (or put in 3.B)
-Brief scepticism: e.g. source, missing info

*3.D Ethics and Ethics Recommendations

-Issue: why is the issue unethical? What principles have been broken?
-Impact on business
-Mention **reputation**
-Brief points on any possible positive outcomes e.g. opportunity in line with company ethos

Recommendations (use **bullet points**)
6-7 points

-**Check facts**, **discuss**, consider **response** (legal advice, social media)
-Not become involved/find alternative

Requirement 3 Planning & Reminder Sheets (Page 2 of 2)

3.E [Other Issues[1] – if needed] (6 ideas per issue)

CAUTION: If the Exam Paper has not asked for any specific other matters to address then **just add more Issue 1 and Issue 2 points to sections 3.B and 3.C and scrap this section**

Use Exam Paper as much as possible in this section

-**Read exam question carefully** to understand requirements
-May be practical, strategic or further detail on the calculations
-Consider following points if relevant:
●Management time
●Costs
●Timing
●Staffing
●Capacity
●Operational disruption

***3.F Conclusions (6 ideas)**

-Refer to results of calculation and consider **significance**
-Query data for calculation: source, evidence
-2 balanced comments on Issue 1 (e.g. one benefit, one risk)
-2 balanced comments on Issue 2 (e.g. one benefit, one risk)
-2 points on each Other Issue(s) if needed
-Comment on each ethics issue
-State whether to **proceed or not**
-Link to business plan/risk review or similar from AI?

Ensure you cover all the above points – this section lays the foundation for the Executive Summary

3.G Commercial Recommendations (7+ <u>bullet points</u>)
[COMPANY NAME] should:
●
●
●
●
●
●
●

●Check inputs
●Market research
●Staffing
●Capacity
●Due diligence on new partners
●Discuss/Negotiate T&Cs
●Consider alternatives

[1] Try to avoid using the heading "Other Issues" – replace this generic label with something more specific once the subject matter is known from your specific Exam Paper. **Always read the Exam Paper question wording very carefully to identify the narrative Tasks required.**

68

Chapter 7   How to Write a Good Executive Summary

Learning Points

After reading this chapter, you must be able to:

1. understand what is, and what is not, required in a good Executive Summary
2. appreciate that repeating yourself without any new ideas is in no way a bad thing
3. recognise the characteristics of a bad Executive Summary
4. understand how the examiners have recently increased the difficulty of the Executive Summary

---

1   Back for good?

At the 2016 ICAEW Tutor Conference, the Case Study examiners set out their plans to remove the Executive Summary from the Case Study with effect from the July 2017 sitting. The examiners had reached the conclusion that the Executive Summary does not add a huge amount of value to the Case Study because the points which must be made to pass the Executive Summary are very similar to the points which have already been made in the Conclusions section to each Requirement.

However, following stakeholder consultation, it was decided to retain the Executive Summary in 2017 and future years. This implies that the imperfections noted by the examiners remain in place – use this to your advantage!

At the same time, it is important to be aware of another comment made at the 2016 ICAEW Tutor Conference – in the interim period before the removal of the Executive Summary (as originally planned), the examiners would gently increase the difficulty of the Executive Summary in order to combat the "lack of value-added" characteristic which it was hoped would be replaced entirely from 2017.

Although the Executive Summary will remain in place for the foreseeable future, we would expect the gentle increase in difficulty (which was started in the 2015 examination papers) will remain in place in order to push this section towards adding more value: this will be the best that the examiners can do to attempt to deal with the known limitations of this part of the examination process.

As explained in further detail in chapter 14, the gentle increase in difficulty is evident from the nature of the markscheme which now has only 4 diamonds available for each Executive Summary markscheme Box (a decrease on the 5 diamonds available in earlier examinations): you must therefore now achieve 3 out of the 4 marks available to pass each Executive Summary Box, which is quite a high "strike rate".

The increase in difficulty is also evident from the ICAEW Marks Feedback forms that we have received from students who failed the examination (not with us) at the November 2015 and subsequent sittings. The Marks Feedback form shows the performance within each element of the examination. We have noticed a considerable number of students who passed all elements of the examination **except the Executive Summary** but who have been failed overall. We have also noticed a number of students

69

who generally achieved good grades in their main report but then had a very low mark in the Executive Summary: whilst these students did fail one other element as well, usually that was a marginal fail whereas the Executive Summary fail is by a larger margin.

We therefore strongly advise you not to disrespect the Executive Summary. Please take some time to review the markschemes **for the examinations held from July 2015 onwards** to see the kinds of points that are now rewarded. Please then also carefully review this chapter, chapter 14 and our Planning & Reminder Sheets presented in chapter 6.

Please do not "fall at the final hurdle" by not incorporating enough time into your preparations to understand how to do the Executive Summary well. No matter how good the rest of your report may be, if you do not pass the Executive Summary, you **will** be failed by the ICAEW examiners.

2 Do not worry about repeating yourself

The Executive Summary is a **summary** – it is not an opportunity to bring in ideas that you did not mention in the main report. You should not worry about the Executive Summary being a mere repetition of what you say in the main report: in fact, repeating your Conclusions from each section of your report is something you should be actively trying to do (see discussion below). It is the role of a summary to repeat points, just in a briefer form, so do not worry if your Executive Summary does not do anything new.

Please also note that the Executive Summary uses "open marking" for the vast majority of its marks – this means that as long as you are offering a conclusion in the right area, then you will get the mark regardless of the specific point made. For example, **anything** sensible on revenue (with a supporting figure) will get a mark in the Executive Summary even if your calculation regarding revenue is incorrect and/or your narrative remark is wrong. Whilst there has been some limited introduction of more specific points which must be matched precisely in the Executive Summary (see below), most marks remain of an "open" or "anything will do" nature and are hence not too difficult to obtain, provided that you are organised and conclude on the correct areas (following our Planning & Reminder Sheets carefully: see chapter 6).

Student 1 stated that he felt that his LL Executive Summary was not adding anything to the report so he tried to develop some further added value advice. After failing and getting a marks breakdown from ICAEW, he gained 5% of the 15% available for the Executive Summary, and this caused him to fail the exam.

Learn from this story – it is another example of good business ideas but very poor appreciation of the markscheme.

Our biggest tip for the Executive Summary is therefore as follows:

> **First make sure you have good Conclusions to each Requirement, thoroughly following the reminders in our Planning & Reminder Sheets, and then heavily (but not exclusively) base your Executive Summary on those Conclusions points.**

70

You may be able to trim down your write up of those same points in the Executive Summary so that you end up with a shorter version of your Conclusions … but **do not leave anything important out** when re-writing the points into the Executive Summary.

If you ensure that you "pull through" your Conclusions points and then add in a couple more "fundamental" or "Big Picture" points (see below) for safety then you should have a good chance of passing the Executive Summary.

It may appear that such an Executive Summary does not add a huge amount of value to your report but this is just how the marking works. The fact that the Executive Summary has been **very** actively considered for removal by the Case Study examiners provides an important implication for the **present** nature of the examination – it confirms that "pulling through" is what the Executive Summary is all about right now (hence the wish of the examiners to change the nature of this part of the examination).

3   Write your Executive Summary as you go

We strongly recommend that you write up the Executive Summary as you go along[22] rather than leaving everything to the end. This way, if your time management goes wrong and your last Requirement (and related Executive Summary element) is rushed then at least you will have 2 elements of the Executive Summary which were done properly earlier in the examination before things went wrong: if you are lucky, this may be enough to pass the Executive Summary even if your final element of the Executive Summary is rushed and weak (or even not attempted at all[23]).

On the other hand, if you leave all of the Executive Summary to the end and your timing is poor, then the **whole** of the Executive Summary will be affected and you will be likely to fail the examination.

---

[22] By this we mean that you complete the main report section of a Requirement and immediately write up the Executive Summary element for that Requirement, and then start the main report section of your next Requirement and write up the Executive Summary element for that Requirement, and so on. The alternative is to leave **all** parts of the Executive Summary until the end, which we believe is less efficient than simply writing up straight after you have done the relevant Requirement.

[23] After discussing with our taught course students following recent Case Study examinations, we know that in the unfortunate event that you only complete 2 sections of your Executive Summary due to poor time management, it is still definitely possible to pass the exam. We have regularly received panicked emails from students in this position straight after the exam only to see them pass the exam easily with a high score. We definitely do not recommend this approach but do not give up if it happens.

4   The 2 Box split – differing levels of difficulty

The Executive Summary ICAEW markscheme does not make any reference to the 4 fundamental Case Study skills areas[24], unlike the markscheme for the 3 main Requirements which uses the 4 skills areas as column headings (hence the approach adopted by some tuition providers of using planning sheets with 4 columns).

Instead, there are just 2 Boxes per Requirement. This is a particularly strong reason to avoid the 4 Column Planning Grid approach in your Executive Summary: the 4 columns/skills areas are not even used in the ES markscheme!

The first Executive Summary Box for each Requirement essentially requires you to "pull through" your Conclusions from the end of each Requirement. This is because both your main Requirement Conclusions (Tasks 1.9, 2.9 and 3.9) and Executive Summary Tasks E.1a, E.2a and E.3a all relate to the same skill – concluding on the main points that the client task asked you to analyse, and including **figures** to support your statements. Therefore, your Conclusions in each Requirement should be written after you have gone back to re-read the precise wording of the Exam Paper to identify the main topics you have to report on. You can then repeat these Conclusions in the relevant Executive Summary section.

For example, if Requirement 1 asks you to analyse "Revenue, Gross Profit and branch performance" then you must conclude **separately and with figures** on all 3 of these issues in your Conclusions section to Requirement 1 in order to pass Task 1.9. If Requirement 2 asks you to "Calculate gross profit under both scenarios and comment on any other issues that X Ltd should consider" then, again, you have 3 issues you absolutely must mention in your Conclusions to Requirement 2 in order to pass Task 2.9: gross profit scenario 1, gross profit scenario 2 and other issues. The same approach should be used for Requirement 3.

Relatedly, if you have been asked to model 2 different years in Requirement 2, then make sure you quote your results for **both** years (i.e. not just a single total): for example, PL (July 2017) required candidates to quote figures for both years (even if incorrect) to obtain a single mark.

Provided that you have done this correctly, Tasks E.1a, E.2a and E.3a should be very straightforward because you are just pulling through your Conclusions remarks from the main body of the report. Doing well in these 3 Boxes could get you a pass in the Executive Summary already and **none of the tweaks recently made by the examiners to gently increase the difficulty of the Executive Summary** (see above) **relate to these 3 Boxes**. This shows the importance of good Conclusions: typically, when we mark or review a paper we can tell that if the Executive Summary is weak then the Conclusions section to each Requirement will probably be weak when we come to read those sections later in the paper.

The second Box/Task for each Requirement element in the Executive Summary is less predictable and thus harder to achieve: it has been made even harder in the recent examinations as it may now

---

[24] i.e. Assimilating & Using Information, Structuring Problems & Solutions, Applying Judgement and Conclusions & Recommendations

contain specific points that you would not necessarily have included in the Conclusions to each Requirement elsewhere in your report.

As a general summary, the second Task/Box tends to be more of an open evaluation Box. However, this Box will **sometimes** have an easy mark for "practical recommendations": we can term this mark "easy" because, unlike Recommendations in the main report, **if** this mark is available in the Executive Summary it does not matter what specific recommendations you make as long as you make **some** recommendations.

More recently, this easy mark has tended to be replaced with a more specific recommendation which you must **match** (particularly in Requirement 1 where specific recommendations in relation to the ET are quite common). This is part of the gentle increase in difficulty discussed by the examiners due to their unhappiness with the current nature of the Executive Summary in Case Study (see above). We therefore recommend that you think about the most fundamental issues resulting from the ET and mention this in your Requirement 1 Executive Summary. You should then think in a similar manner about the "fundamental" or "Big Picture" points in Requirements 2 and 3 as we would expect a greater emphasis on matching specific points in these parts of the Executive Summary: this will continue to provide the gentle increase in difficulty which the examiners have talked about.

As the gentle increase in difficulty officially began in 2015, we strongly recommend that you look at the Executive Summary markschemes **for all examinations from July 2015 onwards**.

For this second Executive Summary Box/Task for each Requirement, it is also advisable to make some scepticism and ethics remarks/recommendations. For Requirement 1, the content of the second Executive Summary Box/Task is less predictable but discussing the extent of the changes in the financial figures, the impact on cash and the impact of this on the business in the longer term would appear to be advisable. Again, please do ensure that you offer a clear recommendation on the ET as well, as this has been rewarded in the last couple of examinations.

We therefore have 2 fundamentally different types of Task to do for each Requirement in the Executive Summary: the first **easy** Box for **repeating** the headline requests and the second **harder** Box for **evaluation**. This is another example where the 4 Column Planning Grid is highly misleading because it suggests that the Executive Summary requires the same breadth of points as elsewhere in the report – it does not: rather, you need to focus on doing 2 specific things (**repetition** and **evaluation**, respectively).

Relatedly, we often see students who include a separate Conclusions **heading** within their Executive Summary. This is not needed: your Executive Summary already **is** a set of Conclusions so no heading is needed. The only heading needed is for your **Commercial Recommendations** (and for your **Ethics Recommendations** in Requirements 2 and/or 3, if these are required): the rest of the Executive Summary can just be written up as a single section without any specific headings. Once again, the final column in the 4 Column Planning Grid, which suggests that Conclusions & Recommendations (as one of the 4 fundamental Case Study skills) are needed in the Executive Summary, is misleading here.

We have allowed for this in our Planning & Reminder Sheets: you will notice that we do not include any headings other than Commercial Recommendations and Ethical Recommendations in our

Executive Summary Planning & Reminder Sheets section – this is entirely intentional as we want you to save time wherever possible and section headings are not needed in the Executive Summary.

5 Inclusion of Requirement 1 and 2 figures – be thorough

We find that a lot of students only mention a few Requirement 1 figures in the Executive Summary, perhaps because they believe that the reader can just go and check the full information in the main report. However, there will be marks for a figure with supportive narrative for **each** of the headline financial figures requested by the client/your partner on the first page of the Exam Paper. Therefore, it pays to be thorough in your presentation of the figures: narrative alone, even if on the right accounts captions, will not be sufficient (and likewise figures with no narrative analysis will also lead to marks being dropped).

Note that the Executive Summary markscheme works by giving you a mark simply for mentioning a figure in support of each key Requirement 1 financial figure: you do not have to have the **correct** answer. All that matters is that you have made an attempt to offer the client **a** figure on the headline areas[25], one which matches your Requirement 1 and related Appendix (whether right or wrong).

Similarly, in the Requirement 2 Executive Summary section, there are marks for quoting the result(s) of your financial modelling exercise. Here you will again get the mark for quoting your result whether or not you have "the" right figure.

So when quoting your Requirement 2 figure, be confident and present it as the correct answer (even if you are feeling uncertain) before then querying the model assumptions to pick up other marks in the first Requirement 2 Executive Summary markscheme Box. We are aware that some students deliberately do not refer to the results of their calculation in their Requirement 2 Executive Summary for fear that they may look stupid if they have the wrong result. However, you will get the mark for quoting your numerical answer even if it is wrong so do not make the mistake of holding back on inclusion of a figure that you know to be wrong – just state it and query the assumptions as there is no point in penalising yourself twice for not getting a tricky calculation correct.

Make sure you quote headline figures for **each** calculation (e.g. year 1 and year 2 if you have done a 2 year forecast or option 1 and 2 if there are different sets of assumptions) – there will generally be 2 separate diamonds in Box E.2a for each of these results and therefore ensure that you are **thorough** so that you pick up both easy marks.

---

[25] To determine what the "headline" figures (our term for tutorial purposes, not official examination terminology) are, always go back to the question wording on the Requirements page of the exam paper where the client or your partner sets out the tasks required: if there is any reference to a figure such as revenue, gross profit, operating profit etc in the wording for Requirement 1 on the Requirements page of the Exam Paper then you must conclude on this in the Conclusions in the main report and, consequently, in the Executive Summary as well.

6 Executive Summary – a reminder of the 6 Tasks

As a basic overview, what you need to do in each Box is as follows:

E.1a*	Review Requirement 1 Appendix figures
E.1b	Evaluation and recommendations on financial performance and ET
E.2a*	Results of Requirement 2 calculations and assumptions
E.2b	Other Issues, scepticism, proceed or not, recommendations
E.3a*	Results of Requirement 3 calculation and 2 main issues
E.3b*	Proceed or not, ethics, scepticism[26], Other Issues, recommendations

We have used a * symbol to indicate the easier Boxes which will normally need to form the basis of a pass.

As explained above, your best guidance is to go back to the first page of the Exam Paper which sets out the client requests and pick out the key requests/question wording within each Requirement. Your Executive Summary must have something to say on **all** of these requests – if what you say can potentially be supported with a figure then you must include a figure or you may not get the mark. Put another way, if it is possible to quote a figure, then do so!

As also discussed above, Task E.1a, E.2a and E.3a essentially "pull through" your Conclusions from each Requirement. It therefore follows that your Conclusions in the main report should follow the same approach of looking back carefully at the question wording and commenting on the main requests – this is all you need to do for Conclusions Tasks 1.9, 2.9 and 3.9.

Picking up these Conclusions Boxes by following our Planning & Reminder Sheets and concentrating on the correct headline points will not only allow you to pass a valuable Box in each Requirement: it will also allow you to quickly draft 3 passing Boxes in your Executive Summary, allowing you to pass that element as well.

On the other hand, get your Conclusions Tasks wrong in the main report and you are very likely to end up with a poor quality Executive Summary.

---

[26] As discussed in much more detail in chapter 12, the amount of credit for scepticism in Requirement 3 has gradually fallen from sitting to sitting in recent examinations yet is still rewarded in some Requirement 3 Executive Summary markschemes such as PL (July 2017). For this reason, we have retained our reference to scepticism in our summary of what to do for Box E.3b but please be careful not to overdo this skills area, either in Requirement 3 itself or in the Executive Summary for Requirement 3.

> **Student 1 says:** *"When I sat LL, I wanted to make my Executive Summary interesting and I used it as an opportunity to include some good points which I had not had time to get into the main report – basically, some strategy ideas and a bit more numerical analysis. When I failed and looked at the markscheme I was sickened – all I needed to do was repeat what I had said in the main report, it really was a case of just **repeating myself**! There was absolutely no credit at all for any new ideas. So just stick to the basics and summarise what you have already done, they seem to like it that way."*

> **Student 2 says:** *"I approach the Executive Summary by literally ticking off every Requirement and ensuring that I addressed every issue in it. This forces you to go back to the question wording and focus on what they want in the Executive Summary. If you try to write the Executive Summary without referring back to the question, there is a danger that you will get distracted into other interesting issues but not what will get the marks.*
>
> *The trick to an Executive Summary is simple – repetition. If it feels boring to write then chances are you are doing the right thing. There is no credit for introducing any new ideas in the Executive Summary. A tip to help with this is to go back to the wording of the Requirements when you are doing the Executive Summary – quickly cover each of the items in the Requirement then Recommend and Conclude. Job done."*

Chapter 8   How to Write a Good Requirement 1

Learning Points

After reading this chapter, you must be able to:

1. appreciate that Requirement 1 is theoretically the easiest Requirement
2. recognise the risk of losing time by trying to do too much in this "comfortable" Requirement
3. recognise the importance of "drilling" Requirement 1 in the run up to the exam
4. understand the 10 Tasks and 6 report sections you should use

---

1   Chapter overview

This chapter is in 2 parts. In the first part of the chapter (sections 2 to 5 inclusive), we review some general advice for Requirement 1. In the second part of the chapter (from section 6 onwards), we work through each of the 10 typical Requirement 1 markscheme Boxes and provide you with advice specific to each Box. Although the chapter is relatively long, please do ensure that you read all sections carefully.

2   The ET (Extra Task[27])

Many students appear to remain unaware that there will normally[28] be 2 Boxes/Tasks available for an additional and less predictable element of Requirement 1 than the straightforward, P&L-focused accounts analysis: we call this extra, unpredictable element the ET or "Extra Task". The ET was first introduced when the new markscheme was brought in for the LL exam in July 2012, presumably to make Requirement 1 a bit less easy to prepare in advance.

Almost every exam since the LL exam has required students to do something "extra" and less predictable than just to analyse the changes in 2 sets of management accounts. Make sure you allow for this in your planning and timing but do not spend too long on this element of Requirement 1.

Unless you are specifically asked to do so (as you were, **exceptionally**, in Palate (July 2013)), do **not** make any adjustment to allow for the ET **before** preparing your general Requirement 1 figures for revenue or gross profit etc – this would require you to amend the management accounts and make all sorts of adjustments which would be too complicated in the time available. To date, no examination other than Palate has required the accounts to be adjusted before beginning your analysis.

---

[27] The term "ET" is an ACA Simplified term which we have developed only for tutorial purposes and for use within our Planning & Reminder Sheets. You should not use this term within your own examination script.

[28] Exceptionally, PL (July 2017) only contained one explicit Box for the ET. However, most of the Recommendations Box (Box 1.10) was reserved for Recommendations in relation to the ET so in this sense there was still plenty of credit. Please see the Foreword to the November 2017 edition of *Cracking Case™* which we have produced in Appendix 3 to this book.

77

Therefore **unless you are given very clear instructions otherwise,** in the main part of your Requirement 1 answer, and in your calculations for revenue changes, GP changes etc, just ignore the ET and then in a **separate** section of your report briefly state how your principal results **might** be affected if the ET is included.

There is normally no need to engage in highly detailed calculations for the ET. You are looking at a maximum of 6 or so calculation lines for Box 1.5, together with some practical narrative advice (which can be achieved even with incorrect ET calculations) for Box 1.8. Other than the ET Boxes, there will be 8 other Requirement 1 Boxes which remain relatively easy to achieve – so do not panic!

A partial exception to the above occurred in the Bod (July 2015) examination. In this examination, the Advance Information clearly indicated that Bod monitored its performance using 3 different KPIs. In the examination, the ET involved analysis of just one of these KPIs (KPI 3) rather than an additional "new project" or "disaster"-style calculation. In this sense, the Bod ET could (and should) have been pre-prepared by practising how to calculate the relevant KPI quickly **and** preparing how to explain any changes in KPI performance.

In our tuition sessions for the Bod examination we advised all our students that KPIs would definitely be tested in the examination and therefore we included testing of all 3 KPIs as part of the financial analysis in Requirement 1 in almost all of our 5 mock exams on Bod. We then included a **further** additional ET in the traditional "new project" or "disaster" style. During the tuition phase, students commented that this created a very time-pressured Requirement 1 and so it was pleasing to see that the examiners recognised this danger and therefore chose not to set an additional ET over and above the KPI analysis.

Whilst the Bod Requirement 1 was clearly a very good opportunity to score well (and quickly) in a relatively easy ET which did not contain anything that could not be rehearsed beforehand, we would expect most examinations to take a more difficult and unpredictable line, particularly if there are no KPIs or similar company-specific financial information. Therefore, please be prudent in your preparations and timing and assume that the ET calculation will generally be less predictable than in Bod. (Having said this, the Bux (July 2016) examination also contained an ET based on further numerical analysis rather than a project- or problem-appraisal so there are some signs that the ET is being made easier. From the Bux Advance Information, there was a definite hint that this might happen from the fact that extensive non-accounting financial information specific to Bux's trade as a publishing company was provided – we commented during our tuition sessions that there must have been a reason why so much of this material was included, and there was! Therefore if you see a detailed discussion of KPIs or similar "non-accounting" financial information in your set of Advance Information then there is a good chance that it may be relevant to Requirement 1 as the ET.)

The PL (July 2017) examination was highly unusual in having no numerical element at all to the ET and therefore only 1 Box was allocated to the ET in the markscheme. We hope that this lack of ET calculations will continue … but somehow we doubt that all candidates will be so lucky (and we note that R4 (November 2017) did have a numerical element, albeit one that was not too difficult)! It should be noted that whilst there was only 1 explicit Box on the ET in the PL markscheme, most of the recommendations in Box 1.10 related to the ET: usually such points would form the second ET narrative Box so in this sense there were, in a way, still 2 Boxes on the ET in this examination.

3 Requirement 1: the most predictable Requirement … but getting harder

Requirement 1 involves review of financial performance, with a focus on the P&L. This Requirement is therefore, for most students, the easiest element of the paper. Although it is obviously good to have a section you will be confident with, be aware of the risk that the easy nature of this Requirement creates: do not spend too long on this element of the exam just because you are so comfortable with the general skill of analysing the numerical aspects of management accounts. **A classic way of failing the exam is to try to do too good a job of Requirement 1** in an attempt to impress from the start or, alternatively, to try to compensate for a lack of confidence in Requirement 2 and 3 by writing and doing too much in this first part of the paper. If you use up too much time, then such an attempt to impress the examiner will be self-defeating when you end up not finishing your script as a whole.

Generally Requirement 1 will ask you to discuss revenue, gross profit and one further key financial matter. We term these the 3 "financial figures". You need be able to do 2 things in your Requirement 1 analysis of these figures: (1) provide some brief **reasons** for changes in the financial figures and (2) spot **patterns** in how the financial figures have moved, both compared to each other and compared to the prior year: for example, have all costs increased or is there only one cost that has increased? Did this year's revenue growth rate beat last year's growth rate? How does the change in revenue mix between products/streams with different margins influence the company's overall gross profit margin? Pattern points like these may seem obvious from your calculations but make sure you **explicitly** state them in your narrative to pick up evaluation marks.

As another example, is there only one revenue stream which has performed badly? If so, say this and compare it to the other streams and the prior year, with some brief reasons for the weak performance. This is what we mean by "**pattern spotting**", a skill which is very important for Boxes/Tasks 1.6 and 1.7.

After reading the Advance Information you should have a pretty good idea of which financial figures could be tested so you should use this to your advantage by preparing **explanations** for why each of these variables may have gone up or down: also start thinking about what possible **patterns** you could be required to spot. We do not know what the information in the Exam Paper will reveal but it is almost certain that the change will either be up or down[29], so you can do some meaningful preparation here. **If you can combine this with as much use as possible of the relevant narrative information in the Exam Paper**, you will be off to a great start[30].

Note that neither the November 2014 (RS) nor November 2015 (CC) Exam Papers provided any information on "events during the year" – instead, all the Exam Paper information for Requirement 1 focused on the ET only. This meant that students could only provide reason points from the Advance Information. Whilst at present this does appear to be a technique restricted to the November sitting, you should prepare yourself well for both eventualities: a Requirement 1 with lots of new narrative information to react to on the day (the usual approach) or a Requirement 1 with no new narrative

---

[29] It is possible that the figure could remain virtually unchanged but this is quite rare. If so, make a brief comment and say whether this is surprising or not e.g. it may be odd if rent has remained unchanged despite an increase in the use of facilities.
[30] As always, it obviously makes sense to do some preparation from the Advance Information but do not go too far and end up with complex points that you force into your answer regardless of whether these are relevant. **Always prioritise the information in the Exam Paper and use this as much as possible**: it is highly unlikely that points based on the information in the Exam Paper will **not** figure on the markscheme but you could be unlucky with respect to points from the Advance Information because there are so many valid points to choose from.

79

information to explain revenue, gross profit and other trends (the recent tendency in some November examinations).

The calculations for Requirement 1 will also be very predictable – you should attempt to drill your calculations and gain as much practice as possible in the preparation of the Appendices using example Exam Paper figures such as our pack of 5 mocks based on the live Case Study. Practice here will save you significant amounts of time to invest in other parts of the paper. We do not think it is excessive for you to practise the preparation of Appendix 1 **at least twice per day** in the final few days before the exam. You will be surprised how much time can be saved through repeated practice and if you can prepare your Appendix 1 in 15 minutes then you will have a huge advantage over other candidates who have been instructed to spend 30 minutes doing so.

We suggest that you set up a draft Appendix 1, using the figures from the Advance Information, which will become the "prior year" figures on exam day. Set this up with nice, clear formatting on the replica ICAEW exam answer pad sheet available from the Free Downloads section at **www.acasimplifiedcase.com** to give you an idea of how you will format the page on the day. Then photocopy a large number of these pre-filled sheets and use these to drill the calculations using example mock exam figures as the "current year" figures – you or colleagues could create these or, even better, you could use our live mock exams.

Although the calculations for absolute changes, percentage changes and margins are easy, you can still get much quicker with practice of your best technique, including use of the memory function on your calculator. You can probably do these calculations in your sleep outside the Exam Hall but if you suffer from the "exam day effect" and lose confidence/time, having the calculations drilled until they are automatic will really help.

In chapter 17, we outline how to prepare a draft Appendix 1 with your "prior year" (i.e. Advance Information) figures pre-filled and formatted to take into the exam with you so that you can then copy across correct figures, in the correct column for your personal formatting of Appendix 1, as one of the first things that you do in the examination (perhaps whilst attempting to calm down during the first few nervous minutes). This will give you assurance that you are pulling through the correct baseline figures and will also speed up your preparation of your Appendix 1. A final advantage of this form of preparation is that it allows you to ensure you are using a nice format, with enough columns and space for what you need to do.

When summarising your Requirement 1 results, make sure you always include 3 elements:

1. a description of the magnitude of the change using a descriptive word such as "marginally", "impressively", "significantly" – this is sometimes necessary to score some of the easier marks often found in Boxes 1.3, 1.4 and 1.5 which require both the correct figure **and** an appropriate descriptive word

2. absolute change in £k

3. percentage change (to 1 decimal place) in brackets

In other words, you will say that "revenue increased marginally by £40k (1.0%)"[31] or "GP increased significantly by £1,432k (8.9%)". You do not need to say (to take a phrasing that we very often see amongst candidates who come to retake the examination with us after failing with another provider) "revenue increased marginally by £40k which represents a change in percentage terms of 1.0%": just use brackets for the "1.0%" rather than wasting so many words!

This is the best way of guaranteeing that you definitely get the mark (since sometimes the markscheme will have a £k change figure and sometimes a % figure). Also there may be marks in the Appendices and Main Report (AMR) section at the very end of the markscheme for using a **mix** of £k and % figures.

Although we still believe that Requirement 1 is potentially the easiest Requirement there is definitely some evidence that the examiners have realised this: hence some examinations have "mixed it up" a little to make Requirement 1 harder. Examples of this include:

- **Palate** (July 2013) – candidates had to adjust the management accounts **before** doing their expected analysis of the financials: hence candidates could **not** rely on any pre-prepared changes, margins or numerical aspects. Candidates were also requested to analyse only 1 of Palate's 3 business lines rather than the expected analysis of the entire business. The ET also involved 2 Boxes on the markscheme because of the complexity of the adjustments.

- **ZM** (July 2014) – candidates had to undertake some analysis of impairment within one business stream: this calculation was, in our opinion, very time consuming and complicated for an ET and hence many candidates would probably have lost time and confidence quite early in the exam. Furthermore, a number of our taught course students were uncertain as to what was being asked in the question: again there was a request to focus on one product line but also candidates were asked to analyse the ZM business as a whole – in practice this meant that 90% of points should have been on the identified product line (Accessories) but candidates should also have analysed the other 2 product lines to some extent. As such, the wording may have made this particular Requirement 1 more challenging than normal.

- **RS** (November 2014) – no information on "events during the past year" was provided by the client so candidates were forced to rely on reason points from the Advance Information: the only Exam Paper information provided related to the ET. Candidates were also asked to analyse the whole Income Statement rather than the more normal focus on 2-3 areas such as revenue, gross profit and operating profit/cash.

- **Bod** (July 2015) – in this examination, the ET did not relate to some kind of project or problem – instead, candidates were simply asked to review performance on a specific KPI which was mentioned extensively in the Advance Information.

---

[31] We recommend that you pre-prepare a standard template sentence which incorporates all the necessary figures (changes in both £k and % terms) and the important descriptive word in a short and efficient style: then stick to similar phrasing **every time**. There are no marks for style of writing or mixing up your phrases to make the narrative more interesting to read: just stick to your same template sentence each time for maximum efficiency and to avoid carelessly leaving anything out by trying to change the sentence structure. Please see page 83 for an example of a standardised sentence structure and phrasing that you may wish to use yourself.

- **CC** (November 2015) – for a second November examination in a row, no information on "events during the past year" was provided so candidates had to use reason points based on the Advance Information only. The only Exam Paper information provided related to the ET.

- **Bux** (July 2016) – for the second July examination in a row, there was no "separate" ET – rather the ET marks were for analysing updated non-financial information i.e. KPIs and detailed statistics on book sales and author recruitment. There was therefore no need to calculate any "disaster" or "project" scenario – rather, a well-prepared candidate could have drawn on their pre-prepared analysis of the non-financial information which was clearly flagged in a particular Exhibit within the Advance Information.

- **PL** (July 2017) – in this examination, the ET did not involve any numbers at all. Instead, candidates were simply asked to review the ethical issues surrounding a problem involving the copying of the company's products by a third party. The lack of numbers caught out many students as all previous ETs had been much harder and required calculations to be performed. However, this form of narrative-only ET represents a great way to accumulate marks without having to spend any precious time on calculations. The following examination (R4 (November 2017)) returned to numerical analysis for some aspects of the ET so we unfortunately cannot conclude that Case Study ETs will now only be narrative in nature. Having said this, the numerical analysis required in R4 (November 2017) was very straightforward and there were plenty of narrative marks for other aspects of the issue so perhaps there is still some grounds for hope regarding the difficulty of the ET in future examinations …

Given these recent changes to the examination of Requirement 1, we strongly advise you not to take this Requirement for granted.

4   Requirement 1 – causes, pattern-spotting and FRP skills

As well as calculating and describing[32] the correct numerical changes (rewarded in Boxes 1.3, 1.4 and 1.5 (if 1.5 does not relate to the ET)), Requirement 1 will reward attempts to **explain** the changes and to spot **patterns** in the changes: these more difficult remarks are rewarded in the "Applying Judgement" Boxes (Box 1.6 and 1.7).

For example, in the LT (November 2013) exam, Box 1.6 contained marks for the following kinds of evaluation:

---

[32] Be thorough here – we frequently see scripts where the student has calculated a figure in his or her Appendix 1 only to fail to mention this in the main report: a typical example would be to mention the gross profit margin of only one revenue stream even though margins for all streams were calculated in Appendix 1. This means you are throwing away easy analysis marks, for which you have done most of the work.

1. Revenue growth lower than the prior year (with figures)
2. Revenue growth driven by volume increase
3. Analysis of revenue per store
4. Closure during a seasonal period (Christmas)
5. Online sales main driver of revenue growth
6. Cost increases not passed onto customers

Looking at these points, we would say that points 2, 4 and 5 are looking at the **reasons** for changes in revenue whilst points 1, 3 and 6 involve **pattern-spotting**: comparisons to the prior year (such as last year's revenue growth rate), comparisons between stores and comparison of revenue changes to cost changes.

As a general rule, we find that students tend to emphasise **reasons** over **patterns** and after discussing this with students, it certainly appears that many other tuition providers are neglecting to mention that marks are available for **patterns**. Please review some recent markschemes to see why we strongly believe that the Box 1.6 and Box 1.7 marks will not just be for **reasons**.

Be **thorough** even if you think the points are boring or obvious – Requirement 1 is the least creative requirement so these are very easy marks and will either be based on pre-prepared analysis of the Advance Information (i.e. your stock answers for revenue up or revenue down, etc) or using points made in the Exam Paper information (better than using the Advance Information as it is more likely the point will be on the markscheme). You can easily drop marks if you do not work through each financial figure properly. Most candidates will be getting most of these marks so you need to do well here to stay in the game.

Make sure you do use the Exam Paper information extensively for this Requirement, as in all Requirements – there will be a lot of irrelevant information in the Advance Information but treat **every** word of the Exam Paper as extremely relevant and potentially very valuable, given that normally most Exam Paper points will be somewhere on the markscheme (which is not the case for the Advance Information, given how long that information is). Make a good impression on the marker at the start by incorporating plenty of Exam Paper points into your answer, showing that you are not relying totally on a pre-prepared approach and are instead capable of thinking on your feet.

Try to use a "2 sentence-3 point" paragraph approach. In your first sentence you state a **fact with a descriptive word** and **reason** – in your second sentence you look for the **pattern**:

> "Revenue from product sales has increased significantly **[DESCRIPTIVE WORD]** by £1,263k (12.0%) **[FACT]** due to competitors leaving the market **[REASON]**. This growth rate is significantly higher than the prior year growth of 6% **[PATTERN]**."

Following this approach you can organise your Requirement 1 narrative around the mnemonic **FRP**: **f**act, **r**eason, **p**attern.

Here the first sentence gets all the marks for numbers and also for explanation: it also includes a brief evaluation and descriptive word "significantly". Hence it covers the **F** and **R** skills very well. The second sentence then tries to get some judgement or deeper issues in, attempting to cover the pattern-spotting or **P** skill.

5   Requirement 1 – overview of Tasks

As an overview (see the remainder of this chapter for further details), the Tasks in Requirement 1 are[33]:

1.1*	Results of Appendix 1 calculations for overall company headlines
1.2	Discuss wider context of performance
1.3*	Basics for financial figure 1 (e.g. revenue (Note)) – F skill
1.4*	Basics for financial figures 2 & 3 (e.g. gross profit and operating profit (Note)) – F skill
1.5	Calculations for ET
1.6	Reasons and pattern spotting for financial figure 1 – RP skills
1.7	Reasons and pattern spotting for financial figures 2 & 3 – RP skills
1.8	Narrative on ET
1.9*	Conclusions **with figures**
1.10	Commercial Recommendations

Note – Our mention of the topics revenue, gross profit and operating profit is based on likelihood and not certainty – you must prepare yourself for testing of other areas and always respond to the question set on the Exam Paper: do not be tempted to write about what you had hoped would be on the Exam Paper.

We have used a * symbol to indicate the easier Tasks which will normally need to form the basis of a pass.

As per our Planning & Reminder Sheets (see chapter 6), we recommend that you apply the following headings for your report sections:

---

[33] There may be minor differences in the order in which the precise Tasks are presented in the markscheme in particular Case Study exams. Nevertheless, the insight that there will always be 10 core Tasks still applies, despite these minor variances.

Requirement 1	Recommended Report Section Headings	
1.A	Context of Performance	[Task 1.2]
1.B	[Financial figure 1]	[Tasks 1.1, 1.3 & 1.6]
1.C	[Financial figures 2 & 3]	[Tasks 1.1, 1.4 & 1.7]
1.D	[ET*]	[Tasks 1.5 & 1.8]
1.E	Conclusions	[Task 1.9]
1.F	Commercial Recommendations	[Task 1.10]

* Do not use the term ET as a heading as this is our term used for tutorial purposes only – instead, refer to the issue itself (e.g. "Receivables issue") for your heading

We recommend that you have a single section (1.C) which addresses both financial figures 2 and 3 in the **same** report section because there is normally just a single **combined** evaluation Box/Task (Box/Task 1.7) for **both** of these figures **together**: hence if you had separate sections for each figure there is a risk that you will write too much evaluation. In most examinations, financial figure 1 has been revenue and this will have its own evaluation Box/Task (Box/Task 1.6) so more FRP points should be made on revenue and hence we allocate this to its own section 1.B.

Note, however, that in the CC (November 2015) examination, Boxes 1.3 and 1.6, which are normally reserved just for revenue discussion, also contained points on gross profit and cost of sales – this was probably because candidates were asked to analyse revenue, gross profit, operating profit and interest cover (4 financial figures!) so do exercise some judgement here. The 4 most recent examinations have returned to the usual heavy emphasis on revenue with both Boxes 1.3 and 1.6 relating to this key part of the P&L.

PL (July 2017) had a Box (Box 1.5) dedicated to analysis of operating profit (rather than this being mixed as normal into Box 1.4 along with gross profit) because the ET did not have any calculations to perform. Therefore, our advice is to beef up your accounts analysis slightly if there are no ET calculations to do … but, as always, do not overcook Requirement 1!

6   Requirement 1 – detailed Task by Task advice

Task 1.1   Results of Appendix 1 calculations for overall company headlines

This Task will be completed quite easily and quickly by quoting your headline Appendix 1 results for the change in overall company revenue, GP, GPM%, OP and so on, which should generally be correct as the calculations are straightforward percentage changes, margins and so on.

Our main tip for this Task is therefore to rehearse your calculations and prepare the "prior year" element of your answer in advance, following the instructions set out in chapter 17.

Task 1.2   Discuss wider context of performance

This Task (which we recommend you address as a separate section entitled "Context of Performance" (CoP) at the start of your Requirement 1 answer) tests your ability to use the Advance Information and Exam Paper to look at the market background which informs the financial results.

Through to 2014, mention of the UK recession would normally have attracted a mark but the examiners appear to have become bored of this point. The November 2016 (TT) and July 2017 (PL) examinations awarded a mark for reference to the uncertainties created by Brexit and we would expect this remark to remain true and therefore relevant to future examinations. (However, please review our discussion in chapter 14 of the examiner comments at the 2017 Tutor Conference for some advice on how to introduce Brexit in the most effective manner.) Note that R4 (November 2017) did not reward any statements on Brexit because the company did not have any export or import operations. We would, however, predict this kind of business to be the exception in Case Study so we would expect Brexit to be a point that you can use in future examinations (but use your judgement, based on the nature of the Case Study business).

To ensure that you are writing relevant points in this section, be careful to make a reference to the client company in each sentence because if you cannot construct a sentence with the impact on the client in that sentence then you are probably writing about something that is too broad an issue.

At the 2015 ICAEW Tutor Conference, the examiners confirmed that making an isolated statement such as "RS competes with companies such as A2A" would not be enough whereas stating that "A2A's strong growth rate appears to be impacting on the revenue growth of RS due to increased competition" would be acceptable: the point is that you are explaining clearly **how** changes in the market are affecting the client company, rather than just dumping in a random fact that you happen to know about the industry.

For this reason, you may wish to complete this Task **after** you have done some of the numerical work, to see what has changed during the year and only then decide what background points to apply. We think that this section should be **placed** at the start of your answer but this does not necessarily mean that you should **write** it first since you may need to get a bit more of an understanding of events during the year before writing your CoP section: in the examination you are given a pad of loose leaf paper so you can easily set up your section heading for the CoP but then leave the page blank and return later to write this section after other parts of Requirement 1 have been written up.

A second advantage of this approach is that it will help you to **avoid repeating any points** – you will not be rewarded twice for the same idea (each point is placed in only one Box on the markscheme, except in the case of the Conclusions Boxes which require you to repeat points made earlier in your answer) so if you first write your answer and then come back to the CoP you can ensure that you are writing as many **different** points as possible, across the answer as a whole, giving you as much opportunity as possible to match the points which have made it onto the markscheme.

You are also welcome to make these points later and "mixed into" your answer: however, we find that if students do not consciously try to write a section-worth of points on these areas then they can end up forgetting about the CoP perspective completely, and hence lose some potentially easy marks.

Checking that your remarks are not "isolated" statements has a second advantage: writing sentences other than isolated ones may also give you a chance of unintentionally scoring a mark in one of the narrative Boxes later in the markscheme (e.g. Box 1.6 or 1.7) if the examiner has allocated a mark for the point there, rather than in Box 1.2: again, if you just say something unconnected to the company such as "Logistics is growing quickly" then there is no chance of getting a Box 1.6 or 1.7 point because these points are always about the impact **on the client company. On the other hand, if you say that "RS should expect to have boosted revenue as the logistics sector is growing quickly" then that is potentially a point that could arise in** either **(but not both) Box 1.2 or Box 1.6/1.7 so by writing in the correct way you can hedge your bets – effectively, you are turning your CoP section into another attempt to gain strategic and evaluation marks.** (See also chapter 16 for more on this issue.)

There will be a similar Background Task in the other Requirements under Tasks 2.2 and 3.2 so be careful to mix your background points up a little in each Requirement. There is generally a slightly different emphasis required for this Task in each Requirement – in Task 1.2, you need to look at the very broadest **industry** and **economy-wide** factors whereas in Tasks 2.2 and 3.2 you should be focusing on the **specific project/opportunity** at issue. We return to this point in later chapters.

As indicated on page 263, we are aware that another large UK tuition provider has been strongly criticising our approach to background industry points by misinforming students that there has been an official announcement by the ICAEW examiners that inclusion of a separate section at the start of a Requirement is not permitted and will result in a zero mark for this section: the other provider has claimed that background points must be included "mixed into" the main discussion. **We have confirmed in writing with ICAEW that no such examiner statement has ever been released**. We also confirmed that use of a separate background section is acceptable by raising a discussion question at several recent ICAEW Tutor Conferences.

As further evidence that our approach is acceptable, please note that one of the example student scripts from the November 2017 sitting that was discussed at the Case Study Workshop at the 2018 ICAEW Tutor Conference contained a separate "Market Background" section and yet was clearly awarded marks for this section by the official ICAEW markers when evaluated within the real November 2017 marking process: in the discussion of this script at the Tutor Conference, the examiners did not comment that the first section had been ignored by the markers and it was clear from the marking grid provided (a copy of the official marking which the script received at the November 2017 sitting) that marks were fully awarded for the introductory section on the industry context (see chapter 14 for further discussion). If incorrect derogatory remarks of this nature are being made about our materials by your tuition provider, please do kindly inform us.

Many of our taught course students tell us that this report section requires quite a lot of thought, thinking back to the Advance Information and spotting the connections and hints in the Exam Paper. As such, it can be inefficient to attempt this section as your first section: (1) the marks are slightly unpredictable so it does not make sense to start with this section compared to the easier and more predictable Tasks discussed below, and (2) attempting the other Tasks will allow you to "warm up" or "get into" the scenario and hence you may find it a lot easier to write about the Context of Performance **after** you have completed the other elements and so have developed a feel for what is happening.

As already explained above, we would definitely consider using this technique of writing the CoP section later into your write up time for Requirement 1 (whilst still presenting it at the start of your report section) as it does not make sense to use up lots of time in thinking at the start of the answer, if this compromises the rest of the Requirement. You can therefore just leave a heading for section 1.A with a blank page, complete the rest of the Requirement and then come back to fill in this element once you have "warmed up" to the scenario and situation. This will also prevent you using repetitive points since you will know what you have said in the other report sections and you can then put **different** points into section 1.A – remember that the marks are awarded regardless of the heading under which you make a point (except for Conclusions which must be under an appropriate heading) so do not agonise over which section to use but do avoid repeating yourself as this will waste valuable time.

On the other hand, if you write section 1.A first then you may end up using the same point again later.

For further discussion of the surprisingly controversial CoP or Market Background matter, please see chapter 16 of this book.

Task 1.3   Basics for financial figure 1 – F skill

This Task requires some further quotation of your numerical results from Appendix 1 in relation to the first financial figure (generally, this will be revenue) but looking perhaps at revenue by stream (including revenue mix) rather than at the overall company-level (which has already been rewarded in Box 1.1). In some examinations, it will also be necessary to use a simple descriptive word such as up "marginally", up "significantly". Although some markschemes do not require a descriptive word (a pure figure will do), we recommend that you hedge your bets and include it anyway, every time.

In this Task you are being rewarded for answering the **fact** question i.e. describing what has happened. The Task should not prove too difficult provided that you are **thorough** in your approach and that you ensure that you make **basic** descriptive points.

Task 1.4   Basics for financial figures 2 & 3 – F skill

This Task is similar to Task 1.3, but with respect to financial figures 2 & 3. Therefore, you might be looking at gross/operating profit margin (rather than gross profit absolutely, which is likely to be rewarded in Task 1.1) or gross/operating profit by stream rather than at the overall company-level (which has already been rewarded in Box 1.1), perhaps with some numerical and basic descriptor references to the direct costs (gross profit) or overheads (operating profit) which may have driven these changes. Again, aim for relatively simple points as explained above regarding Task 1.3. Note that sometimes discussion of direct costs or overheads could be rewarded under Task 1.7 below.

Task 1.5   Calculations for ET

In most recent examinations, the examiner has moved away from a third Box on the relatively easy matter of financial analysis so that Task 1.5 can become the first of 2 Boxes relating to the ET. Task 1.5 therefore now tends to award marks for correct calculations regarding the ET whilst Task 1.8 deals with the narrative side of the ET.

As advised elsewhere in this book, please do not spend too long on the ET as there are plenty of other easier Boxes in Requirement 1 and the related narrative and evaluation marks for the ET can be obtained even if the calculations go wrong. Therefore give this Box your best shot but move on soon.

Task 1.6   Reasons and pattern spotting for financial figure 1 – RP skills

As with all Requirements, the X.6 and X.7 Tasks are the hardest Boxes of all. These require you to demonstrate the skill of evaluation, which is a higher level skill and the marks are accordingly less predictable because there are many valid evaluative points you could make but only a select few points will be on the markscheme.

In these Tasks you are moving beyond the merely descriptive **fact** question to address the **reason** and **pattern-spotting** marks. As such, these evaluation Tasks 1.6 and 1.7 are asking you to look at the "RP" elements of our recommended FRP answering structure (please see the discussion above regarding pattern-spotting for discussion of the kinds of point to consider including).

We recommend that you review the markschemes for the recent Case exams to get an idea of what types of point will score here. We have included some reminders within our Planning & Reminder Sheets in chapter 6 to assist.

Task 1.7   Reasons and pattern spotting for financial figures 2 & 3 – RP skills

See Task 1.6 above. You should apply the same technique and focus as under Task 1.6 but this time with respect to financial figures 2 and 3.

Task 1.8   Narrative on ET

This Task requires you to provide some narrative analysis regarding the ET. Provided that your calculations for the ET are broadly correct, you should be able to pick up marks here by providing some narrative points on our 3 recommended "**PSS**" areas: practical impact, strategic impact and scepticism.

Make sure you are including enough points in the **narrative** as a natural hedge against the fact that your **calculations** may not go so well: it is often possible to pass Task 1.8 even whilst failing Task 1.5 on calculations. (In practice, very few of our taught course students get the correct results in their

ET calculations in our mock exams but they then go on to pass the real exam very easily so learn from this lesson.)

Our other main tip is: **do not spend too long on the ET**. It is not worth it in the overall scheme of things and many students effectively make themselves fail the exam by spending so long on this aspect that they can never recover the time later, giving up subsequent Requirement 1 Boxes/Tasks which are in principle significantly easier to pass whilst also compromising your attempt at the other 2 examination Requirements and at the Executive Summary.

We would recommend commenting on some of the following issues to obtain the Task 1.8 marks:

- Significance of the ET – is it actually material?
- Reasons for the issue arising
- Brief scepticism points – do the adjustments appear reasonable or are the numbers excessive?
- Future impact (looking particularly at the impact on the **reputation** of the business)
- Mitigation – is there anything we can do to avoid this problem?

Your bullet-point Recommendations in relation to the ET in report section 1.D may also help gain credit in Box 1.8 (see chapter 6).

Task 1.9   Conclusions with figures

The Conclusions Task is definitely one of the "banker" or key Tasks in each Requirement, always being based on the same 5-6 main points (supported by figures) every time: see our Planning & Reminder Sheets in chapter 6 for reminders of what these points are.

You should return to the wording of the question on the first page of the Exam Paper (client or partner requests) and identify the key areas you have been asked about: in Requirement 1, this will most likely be revenue, gross profit, a third financial figure, the ET and then add a comment on general performance in the year and a comment about cashflows (or the cash balance if this seems more relevant). Please do not forget to support **every** narrative point in your Conclusions section with an appropriate supporting **figure**.

We see a lot of scripts where the candidate has clearly been uncomfortable with just repeating points made already earlier in the report but for the Conclusions Task in each Requirement this is all you need to do: starting to look at new areas or coming up with creative solutions is very likely to lead you away from the markscheme.

You should then go on to recycle these points into the Executive Summary as well so do not be afraid of reusing ideas or texts: this will again earn more marks than new ideas.

Task 1.10   Commercial Recommendations

Like all Recommendations Boxes, there is an element of luck in passing this Task because there are a large number of reasonable and commercial Recommendations which could be made but in the end only 6-7 points will make it into the "acceptable" answer list. The Box always has one diamond for your own response so you should automatically gain one mark but the others are unfortunately subject to an element of luck.

In Requirement 1, there will generally be at least 2 Recommendations that relate to the ET so this is why we advise having a Recommendations sub-heading within your ET section. If the ET Recommendations are given credit in Box 1.10, then you will gain this credit regardless of where you stated your Recommendations so there is no need to repeat your ET Recommendations at the end of your report section – you should instead look at providing non-ET Recommendations in your end-of-section list so that you provide the broadest possible range of Recommendations across your answer as a whole.

ICAEW have stated (see chapter 14) that bullet points are acceptable for your Recommendations, provided that the meaning is clear. We would advise you to avoid writing extremely short points (we have seen scripts with just 2 words, for example, such as "boost sales") as this is probably a little cheeky but at the same time lengthy paragraphs and detailed explanations are not required. The examiners are interested in **range**, not **depth**, so they fully understand that it is only possible to provide a good range of ideas in the time available if the points are short (see page 188 for comments from the ICAEW examiners on this).

As a tip, we think that it is very useful to write up your Commercial Recommendations section as you go along in the question, noting down any ideas as you have them whilst writing the main body of Requirement 1, rather than leaving the development of your Commercial Recommendations to the end as a separate activity. This should save you time and ensure that you are making points which are relevant to the scenario. If you leave this work as a separate activity at the end, you may waste time if you struggle to think of points or you may come up with ideas that are too generic in nature because you have not written the points at the same time that the underlying issues were considered and so you will not be making any points that link back to what is unique about the Exam Paper scenario information.

7   Requirement 1 Executive Summary elements

Rather than writing your Executive Summary as a separate exercise towards the end of the examination, we recommend that you write up the Requirement 1 elements of the Executive Summary as soon as you have finished Requirement 1 in your main report. This will be easier to do whilst the points are fresh in your mind.

You are aiming to complete 2 Tasks/Boxes for the Executive Summary element of each Requirement: in Requirement 1 (but not the other Requirements), the first of these (Task E.1a in our terminology) is **much** easier than the second, as we shall now explain.

Task E.1a   Review Requirement 1 Appendix figures

This Task can be completed relatively easily by pulling through your Conclusions from Task 1.9. You need to make a statement, **including supporting figures**, on each of the key financial figures in the question and then follow this up with some ET points with figures. You should have done all these things already in Task 1.9.

Prior to the RS (November 2014) examination, there was a mark available for a "wider context" point as well but this has not appeared in any examinations since so we would advise you only to include such a point (which is definitely not needed in the underlying Conclusions section of your main report section on Requirement 1) in the Executive Summary if you can spare the time.

Task E.1b   Evaluation and recommendations on financial performance and ET

This is a harder Task as it is more evaluative and therefore quite open-ended in nature, with more of a luck element than Task E.1a. Try to aim for **reason** and **pattern-spotting** points and also make a few points on the ET, including some recommendations on how to deal with the ET issue. We also recommend that you consider how to deal with any cashflow problems facing the business.

We recommend that you comment on any specific metric emphasised in the live Advance Information (for example, a target level of interest cover, provided that the Advance Information refers to this in detail with example figures: if not, do not waste time on calculating such figures): the examiners will make it clear in the Advance Information if such a specific metric is going to be relevant.

It used to be possible to obtain credit for any sensible Recommendations at all in this Task but starting with the November 2015 paper (CC), there has been a move towards greater emphasis on specific Recommendations relating to the ET so make sure you have plenty of ET-related Recommendations (ideally, around 4 or so). The examiners have also stated that they want to see Recommendations on the "fundamental" or "Big Picture" issues facing the business so please do prioritise the making of Recommendations on these areas.

E.1b is the least predictable of all Executive Summary Boxes so whilst we obviously advise you to make your best attempt, it is safer to base your pass on doing well in the other 5 Tasks of the Executive Summary.

8   Requirement 1 – common errors

Based on what we have observed during our tuition courses and within scripts marked under our Technique Improvement Service (TIS), the most common mistakes of failing candidates are:

- spending too long on Requirement 1 just because it is a "comfortable" Requirement focusing on accounts analysis

- worrying about getting the ET calculation completely correct (difficult to get the marks) and therefore running out of time to write good ET narrative points (easier to get the marks)

- not being thorough – doing a good job of reviewing revenue and gross profit but then making only a few brief remarks on the third financial figure, throwing away easy marks

- not providing £ **and** % figures for the changes **as well as** a descriptive word such as "significantly", "marginally" or similar **every** time that figures for the changes are quoted

- not attempting the Context of Performance Task (1.2) by concentrating only on the figures and not the narrative background or context

9   Requirement 1 – a reminder of the 10 Tasks

We hope that the analysis of this chapter will have given you a better understanding of what you need to do to pass Requirement 1 without spending too long on this part of the exam.

As a basic summary, we now provide a list of what each of the 10 Tasks requires and we then explain the 6 section headings which you should use in your report section to obtain good coverage of the points required. These are just quick, end-of-chapter reminders to consolidate your knowledge: we would not expect you to use these pages in the examination itself as you should instead be using the Planning & Reminder Sheets found in chapter 6 for more specific guidance and reminders.

1.1*	Results of Appendix 1 calculations for overall company headlines
1.2	Discuss wider context of performance
1.3*	Basics for financial figure 1 (e.g. revenue (Note)) – F skill
1.4*	Basics for financial figures 2 & 3 (e.g. gross profit and operating profit (Note)) – F skill
1.5	Calculations for ET
1.6	Reasons and pattern spotting for financial figure 1 – RP skills
1.7	Reasons and pattern spotting for financial figures 2 & 3 – RP skills
1.8	Narrative on ET
1.9*	Conclusions **with figures**
1.10	Commercial Recommendations

Note – Our mention of the figures for revenue, gross profit and operating profit is based on likelihood and not certainty – you must prepare yourself for testing of other areas and always respond to the question set on the Exam Paper: do not be tempted to write about what you had hoped would be on the Exam Paper.

We have used a * symbol to indicate the easier Tasks which will normally need to form the basis of a pass.

We recommend that you address these 10 Tasks via the following 6 report sections:

Requirement 1	Recommended Report Section Headings	
1.A	Context of Performance	[Task 1.2]
1.B	[Financial figure 1]	[Tasks 1.1, 1.3 & 1.6]
1.C	[Financial figures 2 & 3]	[Tasks 1.1, 1.4 & 1.7]
1.D	[ET*]	[Tasks 1.5 & 1.8]
1.E	Conclusions	[Task 1.9]
1.F	Commercial Recommendations	[Task 1.10]

* Do not use the term ET as a heading as this is our term used for tutorial purposes only – instead, refer to the issue itself (e.g. "Receivables issue") for your heading

Chapter 9   How to Write a Good Requirement 2

Learning Points

After reading this chapter, you must be able to:

1. appreciate the importance of querying assumptions in Requirement 2
2. understand the subtle change in how the querying of assumptions is now rewarded in the markscheme
3. understand the markscheme balance between numbers and narrative Tasks in Requirement 2
4. recognise that the calculation in Requirement 2 is not particularly important to passing
5. understand the 10 Tasks and 6 or 7 report sections you should use

---

1   Requirement 2 – overview

In terms of Tasks, Requirement 2 will generally have a split between 2 numerical Tasks and 8 narrative tasks. It is therefore theoretically **possible** to pass the Requirement even if you get all the **numbers wrong** (passing at least 5 of the 8 remaining narrative Boxes) but **impossible** to pass the Requirement just on the basis of getting the **numbers correct** (since most recent examinations have only had 2 Boxes relating to the financial model)[34].

As an overview (see the remainder of this chapter for further details), the Tasks in Requirement 2 are[35]:

---

[34] We find that this is particularly a problem for non-UK students: often non-UK students will perform better than average in the calculations for Requirement 2 (sometimes even achieving perfect results) but they will nevertheless fail the Requirement (and therefore the examination as a whole) because they do not write enough on the non-calculations Tasks.

[35] There may be minor differences in the order in which the precise Tasks are presented in the markscheme in particular Case Study exams. Nevertheless, the insight that there will always be 10 core Tasks still applies, despite these minor variances.

95

2.1*	Outline contract terms & strategic and operational context OR model inputs[A]
2.2	Discuss wider context and make R1 linkages regarding relevant revenue stream
2.3[A]	Correct results for calculation 1 with brief discussion
2.4[A]	Correct results for calculation 2 with brief discussion OR Other Issue
2.5*	Query and evaluate assumptions
2.6	Discussion of calculation results or Other Issue
2.7	Other Issue (may be ethics)
2.8	Assumptions extension point OR ethics recommendations
2.9*	Conclusions **with figures**
2.10	Commercial Recommendations

We have used a * symbol to indicate the easier Boxes which will normally need to form the basis of a pass. Tasks marked with the [A] symbol (for "Appendix") are Tasks which are primarily completed by your numerical work in Appendix 2, together with a **brief** write up of the results: as such, these Tasks do not require the same amount of narrative as most marks are for quoting the calculations.

In respect of Task 2.1, sometimes (such as PL (July 2017) and TT (November 2016)) the marks are for narrative points which need to be discussed within your main report whereas in other examinations the marks are given simply from identifying the correct inputs to the Requirement 2 model: in the latter case, the marks are awarded based on your Appendix 2: you do **NOT** have to write about the inputs in your main report.

In respect of Task 2.4, this would only be answered by your Appendix 2 if the Task is a second calculation: if there is only one calculation to perform, then Task 2.4 will be a narrative Task which must be written up in your main report section and will not be addressed in your Appendix 2.

The above listing follows the order in the markscheme. As set out in our Planning & Reminder Sheets in chapter 6, we recommend that you attack Requirement 2 under the following report section headings, assuming as a first possibility that ethics is NOT tested in Requirement 2:

2.A	Strategic and Operational Context	[Task 2.2 and possibly also Task 2.1]
2.B	Results of financial model	[Tasks 2.3, 2.4 & 2.6]
2.C	Evaluation of assumptions	[Tasks 2.5 & 2.8]
2.D	[Other Issues*]	[Tasks 2.6 & 2.7]
2.E	Conclusions	[Task 2.9]
2.F	Commercial Recommendations	[Task 2.10]

* Try to use a more specific heading than "Other Issues" once the requirements are known: the heading "Other Issues" is just our generic placeholder text as unfortunately we do not yet know what is on the Exam Paper!

In the event (which is more likely) that ethics is tested in Requirement 2, then you should use the following report section headings:

2.A	Strategic and Operational Context	[Task 2.2 and possibly also Task 2.1]
2.B	Results of financial model	[Tasks 2.3 & 2.6]
2.C	Evaluation of assumptions	[Task 2.8 and possibly also 2.5*]
2.D	Ethics and Ethics Recommendations	[Task 2.4 or 2.5 & 2.8]
2.E	[Other Issues**]	[Tasks 2.6 & 2.7]
2.F	Conclusions	[Task 2.9]
2.G	Commercial Recommendations	[Task 2.10]

* There is some variability in practice regarding exactly which Boxes the Ethics and Assumptions points will be put into so the above Box numbers are indicative only. Ethics and Assumptions Boxes will definitely be present somewhere on any Requirement 2 markscheme.

** Try to use a more specific heading than "Other Issues" once the requirements are known: the heading "Other Issues" is just our generic placeholder text as unfortunately we do not yet know what is on the Exam Paper!

We have reflected both possible sets of section headings for Requirement 2 in our Planning & Reminder Sheets by creating 2 possible Sheets for Requirement 2, depending on whether Requirement 2 requires discussion of ethics or not. The question wording on the first Requirements page of the Exam Paper will always clearly and fairly indicate whether ethics will be rewarded in Requirement 2: the examiners are not trying to catch you out in this respect.

97

2   Requirement 2 – detailed Task by Task advice

Task 2.1   Outline contract terms & strategic and operational context OR model inputs

In 2 recent examinations (TT (November 2016) and PL (July 2017)), Box 2.1 was allocated to an outline of the basic contractual terms of the project, details of the parties who will be involved and consideration of practical matters. We therefore recommend that you ensure that terms such as any £ or % figures, contract length and other basics are definitely mentioned somewhere in your answer. Then please also ensure that you describe some relevant facts about what we already know about the companies and individuals involved (from both the Advance Information and the Exam Paper information). Also consider the practical implications of the project for the business.

As always with background sections, ensure that you are making the **impact** of your points clear to the reader: do not simply list out facts simply because you know them (see chapter 16 for more advice here).

Prior to the TT (November 2016) examination, Box 2.1 was generally allocated towards marks for correctly using the inputs to the financial model (primarily taken from the Exam Paper but also using the Advance Information where relevant). In most of these examinations, there was only one calculation to perform and this was rewarded in Box 2.3 so combined with application to the inputs in Box 2.1, this meant that there were generally 2 Boxes for the numerical aspects of Requirement 2. R4 (November 2017) is another example of this format of Requirement 2 markscheme.

In TT (November 2016) and PL (July 2017), there were 2 calculations to perform and these were rewarded in Boxes 2.3 and 2.4: Box 2.1 was therefore allocated to a description of the contract terms, as discussed above. Perhaps the examiners thought that having the usual Box 2.1 for model inputs when there are 2 calculations to perform (rewarded in Boxes 2.3 and 2.4) would mean that there would be too much emphasis (3 Boxes in total) on calculations in Requirement 2. Therefore Box 2.1 was instead allocated to a description of the contract terms and strategic and operational factors.

The learning point therefore seems to be that if there are **2 calculations to perform**, then Box 2.1 will **not** be allocated to identification of **model inputs**: instead, some **narrative** points on the strategic and operational context will be given credit. However, if there is **only 1 calculation to perform**, then Box 2.1 may be allocated to identification of the model **inputs** and for this reason we have retained below our advice in such a case. The most recent examination at the time of writing (R4 Limited (November 2017)) appears to support this hypothesis since it contained only 1 calculation to perform in Requirement 2 and allocated Box 2.1 to inputs, returning to the pattern seen before TT (November 2016) and PL (July 2017) which, as mentioned above, both had 2 calculations to perform and therefore a narrative style of Box 2.1.

If Box 2.1 is related to inputs, then the Box is relatively straightforward. You must work through the Exam Paper narrative and attempt to identify the main inputs to your calculations i.e. the numerical assumptions stated. Typically, these will relate back to a calculation or model that was strongly hinted at in the Advance Information (hopefully through a pro-forma calculation that you can practise extensively, including via our mock exams, as part of your preparation process).

Once the inputs are identified, include these in your Appendix 2 calculation – **you do not need to waste time listing out each input in the main text of your report to pick up the marks in Box**

2.1: inclusion in your Appendix 2 is sufficient to gain all the marks available for Task 2.1. You should **criticise** those inputs in your main report (see below) but do not waste time simply **stating** the inputs in report section 2.B on the financial model (or, indeed, in any other report section in Requirement 2).

You should generally aim to score a passing grade in this Box by identifying at least 6-7 key inputs. Be thorough in your approach to ensure that you definitely pass the Box: in some cases, there may be only one diamond for identifying a **group** of related inputs[36] so it makes sense to search for 6 to 7 inputs. This will also make it more likely that you can score marks for the results of your calculation in Task 2.3 (and Task 2.4 if this is allocated to calculations: please see below).

Task 2.2   Discuss wider context and R1 linkages regarding relevant revenue stream

Our Planning & Reminder Sheets (chapter 6) suggest that you should allocate a dedicated report section "2.A Strategic and Operational Context" (SOC) to this Task – although you can still score the marks if you make the relevant points in passing or "mixed in" elsewhere in your answer, we feel that it is advisable to create a **dedicated** section to force you to make points of this nature and to avoid the risk of forgetting to mention ideas of this type later on when you get into the specific question. **To ensure that you are writing relevant points, be careful to make a reference to the client company in each sentence because if you cannot construct a sentence with the impact on the client in that sentence then you are probably writing about something that is too broad an issue.** Please refer to page 86 for clarification on this issue. Please also see chapter 16 for further detail.

Performing this check may also give you a chance of unintentionally scoring a mark in one of the narrative Boxes later in the markscheme (e.g. Box 2.6 or 2.7) if the point is in fact placed there, rather than in Box 2.2: again, if you just say something unconnected to the company such as "Logistics is growing quickly" then there is no chance of getting a Box 2.6 or 2.7 point because Box 2.6 and 2.7 points are always about the impact **on the company.**

Aim for points which relate to the **specific project** under consideration (in contrast to Requirement 1 where broader market- and economy-wide points should be made), indicating the operational and strategic impact of your points on the Case Study company.

Other marks in Box 2.2 are often available for linkages back to the revenue and gross profit performance of the revenue stream involved in the proposed project. Therefore, it is worth having another look back at your Appendix 1 and commenting on the performance of the relevant stream: for example, if revenue has been declining for the stream in question, you might query whether there is a chance of the project performing well whilst also noting that there may well now be capacity within the stream – if the gross profit margin of the stream is not too high, you might note that there may be better opportunities than the proposed project whilst observing that the absolute gross profit contributed by the stream is significant to the business (if that is the case, of course!). These are just

---

[36] For example, in LT (November 2013) there was only one diamond for identifying **various** inputs in relation to volume figures for all 3 years of the calculation. A separate diamond was then awarded for identifying the **single** matter of fixed one-off costs.

99

example points based on hypothetical performance figures and relationships – always make points which are specific to your examination.

Another Requirement 1 linkage which may be worth making relates to the cash position of the business, particularly if the Advance Information has hinted that the company is struggling for cash (or (perhaps less likely in Case Study) is in a very strong cash position, making investment easy to fund).

Prior to the RS (November 2014) examination, there was always a mark for making reference to the "recession" but we did inform our taught course students that at some point this would change as the UK recovers and/or as the examiners get bored of seeing this point: the point has not been rewarded in any recent markschemes so please look for something more interesting to say! The issue of Brexit now seems more likely to be relevant and was rewarded in TT (November 2016) and PL (July 2017) as a specific point (although not in R4 (November 2017) as this company did not engage in importing or exporting), provided that some kind of implication other than "uncertainty" was noted (see chapter 14 for examiner advice on how to refer to Brexit in your answer). However, your points need to be more project-specific than in Requirement 1.

Aim for points in relation to the strategic fit of the **opportunity** by looking at the key contract terms proposed (including timescales) – this kind of point could then also alternatively score in Boxes 2.6 or 2.7 which are often connected with the practical and strategic aspects of the project.

Look out for relevant figures and statistics other than those you have used in the calculation. For example, in RS (November 2014), there were marks for citing the average market wage (referred to in the Advance Information). Hence if there are any contextual figures **not** used in your calculation, consider including them in your SOC Task (report section 2.A).

Please see page 87 for an argument that you should not necessarily plan or write up this section first but should instead address it after you have "warmed up" by writing up the rest of your answer, thus reminding yourself of the context and also avoiding any risk of repeating your points in both this section and later in your main answer: you will not be rewarded twice for the same point.

Tasks 2.3 and 2.4   Correct results for calculations with brief discussion OR Other Issue (for Task 2.4)

These Tasks often relate to your calculation of the results of the financial model. The marks here are primarily awarded for your work in Appendix 2 – this includes marks for figures produced part of the way through the calculations, even if you do not arrive at "the" correct result. However, to pass the Box you will almost always have to arrive at **the** correct final result and as there are no follow through marks available then this is tough to do.

Given this, do not spend any time or words explaining what you have done: simply present the **results** of your calculations in the text. You will not be rewarded for detailed discussion of your approach so ensure that your workings are easy to follow and leave these as a series of purely numerical steps with very minimal narrative in your Appendix 2.

In terms of difficulty, it is relatively hard to pass both of these Boxes as this will generally require you to get quite close to **the** right numerical answer and there are various points along the way where you may make a careless error or interpret the information in a different way to the examiners.

Therefore, our biggest tip is not to worry about these 2 Boxes – most passing candidates will not pass both but many failing candidates will spend too long on this element and/or lose confidence if they do not believe that they have **the** right answer. Even if you get the calculation completely wrong, you still have 8 other Tasks which are not connected to the calculations and therefore 8 other unaffected opportunities to score the 5 passing Boxes you need.

Considering that Tasks 2.1 (SOC or Inputs), 2.5 (Assumptions – Basics) and 2.9 (Conclusions) are relatively easy, you should normally be on 3 Boxes by default, particularly if you follow the advice contained in this book, including our Planning & Reminder Sheets. This means that you need 2 further Boxes from the remaining 5 Boxes available[37] i.e. a 40% strike rate. **The Boxes for calculations do not have to figure in these 2 remaining Boxes.**

In many examinations, there has only been one calculation (all recent exams other than TT (November 2016) and PL (July 2017) follow this pattern). If this is the case, there will be an empty Box 2.4 which the examiners need to fill.

In Palate (July 2013) and LT (November 2013), Task 2.4 was filled with marks for sensitivity or breakeven analysis even though this was not specifically required by the question wording.

Before you worry that this means you now have to do a further type of calculation, bear in mind that unlike Task 2.3, the marking for sensitivity/breakeven in Box 2.4 in these examinations was relatively open – the markschemes did not require you to arrive at any particular numerical figure to get the marks since there are many valid alternative ways of performing the sensitivity or breakeven analysis: you should therefore pick up the marks simply for trying.

Hence provided that you make a good attempt and produce some sensible figures for priority areas you should pick up the passing diamonds you need – in other words, the skill here is to **remember to do** the sensitivity/breakeven analysis in the first place, rather than about arriving at particular numerical results. Remembering to do the sensitivity/breakeven analysis will put you ahead of many other candidates who will understandably not look at this area, given the lack of specific mention in the question wording.

In the case of the other recent examinations with only one calculation to perform, Task 2.4 was filled with narrative marks based on an additional request included in the wording of Requirement 2. This should have been relatively easy to identify in the question wording so most candidates ought to have attempted the relevant narrative. Look out for any hint on this specific issue in the question wording as it may determine whether you need to do sensitivity/breakeven analysis or, alternatively, some additional narrative analysis on a specific area.

---

[37] Explanation of this calculation: there are 10 Boxes available but discounting the 2 Boxes for correct calculations leaves 8 Boxes and then deducting the 3 Boxes which we consider to be relatively easy leaves a balance of 5 Boxes. Specifically, these are Tasks 2.2 (Wider Context and R1 Linkages), 2.6 (Discussion of calculation results or Other Issue), 2.7 (Other Issue (may be ethics)), 2.8 (Assumptions extension point OR ethics recommendations) and 2.10 (Commercial Recommendations).

Based on the above information, there has been no detailed reward for sensitivity or breakeven analysis since the November 2013 examination so it seems unlikely that this is what the examiners are looking for to fill Box 2.4: instead, it is much more likely that you will be given a specific additional narrative Task to complete.

Task 2.5   Query and evaluate assumptions

This Task does not normally cause problems for students: simply work methodically through the key assumptions within your model, including the inputs you have been asked to use, and raise some doubts as to whether these figures or assumptions are likely to be accurate, **given what we know from the Advance Information and the Exam Paper information**. Stick to figures you have been given: Task 2.8 (which is harder to pass) is where you may be rewarded for considering whether further data is needed, owing to key figures being missing.

Note that in Bod (July 2015), there were **2** Boxes relating to a set of assumptions specifically listed out in bullet point format in the Exam Paper itself (normally it will take more work to identify the assumptions): the first Box was for saying that the assumption was only an estimate or could have been wrong and then the second Box was for comparing the assumed estimate to figures known from the Advance Information or Exam Paper (as we have already advised you to do anyway above).

Other recent examinations have generally been more in line with the Bod approach, suggesting that it is worth reflecting in detail on each assumption, rather than simply saying that the figure might be "different" or "higher" or "lower" – **try to add a second comment which is more interesting than this, either by comparing to the Advance Information or making some kind of commercial/practical point**. This may then attract credit in Box 2.8 if the point is not in Box 2.5. See below for further discussion of Box 2.8.

As the area of Requirement 2 assumptions has been the most variable element within the recent Case Study markschemes, we have reviewed the matter in more depth in chapter 12 so please combine our discussion of Task 2.5 and 2.8 here with that later chapter.

Tasks 2.6 and 2.7   Discussion of calculation results or Other Issue (Task 2.6) and Other Issue (may be ethics) (Task 2.7)

These Tasks form part of the "Applying Judgement" element of the markscheme. As such, they are some of the hardest marks to obtain partly because this is a higher skills area and partly because the diamonds are relatively unpredictable. These 2 Tasks, and their equivalents in Requirement 1 and Requirement 2, have probably attracted more student questions than any other Tasks in our tuition sessions.

Your best guide as to what to do in these sections is always going to be the instructions for Requirement 2 on the first page of the Exam Paper: look for any text after the instructions regarding the financial model – is there any specific request to discuss "commercial", "practical" or "strategic" issues? Is there a request to consider any "other" issues[38] or perhaps to comment on one of the financial aspects of the model (e.g. revenue by stream)?

On this last point, we have noticed that in both the 2015 examinations and in Bux (July 2016), Box 2.6 contained marks relating to the results of the financial model – therefore, do consider writing a few points on the financial impact of the revenue, profits and cash revealed by the financial model, commenting on how significant these are, in light of what you already know about the business and its general profitability. We note that no examination since Bux (July 2016) has dedicated Box 2.6 to discussing the results of the financial model so do not overcook your discussion (particularly given that your financial model results may well not be correct …).

With respect to Requirements 1 and 3 (see chapter 8 and chapter 10), we are generally more relaxed regarding these 2 evaluation Tasks because there are more than enough other simpler Boxes to pass. However, in Requirement 2, we noted above that Tasks 2.3 and 2.4 may be calculations Boxes which are quite hard to pass. It therefore follows that Tasks 2.6 and 2.7 are relatively more important to do well in because Requirement 2 has fewer remaining easier Boxes.

To help with these 2 Boxes, we recommend that you review chapter 11 carefully. In chapter 11, we analyse the practical issues which tend to be rewarded on the markscheme and we conclude that there are seveal key types of issue that should be used to increase the probability that your points in report section 2.D will cover Tasks 2.6 and 2.7. In terms of specific advice for **Requirement 2 practical issues**, points relating to reputation, cash, timing, capacity, impact on other streams, management time and staffing are always likely to be relevant.

It is also possible that one of these Boxes could relate to ethics. In this case, our advice on ethics in Requirement 3 (see chapter 10) would be the correct method to apply here too in Requirement 2.

Notwithstanding our general advice that it is possible to pass Requirement 2 (and the other Requirements) without passing these 2 difficult X.6 and X.7 Boxes, it is still worth trying to have a good go at passing Tasks 2.6 and 2.7 in Requirement 2: as explained above, the Boxes for correct calculations (Box 2.3 and possibly also Box 2.4) are difficult to achieve and if you give up completely on Boxes 2.6 and 2.7 then you are effectively aiming to pass 5 of the remaining 6 Boxes[39] – not good odds!

We therefore analyse below the recent Case markschemes to try to understand what has been rewarded in Boxes 2.6 and 2.7 in the most recent papers.

In the analysis below, a ♦ symbol means that this area was rewarded in the relevant exam. The most recent examination (R4 (November 2017)) is included in the lefthand column and we then work backwards in time as we move rightwards across the page.

---

[38] If the question text just says "other issues" then this is probably the worst outcome as it does not provide very clear guidance. In this case, the best approach is to look at (1) practical issues and (2) strategic issues to fill report section 2.D.
[39] Being Boxes 2.1, 2.2, 2.5, 2.8, 2.9 and 2.10.

Recent Exams: Boxes 2.6 and 2.7

	R4[40]	PL	TT	Bux	CC	Bod	RS	ZM	LT	P	FS	LL
Impact on profit	♦		♦	♦	♦	♦		♦	♦	♦	♦	
Impact on cash			♦	♦	♦			♦	♦	♦	♦[41]	♦
Timeframe		♦	♦	♦	♦	♦	♦	♦		♦	♦	♦
Reputation/Brand				♦			♦		♦	♦	♦	
Staff: pay, hours		♦	♦				♦	♦	♦	♦		♦
Management		♦						♦	♦	♦		♦
Repeat business			♦						♦	♦		
Other streams[42]							♦		♦		♦	♦
Capacity			♦			♦		♦	♦	♦		
Other costs	♦	♦			♦	♦	♦	♦			♦	♦
Margins		♦						♦			♦	
Risks	♦		♦	♦	♦			♦			♦	
KPIs/targets	♦					♦						
Free response[43]									♦			

We can see that only LT offered a "free response" for these Boxes – generally, then (and as usual), you will have to make the **specific point** mentioned in the markscheme to score the diamond.

Based on this review, discussion of **profit**, **cash**, **timeframes**, **reputation**, **management time** and the **impact on other revenue streams** are the points which are most likely to be rewarded.

Task 2.8   Assumptions extension point OR ethics recommendations

Before we review the potential second Box on Assumptions, please note that 2 recent examinations (TT (November 2016) and PL (July 2017)) allocated Box 2.8 to recommendations on how to resolve ethical issues: the marks for Assumptions were then allocated to just a single Box because the examiners needed a second Box for ethics purposes. We have retained below our detailed discussion of how to tackle Box 2.8 if it is a second Assumptions Box in case your examination does not follow this approach to Requirement 2 but note that the most recent examination (R4 (November 2017)), as well as some earlier examinations such as Bux (July 2016) have allocated 2 Boxes to Assumptions and 2 Boxes to Ethics in Requirement 2, so you will need to be flexible with your approach.

As indicated above regarding Task 2.5, the Assumptions Boxes have definitely been subject to change in recent sittings. Task 2.8 may sometimes contain marks for comparing an input back to the

---

[40] The R4 (November 2017) examination had 2 Boxes for Ethics and 2 Boxes for Assumptions in Requirement 2 so there was only space for 1 Box (Box 2.6) on "commercial issues". This Box in fact contained a further Assumptions point (changes in assumptions will affect the results of the model). As such, there are not as many Box 2.6/2.7-style points as usual to add to our table here in relation to R4 (November 2017).

[41] Note that in FS (November 2012) there were 5 diamonds in Task 2.6 simply for discussing cash, including the balance available, timing in different quarters and years and the impact of assumptions on cash: this examination was unusual in having quite so much emphasis on cash.

[42] This means the fact that the project will have an impact on other revenue streams in addition to the stream considered in the question.

[43] A "free response" diamond or mark is a very rare opportunity to score a mark regardless of what you say. In other words, it is a rare exception to the normal rule that you must match the precise point on the markscheme to score the mark. In recent examinations, a "free response" diamond has unfortunately only been found in the Commercial Recommendations Boxes (Boxes 1.10, 2.10 and 3.10).

benchmark set out in the Advance Information (if such a point has not already been awarded in Task 2.5, where it sometimes will be). Task 2.8 could also contain marks for scepticism (see below) and/or for practical points in relation to the assumptions: for example, if the input is correct, can the business cope?

For this reason, we strongly recommend that you work through chapter 12, which we added for the first time to the July 2017 edition of the book and which has been updated as required for this edition. Unfortunately, it is not possible to summarise all the possible points that could be in Box 2.8 here – we need a full chapter to explain things properly so please consult chapter 12 for full details.

In summary:

> Task 2.5 on assumptions involves carefully working through the information **which is given** and querying it; Task 2.8 may involve looking for information which is **not** given (unknown or missing information) and commenting on this omission. Task 2.8 also means looking for reasons for **bias or lack of knowledge** in the information (e.g. the information is from a press report or an ex-employee with a grudge against the company) and assessing problems/concerns with the **methodology**.

When attempting to pass Task 2.8 it is also worth going briefly into other areas such as sensitivity and breakeven, the length of time involved in the forecast (too short or too long), lack of consistency with information previously given in the Advance Information and assumptions regarding the availability of human, material and financial resources. You can see that this second set of ideas for Task 2.8 overlaps with the first Assumptions Task (2.5) to a certain extent and this is why we advise building the core of your Scepticism discussion around **unknown** factors as there is more certainty that diamonds will be available for this.

RS (November 2014) was somewhat unusual in allocating the whole of Box 2.8 just to the potential weaknesses of payback as a project appraisal method, rather than the more typical scepticism points. This was clearly indicated to candidates by the inclusion of a specific request to evaluate payback in the question wording on the first page of the examination paper. In a more typical exam, some "banker" or standard points to put into Requirement 2 scepticism would be (please also see the Planning & Reminder Sheets in chapter 6):

- Changing the assumptions will change the results of the model
- Querying the forecasting period – is it too long or too short?
- Look for potential bias from the provider of the information
- Look for several unknown costs or revenues to consider
- Consider whether the business has the resources for the activity
- State that forecasts are inherently uncertain
- Look at timing issues: does the model assume that we can suddenly earn revenue or save costs immediately – is this realistic?

We would advise you to **always** quickly make some of the above points in any examination and then to look for further points that are not so generic, for safety. (In practice, if you review recent markschemes you will see that the above generic points are generally rewarded. An apparent exception may be RS (November 2014) which focused more on the specific issue of the "payback" investment appraisal method, as was very clearly requested by the wording on the first Requirements page of the Exam Paper: even so, whilst focused on this methodology, the points in RS were of the same nature in terms of looking at the timeframe, looking at issues not included and also the last point on assuming that the project has an impact immediately.)

As discussed elsewhere in this book, TT (November 2016) and PL (July 2017) contained 2 Boxes for ethics in Requirement 2: each time, the second Assumptions Box (Box 2.8) was scrapped to provide the necessary emphasis on ethics in the markscheme. Although the most recent examination (R4 (November 2017) allocated 2 Boxes to ethics and 2 Boxes to Assumptions, it is possible that ethics may "trump" Assumptions in the markscheme allocation (as in TT (November 2016) and PL (July 2017)) so if there are quite a few ethics issues to discuss then we would advise you to **first** complete your ethics sections in Requirement 2 to a good standard before starting your Assumptions section (and also to spend more time on your ethics sections than on your Assumptions section). Remember to include in your ethics section a separate set of bullet point Ethics Recommendations so that you can capitalise on the opportunity to save time by writing bullets for this element of your report. There is no need to repeat your ethics Recommendations at the end of your Requirement 2 report section: even if Box 2.10 were to contain marks for ethics Recommendations, such marks would be awarded regardless of where you have stated your ethics Recommendations so there is no need to repeat your ethics Recommendations at the end of your report section as this will simply waste time.

However, if there is no ethics element to Requirement 2, then we would expect a return to the 2 Box approach to Assumptions. It therefore obviously follows that you should spend more time on Assumptions as there will not be any ethics analysis to do!

Task 2.9   Conclusions with figures

As with the other Requirements, this is one of the most straightforward Boxes. As long as you thoroughly work through the same standard points noted within the reminders on our Planning & Reminder Sheets you should pass this Box with no problems. You should definitely take this opportunity to gain an easy Box because most passing students will be doing so.

The points to make are:

1. Conclude on the modelling outputs specifically requested by the client[44] **with figures**, considering whether the project would (or would not) make a **significant** contribution to revenue/profit

2. Conclude on assumptions and scepticism

3. Conclude on Other Issues

4. Conclude on whether to proceed or not

Remember that under the new marking approach applied since July 2012, you no longer have to reach the same Conclusion as the examiners to score the mark. Therefore as long as you offer **a** conclusion on profit, you score the mark; as long as you reach **a** conclusion on the assumptions, you score the mark, and so on.

The only exception to this occurred in Bod (July 2015) where the project related to a really key client and so the examiner **required** candidates to reach the conclusion that Bod should **proceed** with the project, in order to be awarded a mark. This contrasts with Bod Requirement 3 where any conclusion on whether to proceed or not was acceptable. The more recent examinations have allowed the candidate to conclude either to proceed or not proceed with a project and therefore returned to a more open marking approach.

Please do not forget to conclude on **whether or not to proceed** with the project! Forgetting to do this (especially when the results make it obvious what the client should do) is a classic mistake and a missed opportunity to gain a very easy mark. Do not leave the reader to work out that a profit of £5m with minimal fixed costs means the client should proceed: you need to spell this out, even if it is very obvious!

We realise that stating whether to proceed or not with a project could be considered to be a "Recommendation" in everyday English but the Case Study markscheme does always seem to allocate this mark to the "Conclusions" Task 2.9 (and 3.9 for Requirement 3) so we recommend that you just play it safe and treat this point as a "Conclusion" for exam purposes, therefore including it under your "Conclusions" heading.

Remember that it is only with respect to the points in the Conclusions Boxes (Boxes 1.9, 2.9 and 3.9) that ICAEW are fussy about where a point is stated: to score in these Boxes, your point must be under a heading labelled "Conclusions" whereas the points in all other Boxes on the markscheme can be made in any section. As the "proceed or not" point is always allocated to Box 2.9 in Requirement 2 (and Box 3.9 in Requirement 3), you must be careful to make this point under a "Conclusions" heading (see chapter 14 for more details).

---

[44] Usually these will be profit, revenue, cashflows etc: go back to the first page of the Exam Paper which sets out the Requirements to confirm.

Task 2.10   Commercial Recommendations

As with the other Requirements, this is one of the harder Boxes to pass, given the unpredictable nature of the marks – there are many relevant Recommendations you **could** make so it is hard to know what **will** be rewarded. We therefore advise our taught course students to make their best efforts at this Box but not to rely on it as part of their pass.

Having said this, note that like the other Recommendations Boxes, there is a "free" mark available for your own response: hence making any sensible Recommendation at all will get you 1 of the 3 marks you need. Also note that the Recommendations Boxes have 6 or 7 acceptable diamonds available (including the "free" mark) so the Task is one of the more open Boxes, albeit unpredictable.

A third reason to have a good attempt at this Task, despite the luck element, is that you are permitted to use a bullet point approach so it is a Task that can be done very quickly indeed in perhaps one third of a page of bullet points at the absolute maximum.

We recommend that you offer at least 7 brief Recommendations and make these as practical and project-specific as possible – do not rely on pre-prepared Recommendations: make sure your points are relevant to the specific project in the Exam Paper. Once again, bullet points are fine for your Recommendations (see page 188 for confirmation from the examiners here).

As we have advised in chapter 8 with respect to Requirement 1, we think that it is very useful to write up your Commercial Recommendations section as you go along in the question, noting down any ideas as you have them whilst writing the main body of Requirement 2, rather than leaving the development of your Commercial Recommendations to the end as a separate activity. This should save you time and ensure that you are making points which are relevant to the scenario. If you leave this work as a separate activity at the end, you may waste time if you struggle to think of points or you may come up with ideas that are too generic in nature because you have not written the points at the same time that the underlying issues were considered and so you will not be making any points that link back to what is unique about the Exam Paper scenario information.

Negotiating or **discussing** with other parties tends to be a point which is rewarded. **Due diligence** is also something to consider if new parties are involved. It is also always worth recommending to perform **market research** and to confirm the validity of the model **inputs**.

Although there can occasionally be some credit for ethics Recommendations in Box 2.10, most of the marks in this Box will be for non-ethics Recommendations: ethics Recommendations will normally be rewarded in Box 2.8. As we recommend that you have a report section dedicated to your Requirement 2 ethics Recommendations earlier into your answer, there is no need to repeat your ethics Recommendations at the end of your Requirement 2 report section: even if Box 2.10 were to contain marks for ethics Recommendations, such marks would be awarded regardless of where you have stated your ethics Recommendations so there is no need to repeat your ethics Recommendations at the end of your report section as this will simply waste time. Additionally, we find that if students do repeat their ethics Recommendations at the end of their Requirement 2 report section, they then forget to include enough non-ethics Recommendations to pick up the points which are much more likely to figure in Box 2.10. This is another reason to keep ethics Recommendations away from the end of your Requirement 2 answer by putting ethics Recommendations into report section 2.D instead.

3   Requirement 2 – summary of the basis of a typical pass

Based on the above review and our work with taught course students, a passing student will generally pass the following Tasks:

2.1   Outline contract terms & strategic and operational context OR model inputs
2.2   Discuss wider context and R1 linkages regarding relevant revenue stream
2.5   Query and evaluate assumptions
2.8   Assumptions extension point OR ethics recommendations
2.9   Conclusions **with figures**

If you can generally pass these Boxes (which do not depend on being correct in **any** calculations) then Requirement 2 should not be a problem for you. You should then obviously try to pass the other Tasks/Boxes to ensure a good margin of safety.

Hopefully you will now be confident that passing Requirement 2 is really not about doing well in the calculations but rather about sensible practical advice and scepticism of assumptions and missing information. At the 2015 ICAEW Tutor Conference, the examiners commented that they do not want the Case Study to be about "crunching the numbers" and that the earlier levels of the ACA examinations provide adequate testing of complex, detailed calculations – the examiners instead want your final examination to be a last check that you have developed **practical business advisory** skills (note the word "practical" here: see chapter 11 for the importance of a practical perspective to your examination).

4   Requirement 2 – Executive Summary elements

It is probably easier to gain 2 passing Tasks/Boxes in the Requirement 2 Executive Summary Tasks than in Requirement 1 because the second Executive Summary Box for Requirement 2 is more predictable than the equivalent section to Requirement 1 and always focuses closely on Other Issues, whether to proceed and Commercial Recommendations. You should be able to make these points every time, particularly if you refer to our Planning & Reminder Sheets (chapter 6).

Task E.2a   Results of Requirement 2 calculations and assumptions

This Executive Summary Task is straightforward. Simply repeat your headline results from the financial model (return to the question wording to pick out the "headline" points that the client wishes to see), make some sceptical points regarding the assumptions and then discuss some practical or operational points.

These are points that you should be able to pull through from your Conclusions to Requirement 2 (Task 2.9). Therefore getting your Conclusions correct in your main Requirement 2 section will help you pass both Requirement 2 itself and this first Box of the Executive Summary on Requirement 2.

Make sure you thoroughly and separately quote your financial model results for each year modelled, rather than just giving an overall total: otherwise you might miss out on some separate marks for quoting each different year (see, for example, the PL (July 2017) Executive Summary markscheme for Requirement 2). Remember that you do not need to quote any model inputs or intermediate workings: just quote the headline results (such as revenue and gross profit achievable) which were requested on the first Requirements page of the Exam Paper.

As noted in our review of RS (November 2014) which starts on p261, and as also noted in the previous chapter, the RS Executive Summary marking was harder than usual with only 4 diamonds available in some Boxes. Box E.2a was one of these, with the usual diamond for "wider context" not being present. All examinations since RS (November 2014) have maintained this approach. As such, it is very important that you look carefully at what is being rewarded in the Executive Summary and use our Planning & Reminder Sheets to help you stay focused on the relatively narrow and prescriptive range of points which attracts marks. There no longer appears to be a mark available for "wider context" points in the Executive Summary so only include such a point if you really do have the time to spare.

Task E.2b   Other Issues, scepticism, proceed or not, recommendations

As explained above, passing this Task involves commenting on practical issues, breakeven or sensitivity, whether to proceed and Commercial Recommendations. Although it is the second Box, it is not really much harder than E.2a (unlike the position for the Requirement 1 Executive Summary Boxes where E.1b is much harder than E.1a). Again, our Planning & Reminder Sheets (chapter 6) should keep you on track here.

Make sure you do not try to do anything too complicated and instead just stick to the core and dependable points.

5   Requirement 2 – common student errors

Based on our work with taught course students, we would say that common student mistakes in Requirement 2 are:

- too much concentration on getting the calculations correct – it is not worth wasting time on this because there are 8 easier Boxes that can be passed without correct numbers

- neither writing a SOC section nor using the alternative method of mentioning SOC points "mixed in" with the general narrative and hence performing badly in Tasks 2.1 and 2.2

- not linking back to key Appendix 1 figures for the revenue stream which is involved in the potential project or key figures such as the cash position if the Advance Information has indicated a particular importance of the company's cash position

- forgetting or not realising that criticism of the model assumptions (ideally with 2 points per assumption under the "extension" approach explained in this chapter and in chapter 12) is always required in Requirement 2 (Tasks 2.5 and 2.8)

- not even attempting Tasks 2.6 and 2.7 for Other Issues, despite the reminder in the question wording not only to perform the calculations but also to (for example) "**discuss any commercial matters** that X Ltd should consider" or "**evaluate the financial and non-financial risks and opportunities** of each set of arrangements" (as in PL (July 2017)) – in other words, not reading the question properly

Whilst it is important to try to correct all these issues, we would note that with the move towards a more narrative-focused Requirement 2 in which there are fewer and fewer marks for the numbers, it has become particularly important for you to avoid the final mistake of not reading the question properly and hence missing the fact that a particular narrative Task is required in the first place – this can lead you to instantly drop a Task/Box and this is not good in Requirement 2, which is normally the most technically challenging for students: looking at general performance according to the examiners, candidates tend to score lower grades in Requirement 3 than in Requirement 2 but we believe that this is probably due to a greater level of time pressure in Requirement 3 as a result of overrunning earlier in the examination rather than any higher intrinsic difficulty for Requirement 3.

6   Requirement 2 – a reminder of the 10 Tasks

We hope that the analysis of this chapter will have given you a better understanding of what you need to do to pass Requirement 2 without spending too long on this part of the exam.

As a basic summary, we now provide a list of what each of the 10 Tasks requires and we then explain the 6 section headings which you should use in your report section to obtain good coverage of the points required. These are just quick, end-of-chapter reminders to consolidate your knowledge: we would not expect you to use these pages in the examination itself as you should instead be using the Planning & Reminder Sheets found in chapter 6 for more specific guidance and reminders.

2.1*	Outline contract terms & strategic and operational context OR model inputs[A]
2.2	Discuss wider context and make R1 linkages regarding relevant revenue stream
2.3[A]	Correct results for calculation 1 with brief discussion
2.4[A]	Correct results for calculation 2 with brief discussion OR Other Issue
2.5*	Query and evaluate assumptions
2.6	Discussion of calculation results or Other Issue
2.7	Other Issue (may be ethics)
2.8	Assumptions extension point OR ethics recommendations
2.9*	Conclusions **with figures**
2.10	Commercial Recommendations

[A] If Task 2.1 awards credit for the identification of inputs to the model, this Task will be "automatically" completed in the most part by means of your Appendix 2 work, rather than by large amounts of discussion in the main body of Requirement 2. In respect of Task 2.4, this would only be answered by your Appendix 2 if the Task is a second calculation: if there is only one calculation to perform, then Task 2.4 will be a narrative Task which must be written up in your main report section and will not be addressed in your Appendix 2.

As discussed above, we recommend that you address these 10 Tasks via the following report sections, assuming that ethics is NOT tested in Requirement 2:

2.A	Strategic and Operational Context	[Task 2.2 and possibly also Task 2.1]
2.B	Results of financial model	[Tasks 2.3, 2.4 & 2.6]
2.C	Evaluation of assumptions	[Tasks 2.5 & 2.8]
2.D	[Other Issues*]	[Tasks 2.6 & 2.7]
2.E	Conclusions	[Task 2.9]
2.F	Commercial Recommendations	[Task 2.10]

* Try to use a more specific heading than "Other issues" once the requirements are known: the heading "Other Issues" is just our generic placeholder text as unfortunately we do not yet know what is on the Exam Paper!

In the event (which is more likely) that ethics is tested in Requirement 2, then you should use the following report section headings:

2.A	Strategic and Operational Context	[Task 2.2 and possibly also Task 2.1]
2.B	Results of financial model	[Tasks 2.3 & 2.6]
2.C	Evaluation of assumptions	[Task 2.8 and possibly also 2.5]
2.D	Ethics and Ethics Recommendations	[Task 2.4 or 2.5 & 2.8]
2.E	[Other Issues*]	[Tasks 2.6 & 2.7]
2.F	Conclusions	[Task 2.9]
2.G	Commercial Recommendations	[Task 2.10]

* Try to use a more specific heading than "Other Issues" once the requirements are known: the heading "Other Issues" is just our generic placeholder text as unfortunately we do not yet know what is on the Exam Paper!

Chapter 10   How to Write a Good Requirement 3

Learning Points

After reading this chapter, you must be able to:

1. appreciate that Requirement 3 involves a lot of writing to cover all necessary sections
2. understand the importance of ethics in Requirement 3
3. understand the changing nature of Box 3.1
4. understand the 10 Tasks and 6 or 7 report sections you should use

---

1   Overview of Requirement 3

As an overview (see the remainder of this chapter for further details), the 10 possibilities to gain a passing grade in a typical Requirement 3 are[45]:

3.1	Outline contract terms & strategic and operational context OR calculations
3.2	Discuss wider context and R1 linkages regarding relevant revenue stream
3.3*	Discussion of Issue 1
3.4*	Discussion of Issue 2
3.5*	Ethics – Issue and Impact
3.6	Further Issue 1 points or Other Issue
3.7	Further Issue 2 points or Other Issue
3.8*	Ethics – Recommendations
3.9^	Conclusions **with figures**
3.10	Commercial Recommendations

We have used a * symbol to indicate the easier Boxes which will normally need to form the basis of a pass.

To identify the focus of Issues 1 and 2 in your own particular Case Study, go back to the question wording on the first page of the exam paper to identify the 2 broad areas which the client/your partner asked you to consider: often this will involve benefits as Issue 1 and risks as Issue 2, but always check. These Issues will normally be the first 2 requests made in the first main sentence of the question wording. You must look carefully for both of these 2 areas as writing about only 1 area will

---

[45] There may be minor differences in the order in which the precise Tasks are presented in the markscheme in particular Case Study exams. Nevertheless, the insight that there will always be 10 core Tasks still applies, despite these minor variances.

114

severely limit your mark. At the same time, in contrast to what many students appear to think, passing Requirement 3 is not **just** about doing a good job on these 2 issues – there are potentially a **further 8 Boxes/Tasks** to be attempted and **at least 3 of these must also be passed** (in addition to the Boxes for the 2 main Issues) to pass Requirement 3 as a whole.

As set out in our Planning & Reminder Sheets (chapter 6), we suggest that you structure your Requirement 3 answer into the following report sections (replacing "Issue 1" and "Issue 2" with something more specific once the exact Tasks are known from your Exam Paper):

3.A	Strategic and Operational Context	[Task 3.2 and possibly 3.1]
3.B	[Issue 1]	[Tasks 3.1 & 3.3 and possibly 3.6]
3.C	[Issue 2]	[Tasks 3.1 & 3.4 and possibly 3.7]
3.D	Ethics and Ethics Recommendations	[Tasks 3.5 & 3.8]
3.E	[Other Issues (if needed*)]	[Tasks 3.6 & 3.7]
3.F	Conclusions	[Task 3.9]
3.G	Commercial Recommendations	[Task 3.10]

* Try to use a more specific heading than "Other Issues" once the requirements are known: the heading "Other Issues" is just our generic placeholder text as unfortunately we do not yet know what is on the Exam Paper! **If you cannot see any other such requirements in the question, this may mean that there are more marks available for further points on Issue 1 and Issue 2: in this case, please drop section 3.E entirely and instead put your time into making further points in sections 3.B and 3.C.**

We have carefully organised this section heading list so that you start with the easier points and leave the difficult "Other Issues" until later in your answer (assuming that "Other Issues" are actually needed in your exam: see below). Since Requirement 3 is quite likely to be the Requirement where you are short of time (assuming that you attempt it last) then we recommend that you read our "Plan B" strategy contained in chapter 13 for more tips on the best order in which to tackle the different Tasks.

2   Requirement 3 – detailed Task by Task advice

Task 3.1   Outline contract terms & strategic and operational context OR calculations

Unlike almost all the other markscheme Boxes, this first Box on the Requirement 3 markscheme has been subject to significant change since 2012. From 2012 to July 2014, Box 3.1 required candidates to spot a linkage back to a specific Advance Information Exhibit: for example, if Requirement 3 asked about the "risks" of a project then references back to a "Risk Register" detailed in the Advance Information would attract credit as these references would demonstrate that the candidate had read and absorbed the Advance Information fully.

In more recent examinations, there has been some credit for this kind of Advance Information linkage in Requirement 3 but not in Box 3.1 (see later in this chapter). From November 2014 onwards, Box 3.1 has instead moved towards rewarding an attempt at a project calculation.

In some examinations such as CC (November 2015), a relatively generous approach has been taken: the results of the financial model in Box 3.1 have not been highlighted in bold in the markscheme, meaning that approximately correct answers would be sufficient. However, TT (November 2016), PL (July 2017) and R4 (November 2017) all use bold text for the calculation results on the markscheme which means that – as in Requirement 2 – correct results must be obtained to gain credit.

Whichever way, please do make some attempt to use the figures provided or you will almost certainly be giving up a whole Box in Requirement 3.

It is important to note that in PL (July 2017), Box 3.1 was extremely similar to Box 2.1 and therefore related to a description of the key contract terms (start date, length, a full refurbishment of all the client's hotels) and recent facts on the client in question. Reward for the calculation was therefore rewarded in Box 3.3 instead. For this reason, it is always worth applying the same approach to the contract outline as you use in Requirement 2 when you attempt Requirement 3 because otherwise you might drop Box 3.1. Note that R4 (November 2017) returned to emphasis on figures in Box 3.1.

Task 3.2   Discuss wider context and R1 linkages regarding relevant revenue stream

Try to look at the strategic and operational aspects of the opportunity in Requirement 3 and see if you can link these back to the Advance Information or Exam Paper information in some way. This is likely to gain the marks. **It is definitely worth considering how the project links back to a specific Exhibit (such as a business plan, strategy document or operational risk review) in the Advance Information, referencing the different numbers within that document (such as "Strategy 4" or "Risk 2", together with details of the strategy or risk), if applicable.**

We have also noticed that recent examinations involve a greater reward for **linkages** back to the Requirement 1 financial "story", looking at the revenue and gross profit performance of the revenue stream involved in the proposed project. Therefore, we would repeat the advice given in the previous chapter in relation to Box 2.2: take another look back at your Appendix 2 and comment on the performance of the relevant stream. For example, if revenue has been declining for the stream in question, you might query whether there is a chance of the project performing well whilst also noting that there may well now be capacity within the stream – if the gross profit margin of the stream is not too high, you might note that there may be better opportunities than the proposed project whilst observing that the absolute gross profit contributed by the stream is significant to the business. These are just example points based on hypothetical performance figures and relationships – always make points which are specific to your examination.

Another Requirement 1 linkage which may be worth making relates to the cash position of the business, particularly if the Advance Information has hinted that the company is struggling for cash (or (perhaps less likely in Case Study) is in a very strong cash position, making investment easy to fund).

Please refer to page 86 for further discussion of the correct approach to this Task and then see page 87 for an argument that you should not necessarily plan or write up this section first.

(Reference to Brexit is likely to be a little too broad for Requirement 3 but if you do decide to make such a reference then please review our discussion in chapter 14 of the examiner comments at the 2017 Tutor Conference for some advice on how to introduce Brexit in the most effective manner. Brexit was not discussed at the 2018 Tutor Conference.)

Task 3.3   Discussion of Issue 1

You should work hard at interpreting the question wording so that you can spot the 2 broad areas on which you need to focus in Requirement 3. As always, we think that the best thing to do is to look at recent markschemes for yourself but here is a quick list of Issue 1 and Issue 2 in the recent exams (we will address both Issues together in the table below (thus anticipating our analysis of Issue 2 later in this chapter) as Issues 1 and 2 are often interrelated):

Exam	Issue 1	Issue 2
LL (July 2012)	Strategic issues	Operational issues
FS (November 2012)	Benefits[46]	Risks
Palate (July 2013)	Issues raised by an assurance company	Implications of issues raised by an assurance company
LT (November 2013)	Benefits – operational and commercial	Risks – operational and commercial
ZM (July 2014)	Benefits – financial, operational and commercial	Risks – financial, operational and commercial
RS (November 2014)	Benefits – financial, operational and commercial	Risks – financial, operational and commercial
Bod (July 2015)	Benefits – strategic, financial and operational	Risks – strategic, financial and operational
CC (November 2015)	Opportunity 1 – financial, operational and strategic issues	Opportunity 2 – financial, operational and strategic issues
TT (November 2016)	Financial issues	Operational and strategic issues
PL (July 2017)	Financial issues	Operational and strategic issues
R4 (November 2017)	Financial issues	Operational and strategic issues

(Bux (July 2016) asked for analysis of financial, operational and strategic issues but (uniquely) spread across **3 issues** rather than the more normal Issue 1 and Issue 2. Hence it does not fit easily into the above table and has therefore been excluded as it represents an exception to the rule.)

---

[46] Unlike in later Case Studies, in FS (November 2012) the markscheme does not specify any particular types of benefit and risk such as financial, operational and commercial: it just says "Benefits" and "Risks", in line with the question wording on the Exam Paper which provided no further specification of the types of "Benefits" and "Risks" to discuss.

We would note that the last 3 examinations (TT (November 2016), PL (July 2017) and R4 (November 2017)) have both allocated a whole Box to financial issues and then a **shared** Box to the combination of operational and strategic issues: this is definitely something to consider in your examination strategy.

Based on the above, we can say, firstly, that benefits and risks are the most likely Issue 1 and Issue 2 but, secondly, that it is always worth checking the question wording carefully: for example, in Palate, Issue 2 was actually an extension of Issue 1. **Always read the question wording carefully because it is vital for you to identify the correct 2 issues if your answer is to be focused appropriately.**

Under this Task, do not aim for in-depth or value-added points – just keep things nice and simple and look at the most obvious points. **Boxes/Tasks 3.3 and 3.4 are actually quite easy to pass – it is the rest of Requirement 3 which is more difficult.**

Be careful not to write too much on Issue 1 and 2 – many candidates understandably assume that these parts of the Requirement are the most important (the question wording on the first page of the Exam Paper would seem to suggest that this is the case) but in fact there may only be 2 Boxes for the most obvious components of the Requirement: in other words, **there are potentially another 8 Boxes for points that do not directly relate to the apparent focus of the question**. You can hence easily cause yourself to fail through too exclusive a focus on these 2 issues if this means that you are neglecting the other 80% of this Requirement.

Task 3.4   Discussion of Issue 2

This Task generally involves looking at the second key element of the Requirement. Follow the same advice that we have given above for Issue 1.

Again, do not assume that you can pass Requirement 3 by doing a good job of these Tasks 3.3 and 3.4 only – you cannot.

Task 3.5   Ethics – Issue and Impact

Traditionally, Requirement 3 has always been "the" ethical Requirement but in many examinations from November 2014 onwards, ethics has been tested in Requirement 2. Even if ethics has already been tested in Requirement 2, we still think that for Requirement 3 you should aim to find **at least** 2 different ethical matters (probably 3 or 4) and then evaluate them under the following IIR framework:

Issue	why is this an ethical problem? what ethical principles have been breached?[47]
Impact	will the impact on our business be serious or not?
Recommendations	are there any practical actions we can take to reduce the impact of the problem?

Your II (Issue and Impact) points will normally attract credit in Box 3.5. Your R (Recommendations) points will be rewarded in Box 3.8 (or sometimes alternatively in Box 3.10). We strongly recommend that you make the most of the opportunity to use bullet points for Recommendations by including your ethics mitigation points as a set of bullets under the heading of "Ethics Recommendations" (within report section 3.D). Remember that you are not allowed to use bullet points in your report except when providing Recommendations.

We would regard the Ethics Boxes as some of the easier or "key" Tasks in Requirement 3 and most candidates will need to pass these Boxes. Provided that you identify at least 2 issues and discuss these in a bit of detail, you have a good chance.

All examinations from July 2014 onwards have had 2 Boxes for ethics in Requirement 3, regardless of whether ethics is also tested in Requirement 2, with the exception of Bux (July 2016) due to Requirement 3 in Bux involving discussion of 3 different projects, meaning that Boxes 3.5 and 3.8 were needed for general strategic and operational analysis: however, all 3 projects in Bux had ethical issues to consider.

As such, the importance of ethics to the markscheme appears to have increased in the last few years and therefore you are advised to ensure that your report section 3.D is of a good standard. This is why we suggest that you attempt these sections quite soon into your Requirement 3 answer, after writing up Issues 1 and 2 (given that we recommend that you return to section 3.A on Strategic and Operational Context later into your answer, even though this will be presented as your first section in your actual script. See chapter 6 for more details).

Please note that, as a significant exception to all previous papers, in Bux (July 2016) it was necessary to change Box 3.5 into discussion of a third Issue (an increase on the usual 2 Issues always previously considered) – therefore Box 3.5 was not dedicated solely to ethics, but did contain some ethics points. It remains to be seen whether this pattern will continue but if only 1 or 2 Issues/projects are mentioned on the examination paper then we would assume that Box 3.5 would **return to being a dedicated ethics Box**. This is certainly what happened in the 3 examinations after Bux (TT (November 2016), PL (July 2017) and R4 (November 2017)).

As a final point on Ethics, we would note that the 2 most recent examinations (PL (July 2017) and R4 (November 2017)) awarded credit for noting the possibility that an issue could be a good ethical fit

---

[47] For example, is the action dishonest, unfair, a breach of confidentiality, unprofessional, lacking in objectivity or something that shows a lack of integrity? Do not just say something is "unethical" as this does not really analyse the problem in a helpful way and is too easy to say – instead, try to spell out what the "unethical" aspect actually is, using ethical language.

with the ethical philosophy of the Case Study company: prior to these examinations, the Ethics marks had always been awarded for identifying ethical problems rather than ethically positive aspects. Therefore, you may now wish to comment briefly on any potential for the issues described in Requirement 3 to fit well with the Case Study company's positive ethics philosophy. At the same time, please note that most of the marks for Ethics in these examinations remained of the usual type (identification of ethical problems) so do not go overboard on the good stuff!

Task 3.6   Further Issue 1 points or Other Issue

To tackle this Box, the first thing to do (as with Requirement 2 and Boxes 2.6 and 2.7) is to return to the question wording from the first page of the Exam Paper where the client or your partner sets out the requirements. Look for any possible hint as to what **additional** matters, other than the more obvious Issue 1 and Issue 2, you will need to look at.

In some examinations, there may in fact **not** be any further issues specified in which case you are advised to **drop** your report section on Other Issues and instead write more ideas on Issue 1 and 2 (probably benefits and risks): Boxes 3.6 and 3.7 will reward further points on Issue 1 and Issue 2, respectively. However, in other examinations, Tasks 3.6 and 3.7 could be completely **separate** from earlier Tasks and so a dedicated report section **is** needed. Please note that we are only using the term "Other Issues" as a generic placeholder, which you should replace in your report when you know what the specific Tasks in the Exam Paper are.

Assuming that Task 3.6 appears to have something of a strategic aspect then try to look at the company-level impact of the opportunity or event. We like to teach our taught course students that strategy is all about considerations at the **Board level**: the next Box (3.7) may then look at more practical issues at the **operational level**. Consider things like the importance of the customer, market segment, reputation and opportunity for future work if you are looking at strategic issues.

Task 3.7   Further Issue 2 points or Other Issue

Again, the first thing to do is check the question wording for any hint as to what the additional Tasks may involve, in addition to the more obvious Issue 1 and Issue 2. As stated above, in some exams, this Task may simply be a matter of writing about further points on Issues 1 and 2 whereas in other Case exams, Tasks 3.6 and 3.7 could be quite **separate** from earlier points.

Assuming that Task 3.7 has a practical character (to pair up with our assumed strategic focus in Task 3.6 above) then it will be helpful to use the list of core practical areas in our Planning & Reminder Sheets to generate ideas. Try to keep to the simplest operational points: issues such as quality, capacity, staffing, time frames, reputation, cultural, forex and similar issues stand a good chance of gaining marks.

The distinction between strategic and practical issues can become blurred. Therefore do not worry too much about the division between the Boxes and plan both areas together: we in fact suggest that you have a single report section (3.E) which aims to cater for **both** Task 3.6 and 3.7: the marker will look for your points anywhere on the Exam Paper so do not waste energy and time unnecessarily worrying about splitting these Tasks if they appear to overlap.

Our biggest tip when tackling Tasks 3.6 and 3.7 is not to worry too much about having to achieve these Boxes to pass Requirement 3: as in the other Requirements, these X.6 and X.7 evaluation Boxes are the hardest Tasks to pass and most passing candidates will not gain both Boxes: many will not even pass one, given the uncertainty as to what will be rewarded and considering that there are 8 other opportunities/Tasks to gain a passing Box.

Therefore our biggest tip regarding these Boxes is … **remember that there are other more important things to do to pass!** We say this every time to our taught course students but still they worry about exactly what to do in these very unpredictable Tasks.

Once again, **always check the instructions for Requirement 3 in the Exam Paper** to determine whether Tasks 3.6 and 3.7 relate to specific extra requests from the client or, if you are sure that there are no specific issues other than Issue 1 and 2 to address, then instead write more points on Issue 1 and 2 as Boxes 3.6 and 3.7 will have to overlap with the same areas. In the latter case, you can drop the report section heading for Other Issues (3.E) as you will simply have longer report sections 3.B and 3.C on Issue 1 and Issue 2.

Task 3.8   Ethics – Recommendations

Marks are awarded in this Box for telling the company what to do in response to the ethical issues identified as part of Task 3.5. In other words, here you are rewarded for ethical **recommendations**. As already mentioned above, we strongly recommend that you make the most of the opportunity to use bullet points for Recommendations by including your ethics mitigation points as a set of bullets under the heading of "Ethics Recommendations" (within report section 3.D). Remember that you are not allowed to use bullet points in your report except when providing Recommendations.

There is no need to repeat your ethics Recommendations at the end of your Requirement 3 report section: even if Box 3.10 were to contain marks for ethics Recommendations, such marks would be awarded regardless of where you have stated your ethics Recommendations so there is no need to repeat your ethics Recommendations at the end of your report section as this will simply waste time.

Prior to 2014, this Box tended to be awarded for scepticism points. ZM (July 2014) was the first of the recent Case Study examinations in which there was no dedicated Box on professional scepticism in Requirement 3. Instead, there were 3 professional scepticism remarks mixed in with Boxes 3.6 and 3.7 (2 points in Box 3.6 and 1 point in Box 3.7). This was because the examiners needed to make space in Box 3.8 for a second ethics Box which primarily looked at how to mitigate the ethical issues. Exams since July 2014 have continued this pattern, with scepticism diamonds mixed into other Boxes and with a lower number of marks for this skill than in the past.

It is still worth exercising a bit of scepticism in Requirement 3 because there may be a few marks available – it is just that they may not congregate into a dedicated Box and this is worth bearing in mind when the marking is based not on how many acceptable points you are making but whether you manage to get up to the important figure of 3 diamonds **per Box**. If there is no longer a dedicated

Box for scepticism, then it follows that it is not worth too much of a focus on this skill as there is no way to get a batch of 3 marks to contribute a passing Box. Once again, it is not the **number** of points alone that matters – the **distribution** of those points is extremely important: as the scepticism marks are spread across different Boxes, it is not possible to gain a Box just for this skill alone and you may well have already passed the Boxes into which scepticism marks are sprinkled, in which case gaining the scepticism marks on top does not benefit your mark. Therefore, always prioritise **ethics** over **scepticism** in Requirement 3.

Please note that, in a similar way to Box 3.5 (and again as a significant exception to all previous papers), in Bux (July 2016) it was necessary to change Box 3.8 into evaluation of a third Issue/project opportunity (an increase on the usual 2 Issues always previously considered) – therefore Box 3.8 was not dedicated solely to ethics, but did contain some ethics points. It remains to be seen whether this pattern will continue but if only 1 or 2 Issues/projects are mentioned on the examination paper then we would assume that Box 3.8 would **return to being a dedicated ethics Box**. This was the case in TT (November 2016), PL (July 2017) and R4 (November 2017), all of which had the **standard** 2 Boxes for ethics.

Task 3.9   Conclusions with figures

As with all Conclusions Boxes, only a narrow range of points will feature on the markscheme (4-5 diamonds) and therefore you must stay focused on making the standard acceptable points. As in Requirement 2, do not forget to include a decision on whether the company **should go ahead with the project or not**. Remember that it is only with respect to the points in the Conclusions Boxes (Boxes 1.9, 2.9 and 3.9) that ICAEW are fussy about where a point is stated: to score in these Boxes, your point must be under a heading labelled "Conclusions" whereas the points in all other Boxes on the markscheme can be made in any section. As the "proceed or not" point is always allocated to Box 3.9 in Requirement 3 (and Box 2.9 in Requirement 2), you must be careful to make this point under a "Conclusions" heading (see chapter 14 for more details).

Another common slip up is to forget to offer any conclusions on **ethics**.

As a calculation is now almost certainly required in Requirement 3, remember to offer a conclusion on the **significance** of the **financial impact** of the project, including a relevant figure (the mark here will be "open" and so does not have to be correct but must match your earlier work).

Use of the Planning & Reminder Sheets set out in chapter 6 should normally be enough to score 3 diamonds for this Conclusions Task: the points to make are always of the same type and you are rewarded just for attempting to make your Conclusions rather than for reaching any specific decisions. Therefore, normally you should pass this Task.

Task 3.10   Commercial Recommendations

As in the other Requirements, this Task is very difficult to pass as it is hard to predict what points will be rewarded. Try to use our set of 8 core practical areas (see chapter 11) as the basis and try to be as practical and business-oriented as you can. **Negotiating** or **discussing** with other parties tends to be a point which is rewarded. **Due diligence** is also something to consider if new parties are involved. It is also always worth recommending to perform **market research** and to confirm the validity of the model **inputs**.

Generally, recommendations on ethics do not appear to be rewarded in this Task even though all papers since July 2014 have required a detailed discussion of how to mitigate ethical problems to obtain the marks in Box 3.8. Therefore we strongly recommend that you view Task 3.10 as being about Commercial or "**non-ethics**" Recommendations: otherwise there is a risk that if you include too many ethical recommendations in your Recommendations section then you will get the ethics recommendations marks in Task 3.8 but you will not score any of the marks within Task 3.10. In any case, based on our Planning & Reminder Sheets, you should have put your ethics recommendations into report section 3.D on ethics before you even get to the Commercial Recommendations at the end of your answer so you should not really be mixing up the 2 types of Recommendation anyway.

You are advised to give this Box your best shot through at least 7 practical ideas but try to ensure that you are not reliant on passing the Task as it is unpredictable by nature: the core of your pass clearly lies in the other Boxes, as in the other 2 Requirements.

As we have advised in the previous 2 chapters on Requirements 1 and 2, we think that it is very useful to write up your Commercial Recommendations section as you go along in the question, noting down any ideas as you have them whilst writing the main body of Requirement 3, rather than leaving the development of your Commercial Recommendations to the end as a separate activity. This should save you time and ensure that you are making points which are relevant to the scenario. If you leave this work as a separate activity at the end, you may waste time if you struggle to think of points or you may come up with ideas that are too generic in nature because you have not written the points at the same time that the underlying issues were considered and so you will not be making any points that link back to what is unique about the Exam Paper scenario information.

3   Requirement 3 Executive Summary elements

In our view, the Requirement 3 Executive Summary Tasks are the easiest Executive Summary Boxes to pass: the marks are the most predictable of all the Requirements.

Task E.3a   Results of Requirement 3 calculation and 2 main Issues

In this first Task, you pull through your points from your Requirement 3 Conclusions (report section 3.F (or 3.E if no "Other Issues" need to be discussed), concluding on Issue 1, Issue 2 and the wider context or project background. It is worth identifying 2 matters from Issue 1 and 2 matters from Issue 2 ("2+2 approach") in order to give you a good range of points. If you have been asked to evaluate the benefits and risks of 2 different projects, for example, it would make sense to include a benefit and risk of project 1 and a benefit and risk of project 2 to fulfil our suggested "2+2 approach". This will provide a good balance of points and if you try to select the fundamental benefits and risks then you will also have a few "shots" at any specific points that you might be required to match on the markscheme (although note that Box E.3a tends to be "open", rewarding any points of the right type, rather than requiring points that are too specific).

Also state your overall view on whether the opportunity/project in Requirement 3 is a significant one or not. As noted regarding Requirements 1 and 2 in chapters 8 and 9, there no longer appears to be a mark available for "wider context" points in the Executive Summary so only include these if you have the time to spare.

Task E.3b   Proceed or not, ethics, scepticism, Other Issues, recommendations

In this Task, you repeat your Conclusions on ethics, other matters including practical issues, say whether to proceed and then finally make some Commercial Recommendations (again, bear in mind that in the case of the Executive Summary, and unlike in the main narrative of the Requirement itself, it does not really matter what your Recommendations are as long as you provide some sensible ideas).

In ZM (July 2014), 3 of the 5 diamonds available in this Box (which will now only carry 4 diamonds: see chapter 14) related to ethics so it really does pay to be thorough here if there are several ethics issues to address.

Although there has been a frustrating move towards requiring students to match specific Recommendations on the markscheme to be awarded a mark in the Executive Summary in Requirements 1 and 2 (see chapter 14), to date the Recommendations permitted in Requirement 3 have generally remained "open" in nature i.e. any sensible Recommendation will be awarded the mark. (However, see the Foreword to this edition of *Cracking Case*™ for some examples of relatively specific Recommendations in the R4 Limited (November 2017) Executive Summary for Requirement 3.) This is another reason why we believe that the Executive Summary for Requirement 3 is easier than for the other Requirements.

We would finally note that there was a mark for scepticism of the information provided in Box E.3b in the PL (July 2017) examination. This forms a contrast with many other recent papers where scepticism was only rewarded in the Requirement 2 element of the Executive Summary but based on this example, which is from a recent examination, we would still suggest adding a scepticism point to your Requirement 3 Executive Summary, just in case.

124

4   Requirement 3 – a reminder of the 10 Tasks

We hope that the analysis of this chapter will have given you a better understanding of what you need to do to pass Requirement 3 without spending too long on this part of the exam.

As a basic summary, we now provide a list of what each of the 10 Tasks requires and we then explain the 6 section headings which you should use in your report section to obtain good coverage of the points required. These are just quick, end-of-chapter reminders to consolidate your knowledge: we would not expect you to use these pages in the examination itself as you should instead be using the Planning & Reminder Sheets found in chapter 6 for more specific guidance and reminders.

3.1	Outline contract terms & strategic and operational context OR calculations
3.2	Discuss wider context and R1 linkages regarding relevant revenue stream
3.3*	Discussion of Issue 1
3.4*	Discussion of Issue 2
3.5*	Ethics – Issue and Impact
3.6	Further Issue 1 points or Other Issue
3.7	Further Issue 2 points or Other Issue
3.8*	Ethics – Recommendations
3.9*	Conclusions **with figures**
3.10	Commercial Recommendations

As discussed above, we recommend that you address these 10 Tasks/Boxes via the following 8 report section headings:

3.A	Strategic and Operational Context	[Task 3.2 and possibly 3.1]
3.B	[Issue 1]	[Tasks 3.1 & 3.3 and possibly 3.6]
3.C	[Issue 2]	[Tasks 3.1 & 3.4 and possibly 3.7]
3.D	Ethics and Ethics Recommendations	[Tasks 3.5 & 3.8]
3.E	[Other Issues (if needed*)]	[Tasks 3.6 & 3.7]
3.F	Conclusions	[Task 3.9]
3.G	Commercial Recommendations	[Task 3.10]

* Try to use a more specific heading than "Other Issues" once the requirements are known: the heading "Other Issues" is just our generic placeholder text as unfortunately we do not yet know what is on the Exam Paper! **If you cannot see any other such requirements in the question, this may mean that there are more marks available for further points on Issue 1 and Issue 2: in this case, please drop section 3.E entirely and instead put your time into making further points in sections 3.B and 3.C.**

Chapter 11   Being Practical – Understanding the 8 Case Themes

---

Learning Points

After reading this chapter, you must be able to:

1. understand why development of "practical" points is a key skill in Case
2. give examples from recent Case exams of "practical" points
3. cite the 8 key areas/points which seem to attract marks under "practical" points
4. develop a strategy to prepare potential practical points in the run up to the exam

---

The skill of developing practical Recommendations and fixing practical issues/problems with proposed strategies is important throughout all sections of the Case Study:

- Executive Summary: 3 Tasks have diamonds for practical or commercial Recommendations

- Requirement 1: 1 full Task for practical or commercial Recommendations and several diamonds for practical Recommendations in the ET Task 1.8

- Requirement 2: 1 full Task for practical or commercial Recommendations plus several other Boxes looking at operational issues with the proposed project

- Requirement 3: 1 full Task for practical or commercial Recommendations then various other Tasks looking at the operational aspects of the strategic proposal

Based on the number of marks generally available within the above Boxes, we have estimated that practical recommendations/issues will typically account for around **17.5% of the marks available** for the examination as a whole.

Given the importance of this skills area, this chapter carefully reviews and analyses the points which will tend to score marks, based on our analysis of past papers. As always, we are looking for **patterns** with a view to working out what kinds of point are more likely to score the marks.

1   Requirement 1

Although Requirement 1 is generally about reviewing financial performance (and especially the Income Statement), and therefore can normally be passed primarily on the basis of good calculations and related discussion, it is still worth analysing how practical matters are tested in this Requirement.

The table below summarises recent examination papers (most recent paper in the lefthand column):

	R4	PL	TT	Bux	CC	Bod	RS	ZM	LT	P	FS	LL
Avoid future reoccurrence	♦	♦	♦				♦					♦
Cash flow	♦		♦								♦	
Check figures/facts	♦	♦		♦			♦					♦
Concentrate on growth areas	♦		♦						♦			
Find new suppliers				♦	♦							
Improve credit control											♦	
Improve quality control					♦					♦	♦	
Investigate poor performance			♦	♦[48]	♦	♦	♦	♦	♦			♦
Monitor compliance with targets	♦											
Negotiate with client/supplier		♦			♦		♦	♦		♦	♦	
Pricing policy review			♦			♦			♦			
Review information or trading terms	♦							♦		♦	♦	
Spread best practice												♦
Staffing issues						♦		♦		♦	♦	

As may be expected for a primarily numerical Requirement, **investigation** of the figures is a common recommendation or practical consideration. **Negotiation** with the client or suppliers is also a common theme. It is also worth making points on streams that are performing very well ("concentrate on growth areas") and very badly ("investigate reasons for poor performance").

2   Requirement 2

Many candidates fail the exam because they do not notice that the Exam Paper instructions for Requirement 2 often ask for comments on "**any other issues** that [Company X] should consider" or, alternatively, give candidates further specific Tasks to attempt. Such candidates think that the calculations are all that matters in Requirement 2. This is not the case – reference to these "Other Issues" is effectively an invitation to look partly at practical issues and these often attract the same reward in terms of Boxes as the calculations.

In the 2014 and subsequent examinations (other than TT (November 2016) and PL (July 2017) which both had 2 calculations to perform), there has been even less emphasis on the calculations with additional Boxes for narrative matters such as operational/practical points. As such, we recommend that you look carefully at the points in the following table (most recent paper in the lefthand column):

---

[48] Bux (July 2016) in fact had 2 different diamonds for this point of investigating problems in performance.

	R4	PL	TT	Bux	CC	Bod	RS	ZM	LT	P	FS	LL
Capacity	♦											
Cash flows/funding methods	♦						♦		♦	♦	♦	♦
Discounting/pricing					♦	♦		♦			♦	♦
Due diligence	♦		♦	♦	♦					♦		
Impact on other streams											♦	♦
Look at alternatives		♦						♦			♦	♦
Management time used		♦								♦	♦	♦
Market research		♦	♦	♦	♦			♦	♦	♦		
Negotiate	♦	♦	♦	♦[49]	♦	♦	♦		♦	♦	♦	♦
Review figures	♦	♦	♦	♦	♦	♦	♦	♦		♦	♦	
Staffing issues			♦			♦	♦			♦	♦	♦
Timing issues		♦	♦							♦	♦	♦

Here we can see that it is worthwhile considering how the project will be **funded**, **pricing** methods and **negotiation** with clients and suppliers. It is also generally worth suggesting that any **input** data used in the financial model should be **reviewed and confirmed**. Reference to **alternative projects**, the impact on **management time** and the proposed **timescale** of the project is also worthwhile.

3 Requirement 3

We strongly recommend that you review our analysis below to help with Requirement 3 but our most important tip remains – please ensure you that you leave enough time to complete this Requirement and do not just assume that it is "the easy one". Here is a review of the practical points which have been rewarded in the recent Requirement 3s (most recent paper in the lefthand column):

---

[49] Bux (July 2016) had 2 different diamonds for 2 different types of negotiation point.

	R4	PL	TT	Bux	CC	Bod	RS	ZM	LT	P	FS	LL
Backup for figures		♦	♦			♦	♦			♦	♦	
Capacity constraints	♦	♦				♦	♦	♦				
Diversification	♦	♦				♦		♦			♦	
Due diligence		♦	♦		♦	♦	♦		♦			♦
Funding methods			♦				♦	♦	♦			
Impact on other streams								♦				♦
Legal advice					♦							
Look at alternatives	♦	♦	♦		♦				♦	♦		♦
Management time		♦					♦				♦	
Market research			♦	♦		♦						♦
Monitor compliance with targets	♦											
Negotiate	♦	♦	♦	♦	♦	♦	♦	♦	♦	♦		♦
Pricing/discounting							♦	♦			♦	♦
Quality controls					♦				♦		♦	
Reputational issues	♦	♦	♦			♦	♦	♦	♦		♦	
Staffing issues	♦					♦	♦	♦		♦	♦	♦

Here we can see that again there is emphasis on **funding** the project, **negotiations**, **reputation** and **staffing** issues/considerations. **Negotiation** is in fact one of the most common points in all 3 Requirements so definitely bear this in mind.

It is worth noting that in Bux (July 2016), many of the recommendations in Box 3.10 related to ethics recommendations. We generally recommend that you include these earlier in your answer in your main ethics section (report section 3.D) as you would still gain credit in Box 3.10 if you do so – then ensure that your Recommendations section at the end of the answer contains practical or commercial points. In this way, you will be covered regardless of whether Box 3.10 has a more ethical or more practical flavour.

4 How to develop good "practical" points: conclusions and summary

Although the practical points skill is probably the most open requirement and hardest to predict, the above review of some of the recent Case Studies will hopefully be enough to illustrate some patterns in terms of what to say.

In our review above we have emphasised the 2 to 3 most commonly occurring points within each Requirement but looking at all 3 analyses as a whole, we recommend that you try to focus on the following general areas (some of which are also included as reminders within our Planning & Reminder Sheets):

1. **Income/Pricing/Discounts**
2. **Reputation**
3. **Timing**
4. **Management time**
5. **Capacity**
6. **Need for further information/market research**
7. **Discuss and negotiate – involve stakeholders**
8. **Due Diligence/perform checks on new supplier/partner**

Please learn the above list of 8 areas and study this chapter well – it is not an exaggeration to say that this could be the most important element of your preparation, given the significance (**17.5%**) of the Boxes which involve practical considerations.

As already advised in chapters 8, 9 and 10, we think that it is very useful to write up your Commercial Recommendations section as you go along in the question, noting down any ideas as you have them whilst writing the main body of each Requirement, rather than leaving the development of your Commercial Recommendations to the end as a separate activity. This should save you time and ensure that you are making points which are relevant to the scenario. If you leave this work as a separate activity at the end, you may waste time if you struggle to think of points or you may come up with ideas that are too generic in nature because you have not written the points at the same time that the underlying issues were considered and so you will not be making any points that link back to what is unique about the Exam Paper scenario information.

5 Comments from students

> **Student 2 says:** *"There are obviously very many possible practical considerations you could raise. The most important lesson I learnt for Case is to "step back" when you get to the recommendations stage. In my Requirement 2 in my first Case sitting, I developed some relatively complex arguments which would indicate that a particular course of action was favourable, and should be followed by doing x, y, and z. I had fallen into the trap of trying to provide some insightful, original advice. Good or bad as it may have been, it was never going to be on the markscheme. Take a step back, and provide **basic**, sensible Recommendations. Don't let the thought that "management would know that already" prevent you from saying something."*

Chapter 12   Assumptions and Scepticism – Evolution in the Markscheme

Learning Points

After reading this chapter, you must be able to:

1. understand how the marking of Assumptions and Scepticism has evolved in recent examinations
2. appreciate that you may need to be flexible in terms of the way you write up your points
3. understand the different Box allocation for these skills between Requirements 2 and 3

The area of Assumptions and Scepticism is unarguably the element of the markscheme which has seen the most evolution in recent examination sittings. We have already noted that starting in July 2015, there has been a marked shift in the amount of marks available for Assumptions and Scepticism and also in the types of points that you need to make to obtain these marks. Additionally, 2 recent examinations (TT (November 2016) and PL (July 2017)) only allocated 1 Box to Assumptions in Requirement 2, in contrast to most other examinations (including R4 (November 2017)) where 2 Boxes have been available. Overall, this area is subject to significant change.

Although we have already discussed Assumptions and Scepticism where relevant in chapters 9 and 10, in light of the fact that this area has been subject to significant but subtle change in recent examinations, we have decided to write a dedicated chapter to explore the best ways in which to attempt the relevant Tasks.

We have also decided to create a dedicated chapter because there will normally be 2 Boxes available in Requirement 2 for these skills and therefore around 20% of the marks available for that Requirement relate to this topic. Whilst the number of marks for Scepticism in Requirement 3 has fallen in recent sittings (see below) and now no longer constitutes a full markscheme Box, the marks that remain available could still be very useful, particularly if you are rushing to complete your Requirement 3 at the end of the examination.

For these reasons, it is not an exaggeration to say that this chapter could save your life in the examination.

1   The good old (predictable) days

Several years ago, it was much easier to explain how to gain the marks for Assumptions and Scepticism in both Requirement 2 and Requirement 3.

In Requirement 2, there always used to be a Box for Assumptions and then a separate Box for Scepticism.

The Assumptions marks were available for working through each input in the financial model and stating that this was only an estimate and could turn out different in reality. In some examinations, this was literally all you had to do to get your Assumptions marks – in other words, you pretty much

132

only needed to say that an estimated input "could turn out differently" and then repeat the same point 5 or 6 times for the various different inputs to score all the points in the Box.

The Scepticism marks in Requirement 2 were then available for making a deeper kind of criticism of the model such as querying where the information had come from, looking at any bias in the information, looking at 3 or 4 unknown model inputs which had not been provided in the information or querying the basic methodology.

During this period, there was thus a very clear separation between Assumptions and Scepticism marks in Requirement 2 and both Boxes had very predictable marks within them.

In Requirement 3 in the "good old days", there used to be a single Box for Scepticism – there was no need for a Box for Assumptions because in those days the Requirement 3 markscheme did not contain any calculations or modelling work so there were accordingly no marks for the querying of model inputs. The single Box available for Scepticism rewarded very similar points to Requirement 2 so candidates had to look at the same sort of areas such as bias in the information, missing information and so on.

As noted above, from July 2015 onwards, the recent markschemes have definitely departed from this pattern. It is no longer the case that you should expect to see separate Assumptions and Scepticism Boxes in Requirement 2 and there is no longer a dedicated Box for Scepticism in Requirement 3.

The best way to explain these changes is for us to reproduce the relevant Boxes from the 2015 onwards examination papers so we will do this next and then analyse the implications for your answer.

2   Requirement 2 in recent Case Study examinations

Bod (July 2015)

This examination had 2 Boxes, both in relation to Assumptions:

Comments on adequacy of working assumptions
♦ Salaries: average may be higher / lower than £40k
♦ Fees: only proposed / not agreed
♦ 8 person-days: estimated figure / actual may be different
♦ Interviews: estimated figures for number and cost / actual may be different
♦ Advertising: estimated figure / actual may be different
♦ Entertaining: estimated figure / actual may be different

Evaluates working assumptions
♦ Salaries: affected by local economy / supply and demand
♦ Fees: upper end of 10-15% industry norm
♦ 8 p-days: Dollond 10 / 9 in 2014 / depends on efficiencies
♦ Interviews: Dollond 30 interviews / £40 each
♦ Advertising: use of internet / social media may reduce £20k
♦ Entertaining: unclear what £40k includes

Here we can see that there was no credit for any broader Scepticism points such as the source of the information or the model methodology used. Instead, everything is quite focused on 6 specific inputs in both Boxes.

The first Box is of the type traditionally seen before 2015 – in other words, the Box is relatively easy as the candidate simply had to say that each input was an **estimate**. A second Box of marks was then available for making a **second** or "extension" point on each of those **same** 6 inputs – here the marks were given in most cases for comparing back to a **benchmark mentioned in the Advance Information** (the reference to "Dollond" is a reference back to a similar project that had run in the past and which was mentioned extensively in the Advance Information).

Therefore, the approach to adopt based on this markscheme would have been to identify the inputs, state that each one is only an estimate and could turn out to be different but then to find a second or "extension" point on each of those inputs which was less generic and which would display knowledge of the Advance Information. The second point (Box 2.8) was therefore not a completely **separate** point and nor about scepticism more generally, as might have been the case in earlier examinations.

CC (November 2015)

This examination had 2 Boxes, both in relation to Assumptions:

Comments on adequacy of working assumptions
♦ Bikes: (3,000) bikes / (300) docking stations may be overestimate
♦ Vehicles: cost seems high (£40k)
♦ Vehicles: appropriateness of docking ratio (1 to 30) / 4-year life
♦ D̶ salary: salary may be high (£40k)
♦ ̶bers: may be high (3)
  ̶0k) / Other (£5k): may be higher/lower

  ̶mptions
  ̶ may not be appropriate basis
  ̶-£30k / already have vans
  ̶ CC dep'n policy

  ̶ costs by £160k
  ̶ cheaper insurance

In this e̶ ̶proach was different to Bod (July 2015) – the first Box was no longer available sin̶ ̶g that something is an estimate and could be different (although note that there was a ma̶ ̶aying this in relation to the final point in the first Box on overheads). Rather, the marks were for saying that the estimate appears to be too "high". Saying something appears to be too high requires more knowledge of the Advance Information than the more generic point that "an estimate could be different" so perhaps the examiners decided to make the first Box more difficult.

The second Box was in some ways similar to the previous examination because some of the points such as the fact that the company's existing vans had cost between £25,000 and £30,000 would require knowledge of the Advance Information. However, we can also see some points which would traditionally have been in a separate Scepticism Box such as saying that the application of a London model to the proposed project (which was in Manchester) was not appropriate, consideration of the

134

impact of rounding in the calculation and the suggestion that there may be missing costs such as overheads or other costs. Overall, this second Box is really a **blend** of the traditional Scepticism Box and some of the changes introduced from the July 2015 paper reviewed above whereas in the July 2015 paper, **every** point in the second Box connected back to the inputs criticised in the first Box.

Bux (July 2016)

This examination had 2 Boxes, both in relation to Assumptions:

Comments on adequacy of assumptions
♦ Liza: vested interest in getting a deal **so** figures could be optimistic
♦ List prices: look high (eg Hardback £20 v £15/£18)
♦ Sales volumes: no track record for Emily **so** could be optimistic
♦ Hardback v paperback ratio: different from company/industry norm
♦ Royalties: Paperback/E-book higher than standard rates
♦ Advance: £50k/25% more than previous highest figure

Evaluates assumptions
♦ Liza: GFR estimate was conservative / was achieved
♦ Average revenue per book: £9.16/£8.40 v 2016 £7.67
♦ Sales volumes: timing capitalises on pre-Xmas sales
♦ HB v PB ratio: comparable to GFR / more PBs in future
♦ Royalties: agreeing high rate may impact other deals
♦ Advance: high impairment cost if book unsuccessful

In this examination, there appears to have been a further subtle evolution in the approach. Similar to the previous examination, some of the marks in the first Box were awarded for stating that an input appeared to be "high". Yet there are also some Scepticism marks such as the reliability of Liza as a source of information and the fact that we have no prior historical data in relation to Emily.

However, it is the second Box ("Evaluates assumptions") which is of more interest here. The first point in this second Box is **very different in nature** to any of the other Boxes we have reviewed so far in this chapter as the mark is awarded here for saying that the estimate appears to be **reasonable** as Liza had previously achieved what she had promised on an earlier project. This is the first time we have ever seen an Assumptions mark for saying that something appears to be **correct** – normally the marks are reserved only for being **critical** of the inputs.

Another interesting mark here is the third point which states that the timing of the book launch would capitalise on pre-Christmas sales: normally, we would expect to see this in the strategic or operational points Box and not in relation to Assumptions. In respect of the issue of timing in the Assumptions or Scepticism Boxes, we would normally expect to see some kind of statement that the proposed timing was not achievable – this would then show some Scepticism as to whether the model was realistic. However, in the July 2016 examination, the timing mark is again for suggesting that the input/model is **reasonable** because high sales would occur before Christmas.

Similarly, the final 2 points in the second Box are also of a strategic or operational nature rather than being criticisms of the model. The first of these 2 points is that if a very high royalty is offered to Emily as a new author, then the company would presumably face requests for similarly high royalties from its existing authors and so there would be a very high marginal cost of engaging Emily. As such, the mark is awarded for reminding the company that the decision in relation to Emily is effectively a decision in relation to all other authors as well. This makes it something of a strategic point rather than a classic Assumptions point because the issue is not that the input is wrong: rather, the point is that there would be significant strategic implications of maintaining the proposed figure for that input. Again, like the first point in the second Box reviewed above, this mark is based on the input potentially being **reasonable** (rather than being a suggestion that the input is not correct, as has been required for all other Assumptions marks in other past papers).

The final point in the Box is an accounting issue which reminds the company that there will be a high impairment charge if the book fails – again, we would normally consider this to be a strategic consideration rather than a classic Assumptions points (as there is no suggestion that the input is wrong). Put another way, the mark is awarded here not for saying that the sales forecasts appear high (which would be a model input or Assumptions mark) but rather for spelling out the implications if the project were to fail in practice (something which has nothing to do with whether the model is reasonable).

Based on the above, hopefully you can see that the second Box on Assumptions in this examination is very different to the other examples. We therefore started to advise our taught course students to take a more careful approach to their Assumptions in Requirement 2 and to include more strategic and operational points, just in case these were actually rewarded in the second Box for Assumptions.

Even so, hopefully you can see that even in this case, the examiners are now clearly asking you to compare the inputs back to the Advance Information and that you cannot get away simply with saying that something is an estimate and "could be different" as you could have done even as late as the July 2015 examination.

TT (November 2016)

This examination had only 1 Box in relation to Assumptions and Scepticism in Requi_ probably because there were 2 Boxes for ethics in Requirement 2 so it was necessary to space. (Note, however, that R4 (November 2017) included 2 Boxes for Assumptions **and** 2 ethics in Requirement 2.) The marks in the single Assumptions Box for this examinatio_ follows:

Evaluates all assumptions
- ♦ £12m: negotiable / minimum / £0.75 v £1 per bottle
- ♦ 16m bottles: volume not guaranteed / may be seasonal
- ♦ Logistics: 25% looks high/low (with **reason**)
- ♦ Personnel: 100% looks high/low (with **reason**)
- ♦ Compares calculated GP% to TT / TP or Alt 1 v Alt 2
- ♦ Changes in assumptions will affect profit/margin

The only Box on Assumptions in this examination contained no points of a broader strategic or operational nature and instead was primarily a case of suggesting that an input seemed high or low, together with the obvious point that changes in assumptions would affect the outcome of the model.

However, note that there was a mark for comparing the profit margin on the proposed project back to the profit margin of that stream for the company as a whole or for comparing the profit margin between the 2 alternative project options within Requirement 2. This suggests that you should try to make some comparative remarks in relation to margin. Presumably the point here is to say whether the proposed margin is out of line with what the company normally obtains for that kind of activity.

You should also note that, as had been the case in other preceding examinations, candidates did have to explain exactly **why** they had said an input seemed too high or too low: notice the requirement in bold text in the markscheme which confirms that candidates had to include a reason for their statement in the above Box. Similarly, the first point in the Box gives a mark if you compared the estimated cost of £0.75 in the model back to the specific benchmark of £1 in the Advance Information. This again shows the benefit of fully explaining **why** you think the figure seems too high or too low, using this as an opportunity to show some knowledge of the Advance Information.

PL (July 2017)

As with the previous paper, as this examination had 2 ethics Boxes in Requirement 2, there was only a single Assumptions Box available. (Note, however, that R4 (November 2017) included 2 Boxes for Assumptions **and** 2 Boxes for ethics in Requirement 2.) The marks available were as follows:

Evaluation of assumptions
♦ Revenue increases may be optimistic eg 5% mkt decline
♦ Inconsistent revenue growth / may be bias in budgeted rev
♦ Eric: £40m may be too easy / budgeted rev exactly £40m
♦ Agency costs low e.g. Thor +£100k-£250k / 2020 increase
♦ Compares calculated returns to target (120%)/each other
♦ Changes in assumptions will affect return % / choice

These points are very much in line with what we have seen above: you do now clearly have to add a bit of detail on each input with the first and fourth points requiring knowledge of the Advance Information, including a broader market trend (the forecast 5% decline in the market, which could also have been referenced in Requirement 1).

We also see reward for a relatively generic point that changing the model inputs/assumptions will affect the output – obviously! Even so, it is worth making this point.

R4 (November 2017)

This examination had 2 Boxes, both in relation to Assumptions (as well as 2 Boxes for ethics):

Assumptions
♦ Activity assumptions provided by OB1
♦ Profile of attendees unknown / mix of recyclate unpredictable
♦ £335: maximum / could be lower
♦ 30,000 tonnage: estimate / looks high / could be lower
♦ MW 60%: recyclate tonnage open to question
♦ May lead to further work if done successfully

Evaluation of assumptions
♦ Possible bias / OB1 may be optimistic
♦ Numbers/tonnage depend on weather/external factors
♦ Compares to 2017 fig (£325) / unknown 2018 market rate
♦ Calcs MRF utilisation 82% / consider monthly capacity
♦ Impact on meeting 2018 LA target (41%)
♦ Any increase in non-recyclate (10%) waste will impact GP

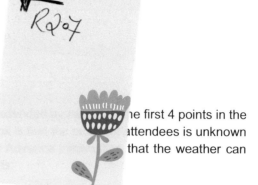

The first 4 points in the first Box in this examination are ⌐⌐⌐⌐⌐⌐⌐⌐⌐ ⌐he first 4 points in the second Box. For example, the second point in the first B ⌐⌐⌐⌐⌐⌐⌐⌐ ⌐ttendees is unknown – this is then extended through use of a point from th ⌐⌐⌐⌐⌐⌐⌐⌐ that the weather can affect the composition of attendees at certain large eve ⌐⌐⌐⌐⌐

The final point in the first Box and final 2 points in the second Box are of a slightly different nature. These points make broader strategic or operational points on the ability to obtain future opportunities (final point of the first Box), the impact on the target specified by a governmental body (penultimate point in the second Box) and the impact of costs on GP (final point in the second Box). None of these 3 points really query the inputs used in the model and so are unlike the "classic" Assumptions points seen in previous years – they are instead broader points that students might actually have ended up making in their SOC section at the start of Requirement 2 and/or in their "Other Issues" discussion of "commercial considerations", as requested by the Exam Paper.

The learning point therefore seems to be that it is always worth extending your Assumptions points by adding a second comment on each input. However, and somewhat strangely, you should also ensure that you include plenty of strategic and operational discussion throughout your answer as it appears that you might then unintentionally pick up credit in the Assumptions Boxes. Although this represents something of a change in approach compared to the "classic" inputs points that always used to be the only kind of points in the Assumptions Boxes, it has long been clear that the Case Study examination is primarily about basic, practical advice and considerations (hence our chapter on how to develop practical points that are likely to score (chapter 11 in this edition of *Cracking Case™* book) has been in this book for several years now). Therefore, in some ways, perhaps it is not a bad thing to find some slightly strange points making it into the second (difficult) Assumptions Box – these are points that you should be making elsewhere in Requirement 2 anyway so now you have a chance of scoring marks that will contribute towards passing a Box which is otherwise quite tricky.

3 General observations on Requirement 2 in recent Case Study examinations

Given the recent evolution and changes in the relevant Boxes, it is hard to reach any definitive conclusions here and you are advised to use a flexible approach which caters for different "styles" of Assumptions Box in Requirement 2. However, here are some patterns:

> If it is possible to **compare the input to some kind of benchmark in the Advance Information**, then **make sure you do so** – there may well be a **second** mark on that input for making the comparison to this information as it will show knowledge of the Advance Information. We have termed this the "extension" mark.

We would still recommend that you are mainly **critical** in your statements regarding inputs – it remains rare to see any statement which says that the input is **reasonable** (see July 2016 for some examples of this exception, however).

We would recommend that you consider the operational and strategic impact of the inputs being true – in the July 2016 examination there were marks in the second Assumptions Box for this whilst in the November 2016 and July 2017 examinations there was only one Box for Assumptions but the relevant operational and strategic impact of the project was rewarded in other markscheme Boxes so you would not have lost out by following this advice.

We would also recommend making some comparisons between the margin of the project and a sensible comparator such as the margin for the relevant revenue stream from Requirement 1/Appendix 1 or any similar existing project mentioned in the Advance Information. This was rewarded in the Assumptions Box in TT (November 2016) but would almost certainly feature somewhere else on the markscheme (probably a background Box such as 2.1 or 2.2) if not in the Assumptions Box as it is an obvious and sensible financial consideration: for example, Box 2.2 in R4 (November 2017) contained credit for comparison to the relevant stream's most recent GP or GP margin from Requirement 1. Therefore, as with our tip immediately above, you should not lose out even if the mark is not in the targeted Assumptions Box (but, at the same time, do not depend on it being in the Assumptions Box i.e. make some other Assumptions points for safety).

Do not simply say that an input **might turn out to be different** – you could get away with that before 2015 but now you must explain **why** you think it is too high or too low (using the Advance Information is probably the best basis for your argument, given our first point in this sub-section). Including the reason may be necessary to obtain the mark if there is only a single Assumptions Box or it could be an element of the "extension" mark if there are 2 Assumptions Boxes. So, either way, it is worth including this kind of point in your answer.

4   Requirement 3 in recent Case Study examinations

Fortunately, we do not need to spend so long explaining how the markscheme for Requirement 3 has evolved as the change is much simpler: there will no longer be a dedicated Box for scepticism in Requirement 3 and instead any important points of a sceptical nature will be mixed into other Boxes in relation to the financial, operational and strategic issues of the project.

We are disappointed to see the removal of a dedicated Box for Scepticism in Requirement 3 for the following reason. If the sceptical points are now going to be mixed into other Boxes which are probably easier by nature, then a candidate may not actually obtain any credit for their Scepticism marks: if the relevant other Boxes have **already** been passed by matching enough points of a financial, operational and strategic nature (the main emphasis of those Boxes), then the candidate does not really obtain much reward for showing the scepticism skill on top.

On the other hand, of course, if the candidate has not made enough financial, operational and strategic points which match the markscheme, there will be considerable benefit from the scepticism marks that are achieved as these could turn those Boxes into passing Boxes.

Based on our review of recent past papers, we would expect to see a total of 3 to 4 sceptical points "mixed into" the other Boxes in Requirement 3. As there will seemingly not be a full Box of assumptions or scepticism marks in Requirement 3, we do not include a dedicated section for this skills area in our Planning & Reminder Sheets (unlike in Requirement 2).

In Requirement 3, based on the markschemes for recent past papers from July 2015 onwards, we would recommend that you look at some of the following points when applying scepticism:

Information has been provided by a third party rather than directly (July 2017)

Costings and capacity requirements appear unrealistic (July 2017)

Data is out of date as based on prior year pricing (November 2016)

Input is only an estimate (November 2016)

Assumptions have been provided by a party with an interest in the project (November 2016)

Exchange rate assumption could be wrong (November 2015)

Cost assumptions not confirmed (November 2015)

Unknown number of placements/sales (July 2015)

Unknown running costs (July 2015)

As you may have noticed, there was not really any credit for scepticism in Requirement 3 in Bux (July 2016) nor in R4 (November 2017). This serves as another reminder not to do too much work on this skills area in Requirement 3 (in contrast to Requirement 2).

As a final matter, since Requirement 3 will definitely contain some analysis of ethical issues, we would recommend that you briefly query the source and reliability of any allegations of unethical conduct (combining this with a recommendation to confirm the facts independently). This may generate 2 useful marks for you in different Boxes since the recommendation to confirm the facts will be in a different Box to the sceptical point on the source and reliability of the information.

5   Conclusion: subtle changes

We hope you have found this chapter useful to understanding some of the subtle but important changes in the way Assumptions and Scepticism are assessed in Case Study. We would suggest that the changes in Requirement 2 are of greater importance to understand since there may be 2 full Boxes of marks at stake and Requirement 2 is relatively difficult to pass.

Remember that, as discussed, if there is an ethics aspect to Requirement 2 then, based on 2 recent examinations (TT (November 2016) and PL (July 2017)), this might "override" the marks available for Assumptions: ethics may take up 2 Boxes and Assumptions will be downgraded to just a single Box if there are 2 calculations to perform. In R4 (November 2017), there were 2 Boxes available for ethics

and 2 Boxes available for Assumptions but there was only 1 calculation to perform so this may be why space was found for so much emphasis on **both** ethics and Assumptions.

Please ensure that you have read this chapter several times before your examination: we have tried to reflect the above learning points in our Planning & Reminder Sheets (chapter 6) but as the issues are relatively subtle, it is difficult to do so in the space available on those Sheets. You must therefore develop your own understanding of the relevant Boxes through a thorough understanding of this chapter.

Chapter 13   Plan B – What To Do If You Screw Up Your Timing

Learning Points

After reading this chapter, you must be able to:

1. understand potential reasons why you might screw up your timing
2. understand how to implement our Plan B to prioritise easier Boxes
3. appreciate that it is possible to salvage a pass even when short of time for your final Requirement

---

1   The importance of good time management

Unlike the other ACA examinations where it is possible to accumulate enough marks early in the paper to compensate for the fact that you did not finish the paper fully, if you fail to complete your Case Study script then there is a very good chance that you will fail the examination as a whole: you must pass **all** 5 elements of the examination (Executive Summary, Requirement 1, Requirement 2, Requirement 3 and the Appendices & Main Report (AMR) Boxes, which assess your presentation, Appendices and use of language: see chapter 4 for more discussion of the AMR Boxes). Unfortunately, it is not possible to compensate for a weak or incomplete Requirement 3, for example, by having an excellent Requirement 1.

Every Examiners' Report and every Tutor Conference emphasises that the **single most cause of failure is poor time management**, usually resulting in a weak Requirement 3 and/or an incomplete Executive Summary.

In this chapter, we therefore present our Plan B, which is a second best approach to be used if you find yourself in the unfortunate position of having overrun in the earlier parts of your script.

In most cases, students will complete the Requirements in order (i.e. Requirement 1 then Requirement 2 and then Requirement 3) so it will be Requirement 3 which takes the hit in terms of a shortage of time. Most of our advice in this chapter therefore relates to ways to economise on your time in **Requirement 3**. However, we know that students complete the examination in a variety of ways and therefore we provide advice for all Requirements.

2   Complete your Executive Summary as you go along

Our first piece of advice is something that you should be doing even if you do not suffer from timing problems: as already advised elsewhere in this book, we strongly recommend that after you complete a Requirement, you then complete the relevant Executive Summary section for that Requirement before moving on to start the next Requirement.

We recommend this approach because it is easier to summarise something which you have just written than it is to write all your Requirements and only come back to the Executive Summary at the end: writing your Executive Summary in one go at the end of the process will require you to re-read a lot of information before you can write anything of a good quality and you will lose valuable time.

However, a second advantage of this advice is that it means you will have completed 2 good quality Executive Summary sections relatively early in the examination i.e. after you have completed your first 2 Requirements. Therefore, 2/3 of your Executive Summary should be of a good standard. On the other hand, if you leave everything to the end then there is a chance that your **entire** Executive Summary will be rushed and poor quality.

After every examination sitting, we are contacted by taught course students who did not complete all 3 parts of their Executive Summary: in many cases, these students did not even start the third part of their Executive Summary. However, in every case where we have been contacted in such a situation, the student has in fact passed the examination with a high grade. This provides evidence that if you complete **2 good quality Executive Summary sections** in the early to middle phase of your examination then these good sections should be enough to secure the 3 passing Boxes which you need to **pass the Executive Summary as a whole**: it appears that you will not be penalised purely for not having completed your Executive Summary if you have enough good quality material to award enough marks to pass the necessary number of Boxes (3 of the 6 Boxes available for the Executive Summary).

3   Plan B for Requirement 1

In almost all cases, students will complete Requirement 1 first and hence very early in the paper. You may therefore be wondering why a Plan B could be needed for this Requirement.

We find that many students spend too much time on Requirement 1, damaging the whole of the rest of their paper. We therefore sometimes recommend to our taught course students that they attempt this Requirement last so that they are not faced with the temptation of doing too much: they will then already have completed the other Requirements and will be forced to stop writing their Requirement 1 when the time expires at the end of the examination. In other words, rather than relying on their own self-discipline to stop them (when completing Requirement 1 first), the invigilator will enforce the discipline by terminating the examination.

Therefore, some students will be attempting Requirement 1 last. However, the following advice is also valid if you attempt Requirement 1 first but find yourself spending too long it in the real examination, perhaps because you are trying to do too good a job of the analysis ("overcooking").

How could your minimum of 5 passing Boxes be achieved if you are under time pressure?

Discuss the wider context of performance (Box 1.2) – this Box is easier to pass in Requirement 1 than in the other Requirements. Make sure you quote any relevant numerical datapoints from the Advance Information (such as the expected industry growth rate) and compare this with the performance of the Case Study company. Also mention any key broader themes on expectations from the Advance Information such as increasing or decreasing levels of interest in the industry's products/services. Then consider any further numerical context such as the cash position or bank loans.

Easy numbers Boxes (Boxes 1.1, 1.3 & 1.4) – we recommend that you look at the past markschemes for these Boxes. You should see that the marks are awarded for relatively straightforward points such as a percentage change, sometimes together with a descriptive word like "significantly", "marginally" or "impressively". This is not rocket science and can be done quickly. In fact, the marks in Box 1.1 are simply for correct calculation results on straightforward areas such as the change in revenue or the change in gross profit (for example), without even requiring any narrative points at all.

Conclusions (Box 1.9) – again, we recommend that you look at past markschemes for the Conclusions Box. Here the marking is open in the sense that you do not have to reach a specified conclusion to be awarded a mark: you only need to conclude on the right general areas, **with a figure** (which does not need to be correct to be awarded Conclusions marks).

Based on the above set of 5 relatively easy Boxes, hopefully you can see that you can pass Requirement 1 without passing the ET Boxes and without trying to gain the evaluation points in Boxes 1.6 and 1.7. You also do not necessarily have to pass the Commercial Recommendations Box (Box 1.10).

As such, our Plan B for Requirement 1 is based on attacking the above 5 Boxes as a priority: as long as you attempt your Context of Performance section and are quoting plenty of figures with descriptive words then you still have a chance of passing.

We actually believe that the biggest risk with Requirement 1 is spending **too much time** on the analysis: being under time pressure and economising on your work could actually be a good thing in some ways.

4 Plan B for Requirement 2

Requirement 2 has typically been the most difficult requirement to pass because of the numerical aspects of the financial model. As outlined in our review of RS (November 2014) (our review starts on page 261), over time the weighting of marks in the Case markscheme appears to be moving away from calculations and towards narrative work so try not to worry about this aspect. This is in line with the recent comments of the examiners at the ICAEW Tutor Conference (see chapter 14)[50].

Here is what we suggest that you do if you are answering Requirement 2 last and are therefore short of time.

Start with your querying of assumptions and scepticism (report section 2.C and markscheme Boxes 2.5 and 2.8 in most examinations[51]) – these elements can be written up before you have done any calculations as it is possible to criticise the inputs and methodology before you have calculated any results. It makes sense to attempt these Boxes first so that at least you can have a

---

[50] At the same time, please note that both the July 2017 and November 2016 examinations involved 2 calculations in Requirement 2.
[51] However, note that the July 2017 and November 2016 examinations (and some earlier examinations) only had 1 Box for the querying of Assumptions.

good attempt at the narrative: otherwise, if you start with the calculations and overrun then you will probably get the calculations wrong and not pass these easier narrative Boxes either.

Identify the easier "Other Issue" Box and attempt this (Box 2.6 or 2.7 and possibly also Box 2.4 if only 1 calculation is required) – many candidates appear to be unaware that in addition to the calculations and some related criticism of the inputs used in the financial model, there will generally be at least 2 further narrative Tasks of a strategic or operational nature to complete in Requirement 2.

Some of these Tasks should be easier than others in the sense that there will be directions as to what to do, whereas other Tasks will be left relatively open. For example, in RS (November 2014), the client/partner request at the start of the examination paper asked for an evaluation of the possibility of funding an investment from working capital as well as comments on operational and ethical issues. In our opinion, tackling the question of funding investment out of working capital would have been a sensible prioritisation as the examination question does clearly set out the focus of this Task, compared to the vaguer request to assess "operational" issues. Alternatively, ethical issues could have been a task to prioritise, given that the ethical issues are normally relatively easy to spot.

Whichever way, this aspect of Plan B involves identifying at least one of the other narrative tasks to address.

If you perform well at this Task, and include testing of assumptions and scepticism (see previous point), then you will hopefully have passed 3 Boxes already.

Ensure that your Conclusions are to a good standard – as the marking of the Conclusions Box (Box 2.9) is "open" in the sense that you do not have to reach a specific conclusion then, provided that you follow our planning sheets and stay focused on the key areas, it should be relatively straightforward to pass this Box. Some students will complete their Conclusions as they go along, having completed the easier tasks mentioned above, since there are Conclusions marks regarding assumptions, scepticism and the narrative issues that you will have tackled already if you follow our Plan B strategy.

Have a good attempt at the calculations, making your inputs clear – in all recent examinations other than RS (November 2014), TT (November 2016) and PL (July 2017), Box 2.1 has awarded marks simply for identifying the correct inputs to the model (even if you subsequently go on to calculate the wrong result). As such, your fifth and final Box required could simply depend on having a clear Appendix 2 where the marker can see that you have found the correct inputs for your financial model.

One more Box for safety – if you have followed the above process, the next step is probably to attempt the "SOC" Box or Boxes by completing the first section for Requirement 2 which you initially left blank. Alternatively, you may possibly decide to attempt another evaluation/narrative Task. Or you might attempt the Commercial Recommendations Task (Box 2.10) and hopefully will be lucky to match at least 3 points in the list: to give yourself the best chance, try to include **as many points as possible in a bullet point format**. (ICAEW have confirmed that bullet points are acceptable as the examiners wish to see a large range of recommendations: see chapter 14).

Requirement 2 Plan B: a summary

The above advice is quite lengthy and therefore we summarise it in the list below:

---

1. Criticise assumptions and show scepticism

2. Identify at least one non-vague narrative Other Issue and attempt this

3. Attempt calculations, emphasising clear presentation of the inputs in your Appendix 2

4. Write up Conclusions, carefully following our planning sheets

5. One more Box for safety: consider SOC, a further Other Issue or Commercial Recommendations

---

5   Plan B for Requirement 3

As explained above, this is typically the Requirement which will be most rushed as normally candidates will attempt this Requirement last: in past Examiners' Reports, heavy criticism is almost always made of students for not completing this Requirement properly.

As such, we definitely recommend that you study our Plan B for this Requirement particularly carefully.

Drop your "SOC" section (Box 3.2 and possibly also Box 3.1) or leave space and come back to complete this section at the end, if you have time – as with Requirement 2 (see above), there are easier and more predictable Tasks or Boxes to attempt in Requirement 3 than the SOC Boxes (Box 3.2 and sometimes also Box 3.1). Given the unpredictability, it does not make sense to start with this section if you are short of time as you could simply be unlucky and spend time writing up good points which are not rewarded.

Identify Issue 1 and Issue 2 and start with these – Requirement 3 will almost always involve 2 main issues. Typically, these will be advantages and disadvantages, or benefits and risks, of a project. Alternatively, you may be asked to evaluate 2 projects with all the benefits and risks of one project being Issue 1 and all the benefits and risks of the second project being Issue 2. These Tasks or Boxes are very straightforward and rely mainly on points from the Exam Paper information.

To identify Issue 1 and Issue 2, you can normally look at the first sentence of the paragraph containing the instructions from the client/partner on the first page of the examination paper. In other words, Issue 1 and Issue 2 will be the first points mentioned by the client or your partner when setting out all the various Requirement 3 Tasks.

If you complete these 2 Tasks well, you will already have 2 of the 5 Boxes or Tasks which you need to have a chance of passing.

Next do Ethics: 2 relatively easy Boxes – most recent examinations have awarded 2 Boxes for ethical issues in Requirement 3.

The issues are normally relatively straightforward to spot so just ensure you are writing enough using our IIR (Issue, Impact, Recommendations) analysis framework. It is no longer necessarily the case that there will only be 2 ethical issues to assess: there could be as many as 4 or 5 matters to recognise. This is why we recommend in our Planning & Reminder Sheets that you address ethics in report section 3.D, rather than leaving it to the end of the Requirement and possibly running out of time: in practice, if you are following Plan B and have left the SOC section (report section 3.A) for later in your answer, then ethics will be the **second** area that you address in your script for Requirement 3, after Issue 1 and 2 (written up in report sections 3.B and 3.C, respectively). This makes sense given that 2 Boxes are available for relatively easy points on ethics.

Remember that the first Box tends to be awarded for **identifying** the ethical issues and the second Box tends to be awarded for explaining the potential **impact** or how to **mitigate** the problem (effectively, your recommendations on the ethical issues). Make sure you are writing enough on **both** types of point: following the section headings in our Planning & Reminder Sheets should force you to do so as we have allocated 2 different headings for the ethics discussion and ethics Recommendations, respectively. Remember to take advantage of the opportunity to use bullet points for your ethics Recommendations.

If you complete the Tasks for Ethics, Issue 1 and Issue 2 well, you should now be on 4 of the 5 Boxes or Tasks which you need to pass.

Conclusions – as with the other Requirements, the Conclusions Box for Requirement 3 (Box 3.9) applies an "open" marking approach, meaning that as long as you are concluding on the correct approximate areas (in Requirement 3, these will be Issue 1, Issue 2, scepticism issues, other narrative issues (if applicable), Ethics and whether to proceed with the project) then you should pass this Box. After following the above advice, you will then hopefully be on 5 passing Boxes.

Check for any specified and clear "Other Issues" – in the same way as in Requirement 2, sometimes the Exam Paper will set a very clear and specific additional narrative issue to consider.

If the content of this Task appears to be clearly specified and something that you think you can attempt well, then definitely consider doing this element, even though you are only using a "Plan B".

In other instances, there may be a relatively vague Task set, in which case consider leaving this Box until later – if it seems a little vague, then chances are you would not have passed it anyway.

A third possibility is that there will not in fact be any further issues beyond the Issue 1 and Issue 2 that populate Boxes 3.3 and 3.4 – always check the question wording to ensure you have not missed something and if you still have confidence that there is no further Task of this nature then this would mean that Boxes 3.6 and 3.7 will contain more points on Issue 1 and Issue 2. Therefore, beef up your discussion of Issue 1 and Issue 2, even though you are only using a "Plan B": the marks tend to be for relatively straightforward points, mainly taken from points raised in the Exam Paper Exhibits.

Based on the above approach, hopefully you can see that it is possible to pass Requirement 3 whilst only effectively passing 5 or so of our recommended 7 report sections, namely:

3.B   [Issue 1]

3.C   [Issue 2]

3.D   Ethics and Ethics Recommendations

3.E   [Non-vague Other Issue, if any]

3.F   Conclusions

If you have any time left, you should now fill in the gaps, perhaps starting with the SOC or some of the other narrative Tasks which are additional to Issue 1 or Issue 2 (or in some examinations which involve further points on those same 2 issues: always check the question wording carefully). Alternatively, you may wish to spin the wheel of "Recommendations Roulette" and see if you are lucky enough to match the points on the markscheme in Box 3.10.

If you are short of time at this point then **be careful not to spend too long on Requirement 3 at the expense of your Executive Summary section for Requirement 3**: if you have done a good job of the 5 report sections listed above then it may be advisable to invest a bit of time in the Executive Summary as opposed to polishing your Requirement 3 too thoroughly, unless you are confident that you have written 2 strong Executive Summary sections on Requirements 1 and 2 already (by following our advice to write each section of the Executive Summary after finishing the related main report section: see section 2 of this chapter).

6   Plan B: a summary

Based on the above Requirement-by-Requirement review, we have highlighted in bold in the table below the sections which should be prioritised in your basic "skeleton" Plan B attempt at each Requirement:

Plan B: Sections to prioritise

Requirement 1	Requirement 2 (with no ethics)	Requirement 2 (with ethics)	Requirement 3
1.A	2.A	2.A	3.A
1.B	**2.B**	**2.B**	**3.B**
1.C	**2.C**	**2.C**	**3.C**
1.D	2.D	**2.D**	**3.D**
1.E	**2.E**	2.E	**3.E**
1.F	2.F	**2.F**	**3.F**
	2.G	**2.G**	3.G

7   Numbering your pages: does it matter?

Around 2 to 3 minutes before the end of the examination, the exam hall will become noisy with a lot of rustling of paper as candidates quickly number all their pages in order to try to obtain a diamond/mark in 1 of the 4 Appendices & Main Report (AMR) Boxes (AMR.3) available at the end of the markscheme for the presentation, use of language and quality of the Appendices in your report.

Provided that you have learned how to count to approximately 30 (most student scripts are 30 pages or fewer), this is indeed a pretty easy mark to obtain. However, if you are suffering from severe timing issues and therefore using our Plan B, you may wish to consider whether it is worth investing the time needed to earn this mark (given that you only need 2 of the 4 AMR Boxes to pass this element of the report) or whether you should instead spend the time writing some more words in your main report sections (e.g. in your Executive Summary).

Looking at the content within the 4 AMR Boxes (see page 48), Boxes AMR.1 and AMR.2 should really be passed by default, provided that you have created a well-presented Appendix 1 and Appendix 2. AMR.4 should then also be easy to pass, provided that you have an appropriate disclaimer, have put the report in the name of your partner (or in the name of the company itself if, exceptionally, your fictional character role is that of a member of staff of the company, rather than (as is normally the case) that of an external adviser) and have avoided any unethical remarks.

Based on this, you should be able to pass the AMR element of the examination based on Boxes AMR.1, AMR.2 and AMR.4 even without doing any page numbering (which is credited in Box AMR.3): remember that you only need to pass 2 AMR Boxes to pass the AMR section as a whole and we have highlighted here that 3 of the AMR Boxes are very easy to pass. However, looking at Box AMR.3 in more detail, provided that you have written reasonable length paragraphs, used section headings (which you really should be doing if you are using our Planning & Reminder Sheets) and written legibly, then you will have passed Box AMR.3 by obtaining 3 diamonds even without doing any page numbering (thereby sacrificing one diamond in Box AMR.3).

For these reasons, we are not quite sure why so many candidates prioritise page numbering at the end of the examination: yes, it is a very easy mark to obtain … but you probably do not even need the mark! In our opinion, it would be far better to spend the time writing another 25 words of your Executive Summary or finishing off part of your main report than to bother with the page numbering.

Remember that after the end of the examination you are not allowed to write anything but you will be given 5 minutes to organise your loose leaf pages into the correct order and to attach the treasury tag that secures your script. Therefore if you did not have time to do the page numbering, or you chose not to do the page numbering and instead wrote some words in another section, you will still have plenty of time to make sure that the pages in your report script are in the correct order and therefore understandable by the examiners.

It may sound a little excessive to consider the apparently minor issue of whether you have numbered your pages as part of an examination strategy for your final examination before qualifying as a Chartered Accountant but on the other hand a minute of writing time saved by not bothering to do the page numbering could be enough to secure 2 or perhaps even 3 diamonds in your Executive

Summary section: these are much more valuable than a diamond in a Box you have quite possibly already passed anyway through clear and legible writing, with sufficient headings.

8 Plan B: final thoughts

We obviously hope that everything works out really well for you on exam day and therefore that this chapter becomes irrelevant to you after you manage your time perfectly and fly through the exam.

However, despite the best intentions and despite ample practice at mock exams, you never quite know what will happen on exam day. Therefore, even if you are confident that you will manage your time properly on the day, we still recommend that you spend some time becoming familiar with the suggestions made in this chapter and add some related reminders to your Planning & Reminder Sheets, just in case …

Our approach is essentially to target the easier Tasks/Boxes first to ensure that you build up a solid base of marks, and then to fill in the gaps in the rest of the relevant Requirement if you have time.

As mentioned, you will need to make a judgement call after you have completed the easier Tasks/Boxes in your Plan B attempt as it may now be time to move on to your Executive Summary section rather than spending too long on difficult remaining Tasks or Boxes in the main Requirement (often Requirement 3 if you complete this last) which you do not end up passing anyway. At the same time, if you have followed our advice to complete the Executive Summary as you go along, it may well be that your Executive Summary is already good enough to pass as a result of 2 strong Executive Summary sections completed before timing issues became a problem on examination day.

Many past users of this book have emailed in after results day to thank us for developing Plan B as they felt that it got them out of a difficult situation in their own examination. Hopefully, by following the techniques in this chapter you will now also know how to take action to fix any timing issues which may occur and hence save an otherwise passing script from failing due to poor performance in only one element of the examination.

Chapter 14   Tips from Recent ICAEW Tutor Conferences

Every February, ICAEW holds a Tutor Conference to which all tuition providers approved under the ICAEW Partner in Learning scheme are invited. This is an excellent opportunity to gain an "inside view" on what the examiners really want you to do when writing your Case Study report.

In this chapter, we present a summary of some useful points from the most recent Tutor Conferences. Given that the Case Study examination has evolved over time, we will start with the most recent Tutor Conference held at the time of writing (the 2018 Tutor Conference) and will then work backwards in time through to the 2013 Tutor Conference. (As the comments made at the 2015 Tutor Conference were very similar to those at the 2014 Tutor Conference we have only created a 2015 section in this chapter, in order to avoid duplication. If a tip was made at both a recent Tutor Conference and at an earlier Tutor Conference, we have not generally included the tip twice by adding it to the discussion regarding the more recent Conference but rather have left in place our original discussion of the point from the earlier Conference: this means that our notes for earlier Conferences are more detailed as we have only added new points to the discussion of more recent Conferences. We have carefully checked all points to ensure that they remain relevant and have amended the text where necessary to bring the remarks fully up to date.)

During the Case Study workshop, the most recent examination paper to have been taken by students is reviewed and debriefed in detail by the examiners. Therefore, as the Tutor Conference always takes place in February, it is the **November** sitting past papers which provide many of the illustrative examples in this chapter.

Although this is a relatively long chapter, please do persevere right to the end as it contains a lot of useful tips and tricks directly from the examiners themselves: as mentioned above, because of the way we have updated this chapter over time, it is the earlier Conferences which contain more tips so this is another reason to read right through to the end of the chapter.

Your time invested in this chapter will be worthwhile – after all, there can be no better source of information on how to tackle the examination than the examiners themselves.

1   Tips from the 2018 ICAEW Tutor Conference

The 2018 Tutor Conference provided a good opportunity to obtain detailed examiner feedback directly from the author of the November 2017 examination, R4. Here are the main learning points raised.

1.1   Change in the assessment of a candidate's Own Research

As already discussed in detail in our review of the R4 (November 2017) examination which is provided in the Foreword to this edition of *Cracking Case*™, possibly the single most important discussion point at the 2018 Tutor Conference related to a change in the way that Own Research marks will be awarded. We have already discussed this issue in detail in our section starting on page 10 so we will not repeat all of the discussion here.

151

In summary, you will now only gain credit for your Own Research remarks if the point that you make overlaps with one of the points in Boxes 1.2, 2.2 or 3.2 … and these are points that you might already have made anyway based on the Advance Information or Exam Paper alone. You are therefore no longer guaranteed to gain a mark for Own Research as you would have done in the past and there is now a risk of duplication of time and effort without any benefit to your mark if you include your Own Research. For these reasons, there is now considerably less benefit in providing Own Research points in your answer and you should therefore consider whether to put your scarce examination time into another skills area.

This represents a significant change from the previous marking approach (and therefore our previous technique advice) so please bear it in mind for the July 2018 examination.

1.2 Implicit confirmation of an error in the criticism of our materials by another tuition provider

As explained elsewhere in this book, since at least 2014 our Case Study learning materials and examination technique have been subject to false and unfair allegations by another large UK tuition provider who has claimed that the ICAEW markers will ignore any introductory paragraphs such as those headed up as "Market Background" or "Project Background". We have repeatedly informed the other provider that this criticism is untrue.

At the 2018 Tutor Conference, one of the real November 2017 candidate scripts which was discussed by the examiners as part of the annual marking training exercise for tutors contained a section headed as "Market Background". The official ICAEW marking grid which had been marked by trained ICAEW examiners as part of the real marking process awarded several marks in Box 1.2 in relation to the section headed as "Market Background". For example, as the first point made in the "Market Background" section, the candidate wrote "R4 should be able to capitalise on forecast 4.9% industry growth to grow revenue". This remark was clearly awarded credit in relation to the second diamond in Box 1.2 ("National growth rate 4.9%").

This provides very clear evidence indeed that there is nothing wrong with using an opening paragraph such as a "Market Background" paragraph and that the ICAEW markers will definitely not ignore such a section when they perform the marking. Although the examiners did discuss several problems with the relevant candidate script, there was no mention whatsoever of any breach of examination regulations occurring through use of a "Market Background" paragraph.

As explained elsewhere in this book, with effect from the July 2018 edition of *Cracking Case™*, we have decided to change the heading of our recommended introductory sections as described below:

Requirement	Old term	New term
Requirement 1	Market Background	Context of Performance
Requirement 2	Project Background	Strategic and Operational Context
Requirement 3	Project Background	Strategic and Operational Context

We emphasise again that this change is simply a change in **terminology** as we have not amended our underlying examination technique in any way whatsoever – instead, after discussion with students on our recent classroom tuition courses, we feel that changing our terminology should help keep candidates focused on points that are more likely to score as the terms "Market Background" and "Project Background" are, in retrospect, potentially not as specific in terms of guidance as we would like.

We have no doubt that the relevant competing tuition provider will attempt to make further criticisms of our materials as a result of this terminology change so we therefore kindly ask for your understanding and professional scepticism of any such remarks.

1.3   The "unusual" nature of Requirement 3 in R4

The examiners noted that many candidates and tutors described Requirement 3 in R4 as "unusual" or "tricky" because it did not relate to a strategic development proposal but rather to a problem that had already arisen at an existing client. As such, in this examination, Requirement 3 was backwards-looking in nature rather than forwards-looking as it normally would be.

The examiners noted that the Advance Information for R4 did not have the usual emphasis on strategic development proposals in a business plan or similar document. Instead, there was a detailed Exhibit which set out a number of different risks facing the business. The examiners commented that this should have provided a hint to candidates that there was a good chance that Requirement 3 (or Requirement 2) would have an emphasis on risks and problems rather than the usual positive strategic development possibilities.

This provides helpful guidance to candidates – if the Advance Information for your examination contains a business plan or similar document with a strategic development emphasis then there is a good chance that Requirement 3 will be "normal" in nature whereas if the emphasis is more on risks and there is a minimal (or no) business plan then you will need to be prepared for something different to happen in Requirement 3.

As a side note, please do note that the R4 Requirement 3 was not the first time that Requirement 3 has had a different form: the July 2013 examination (Palate) was actually quite similar to R4 in that it required the candidate to deal with problems which had already arisen at a client. We mentioned this to candidates on our November 2017 classroom tuition course and explained that even when Requirement 3 is unusual in this way, the allocation of markscheme Boxes is exactly as set out for a "normal" Requirement 3, as described in detail in the rest of this book. Therefore, whilst the Requirement might seem different on the surface, underneath the markscheme will be the same as normal and we would not advise you to do anything too significant in terms of changing your examination technique.

1.4 Reference to depreciation in Requirement 1 Extra Task

The examiners noted that many candidates did not deal well with the Extra Task in Requirement 1 which required candidates to discuss the depreciation charge for the year with the Board.

The examiners noted that Case Study does not require detailed technical knowledge of accounting rules so perhaps candidates might therefore have assumed that depreciation would not be discussed as it does not relate to the practical and strategic matters which form the main focus of Case Study. However, the examiners stated that there were 2 major hints that depreciation would be tested.

Firstly, the Advance Information stated that some members of the Board questioned how the depreciation charge was calculated. It was also stated in the Advance Information that some members of the Board were not confident regarding the "bridges" between the different financial statements (Income Statement, Statement of Financial Position, Cash Flow Statement). The examiners therefore noted that the Advance Information did give a hint that depreciation would be significant.

Secondly, the Advance Information indicated that the depreciation charge was a very large figure in the accounts. As Case Study is all about looking at the most important issues affecting the business, it would therefore follow that depreciation was potentially something that could be tested.

As a further hint, we would also note that the Advance Information provided a separate statement of the proceeds on disposal of fixed assets: this kind of detailed information is not normally provided in the Advance Information. This information again related to the area of depreciation as the Advance Information indicated that R4 was consistently making losses on disposal and therefore had apparently not been depreciating its fixed assets at an appropriate rate.

Hopefully, the above will provide some hints as to when particular technical points such as depreciation will be tested – in the absence of such hints, please ensure that you stay focused on more practical and strategic points as Case Study is not intended to be a financial reporting examination. Depreciation had not been tested in Case Study for several years before the R4 examination so you should certainly not assume that this technical concept will always be something that attracts marks.

As a final note on depreciation in the R4 examination, a tutor from another tuition company queried why the R4 markscheme did not provide any credit for a recalculation of the depreciation charge to confirm whether the R4 figure was correct. The tutor suggested that this would demonstrate the key Case Study skill of professional scepticism. The examiners responded that it would be possible to provide the requested advice on the impact of the depreciation charge on the accounts (the focus of the Extra Task) without going into the detail of what the revised charge should actually be. Therefore, the marks were for the discussion of the possible impact of the charge rather than for recalculating the charge itself.

154

Once again, this shows the importance of not adopting too technical an approach in Case Study: the examination is not a financial reporting or auditing examination so the most important thing to do is concentrate on the practical and strategic impact of issues rather than adopting too much of an "accountant's" perspective.

1.5   Recommendations – bullet points and length

In response to a question from one of our tutor team, the examiners confirmed that candidates can use bullet points for their ethics Recommendations in exactly the same way as for their other non-ethics Recommendations.

As explained elsewhere in this book, we strongly advise you to make the most of this opportunity to save time. Our Planning & Reminder Sheets suggest that you have a subheading within your ethics discussion which is dedicated to your ethics Recommendations – this will ensure that you provide a good number of ethics Recommendations in the middle of your report section and you can then provide Recommendations in relation to areas other than ethics in a bullet point list at the end of your report section. This will give you a good range of different types of Recommendation point across your answer as a whole.

At the same time, the examiners reminded candidates not to be too "cheeky" in the use of bullet points. Some points such as "increase sales" would be considered too brief to attract credit. The examiners stated that there is no specific rule on the number of words that are required for a Recommendation to attract credit but in general candidates should aim for around 4 or 5 words, assuming that this both makes the Recommendation and also provides some non-generic points which are specific to the scenario. So, for example, saying "increase high margin SEWCO[52] sales" would attract credit as the candidate would have had to have observed the margin for this revenue stream in Requirement 1 before making such a point. This will be a much better Recommendation than simply saying "increase sales".

For this reason, whilst we strongly advise you to use bullet points for your Recommendations (and, again, you can do this for both ethics and non-ethics Recommendations), be careful of the potential for a "false economy" if your points are extremely brief.

1.6   How many past papers should candidates attempt before the examination?

In response to a question from a member of the tutor team at another tuition provider, the examiners suggested that the 4 most recent Case Study past papers would be the best source of information on how the examination is tested. The examiners stated that Case Study has subtly evolved over time so candidates should always be advised to look at recent past papers.

---

[52] The term "SEWCO" relates to one of the R4 revenue streams and is therefore specific to the November 2017 examination. Please do not use this specific term in your own examination answer.

We would definitely agree that the examination has evolved over time and this is one of the reasons why we always try to create a new edition of *Cracking Case™* ahead of each examination sitting: this allows us to update our examination technique for the latest learning points.

We would therefore agree that the 4 most recent Case Study past papers are the best source of evidence before the Advance Information has been released. However, it would certainly be a significant investment of time to sit all 4 past papers as preparation as you would need to read, absorb and analyse 4 different sets of Advance Information to sit each of the relevant papers.

It is for this reason that we provide 5 Mocks based on the live Advance Information because this provides you with an opportunity to practise your examination technique 5 times whilst only reading one set of Advance Information (and a set of Advance Information which is obviously very important to your own examination!). Please see page 6 of this book for further information on our live Mock Exam Pack.

1.7   The importance of linkages between Requirements

The examiners noted that the review of assumptions for Requirement 2 did require some knowledge of the points made in relation to Requirement 1. For example, the Requirement 2 financial model applied unchanged 2016 sales prices but Requirement 1 indicated that sales prices had risen.

The examiners therefore advised candidates to ensure that they look for linkages between Requirements. As explained elsewhere in this book, we have noticed that the number of marks available for linking backwards from Requirement 2 and/or Requirement 3 to Requirement 1 definitely seem to have increased at recent sittings. Our Planning & Reminder Sheets therefore remind you to consider this perspective in your own attempt.

The examiners clarified that they would not expect candidates to recalculate the Requirement 2 or Requirement 3 model based on a better source of data on inputs such as Requirement 1 as this would be too much work in the time available. Instead, candidates should simply comment in their narrative discussion on the limitations of the information provided in Requirement 2 or Requirement 3 if the Requirement 1 information provided more up-to-date data.

1.8   Are Requirement 2 and Requirement 3 now just the same?

The examiners noted that some tuition companies (not us!) have now advised candidates that they should take the same approach to Requirement 2 and Requirement 3 as these Requirements are now basically the same in nature. This advice is based on the fact that, just like Requirement 2, Requirement 3 will now always include a calculation whereas a few years ago Requirement 3 did not include any figures to work with.

The examiners stated that they do not agree with this advice. The examiners stated that Requirement 2 is designed to lead to a relatively straightforward "yes or no" decision whereas Requirement 3 is likely to be a more nuanced and more balanced Requirement which has a more complex answer.

Additionally, the calculation of the Requirement 2 should generally be relatively straightforward and may be heavily based on a pro-forma in the Advance Information whereas the Requirement 3 calculation will normally be less formulaic and will require students to think on their feet a little bit more.

1.9 Hints from the provision of an analytical commentary

The examiners noted that the R4 Advance Information included a detailed analytical commentary which explained how all the main accounting figures worked for the company in question.

The examiners indicated that a good candidate would have to familiarise themselves with such a commentary as it would explain how certain company- or industry-specific figures were calculated.

Additionally, whilst the Case Study examination would not require candidates to go through **all** the figures in the accounts and therefore would not require discussion as detailed as the analytical commentary in the Advance Information, for those parts of the accounts that did require discussion, the examiners stated that the Advance Information analytical commentary would provide a good model of the types of sentence and points to discuss in a candidate's answer. In other words, the Advance Information analytical commentary could provide a useful "skeleton" for a candidate's discussion of the relevant points.

1.10 The importance of describing the numerical change

The examiners reminded candidates and users that it is not correct simply to drop in lots of figures in Requirement 1 – rather, the candidate must always describe the change and provide a few words of commentary or explanation. Otherwise, the candidate is likely to be dropping marks.

We would strongly agree with this advice because the markscheme often provides relatively easy marks for descriptive words such as "significantly" or "marginally" and also for reasons (which can often be any sensible reason rather than a specific reason). Our Planning & Reminder Sheets therefore provide plenty of reminders to include such straightforward narrative points in your answers every time. Please see our discussion in chapter 8 for more on this point.

1.11 Computer-based assessment for Case Study

At the end of the Case Study workshop at the 2018 Tutor Conference, the examiners noted that, from 2018 onwards, all ACA subjects other than Case Study will be examined using the ICAEW computer-based assessment software.

The examiners confirmed that Case Study will definitely not apply a computer-based assessment method until 2019 at the earliest. The Case Study workshop therefore ended with a discussion of how computer-based assessment might work for Case Study.

Overall, we expect that the move to computer-based assessment software could lead to some significant changes in Case Study examination technique. 2019 is therefore likely to be a transitional year for both tuition companies and candidates.

Therefore, although you are probably very keen to pass the examination in 2018 anyway, we think it would definitely be in your interests to ensure that you have passed Case Study under the current handwritten method to get things out of the way before any "transition disruption" occurs in 2019.

2   Tips from the 2017 ICAEW Tutor Conference

The 2017 Tutor Conference provided a good opportunity to obtain detailed examiner feedback directly from the author of the November 2016 examination, TT. Here are the main learning points raised.

2.1   Performance in Requirement 1

It was noted that many candidates spent too long on Requirement 1 and went into far too much detail on the financial performance of TT. The examiners stressed the importance of focusing only on the most important changes during the year rather than trying to analyse and explain everything. The point of Requirement 1 is simply to check that the candidate can summarise the "Big Picture" rather than to see whether they can analyse every single figure in the accounts.

The examiners noted that Exhibit 6 in the Advance Information provided a summary statement of revenue stream performance and was a relatively unusual Exhibit as normally a summary overview would not be provided. The examiners stressed that if a main numerical Exhibit was unusual in nature, it would have been provided for a reason – in this case, it should have forewarned candidates that they would have to comment on the business as a whole rather than focusing on individual streams. Therefore, candidates should not have wasted time pre-preparing detailed, stream-specific reasons. Our response would be that whilst the Exhibit was indeed unusual, it is not clear how a candidate sitting the TT examination as their first attempt at Case Study would have any way of knowing this as they would lack any comparator (unless several past papers had been attempted). The "unusual" nature of an Exhibit should therefore be something which tuition providers must point out.

In the TT Advance Information, it was possible to analyse the company's cost of sales in detail because a breakdown of each cost heading was given (not always the case in the Advance Information). However, the examiners stated that if this level of detail was required, then the Exam Paper would explicitly have requested it since it would require a lot of work and perhaps not really be easy to do in the time available. Please bear this in mind for your own examination as we did receive a large number of queries before the TT exam as to whether a detailed cost of sales analysis should be included – the examiners have now said that they would only expect this if it was **specifically requested**.

Candidates were advised to concentrate on what is **changing** in Requirement 1 and not to spend too long looking at the general background of all streams or at margins which were not moving around very much.

According to the examiners, the Big Picture that they wanted candidates to spot was simply that performance in the Orange Juice division was poor, excess capacity consequently existed and there could potentially be a future impact on cash – that was it! If the candidate basically spotted this position and illustrated it sufficiently with enough comments and supporting figures, then they would pass Requirement 1 – they did not have to explain every movement in the accounts figures.

Around half of candidates did not even attempt to perform the additional calculation (which we term the ET) in Requirement 1. This meant that 2 Boxes were essentially thrown away by half of the candidates attempting the examination. The examiners suggested that this was not sensible.

Even so, performance in TT Requirement 1 was good and slightly above average for a Case Study examination.

2.2 Performance in Requirement 2

Here the examiners noted that Exhibit 9 in the Advance Information suggested that in the example contract, TT incurred costs of roughly £1 per bottle in its existing Toll Processing operations. This figure should therefore have been used as a sensecheck when performing the calculation for the proposed new Toll Processing project in Requirement 2 in the examination itself – as this related to output of 6 million bottles, it would be expected that costs would be approximately £6 million and anything greatly different from this figure would indicate that a mistake had been made.

The examiners recognised that there were different reasonable approaches to the calculation of the costs figure and therefore the markscheme did award marks for a **range** of reasonable estimates. Candidates should therefore not obsess about getting the single correct answer if they genuinely feel that different approaches are valid – the examiners will be fair and will take this into account.

2.3 Comments on Requirement 3

It was again confirmed by the examiners that a candidate's calculations in relation to Requirement 3 do not have to be in a separate Appendix 3 – the calculations can be performed in the main report or there can be a relatively informal calculation provided at the end of the report.

It was emphasised that only Appendix 1 and Appendix 2 are formally evaluated in terms of presentation and structure within the markscheme.

2.4 Ethics can arise in any Requirement

It was emphasised that ethics is not the preserve of Requirement 3 only – many candidates missed the request to review ethical and business trust issues in Requirement 2, presumably because they have been taught that Requirement 3 is "the" ethics Requirement. The examiners strongly advise against this assumption.

2.5 Use of historic figures from the Advance Information

The examiners advised candidates to concentrate on the prior year figures only (in other words, the latest figures given in the Advance Information which then become the prior year figures once the Exam Paper has given you new figures from the latest set of accounts). Candidates should not go any further back into the past, even though the Advance Information will provide several years of data.

In the TT exam in particular, the examiners noted that the Advance Information had already referred to 2014 as a year of transition in which the company had fundamentally changed its business model. This should have acted as a further indicator to candidates not to go into the details of 2013 as these figures related to a different way of running the business. Neither should candidates have spent time looking at the figures for 2014 as this was an exceptional year of transition rather than a sensible underlying comparator year.

However, even without these exam-specific hints not to go too far back in time, the examiners generally advised candidates to look only at the most recent data in Case Study. We would ourselves recommend that students only consider the most recent year of accounts figures in the Advance Information as this will provide the prior year comparatives to the information given to you for the first time on exam day: there are not really any marks for looking at years other than these 2 years (Exam Paper for the most recent year ended and Advance Information for the "prior year" comparatives).

2.6 Sensitivity testing in Requirement 2

A common question on our taught courses is to ask when a sensitivity analysis should be performed in Requirement 2. The examiners commented that in TT the candidate was required to perform 2 financial modelling calculations, considering alternative outcomes of the project. It was therefore noted that a form of sensitivity testing had already been carried out simply from the fact that there were 2 calculations to perform. Therefore, it seems that sensitivity testing would not normally be required if there are 2 calculations in Requirement 2.

Unfortunately, as discussed elsewhere in this book, it has been relatively rare in the recent Case Study examinations to see 2 financial model calculations in Requirement 2. Therefore, we would expect most examinations to continue to have only one modelling calculation to perform and so the examiners' comments above do not really help us to resolve whether sensitivity testing is required in other types of examination.

2.7 Read the question wording and Advance Information wording carefully

It was noted that a very high proportion of candidates misread the statement in the Exam Paper that the level of sales to existing customers under one alternative would be "reduced **to** 30%" as saying that output would be "reduced **by** 30%". Not only did this obviously have a big impact on the results of the financial model, it also meant that candidates would have missed the point that reducing sales

160

to existing clients by well over 50% was not a sensible idea. Various practical, strategic and scepticism marks would therefore also have been lost by misreading "**to**" as "**by**".

As such, always read the question wording very carefully – the examiners accepted that it would probably be more common to see a reference to a reduction of something "by" 30% because a reduction of 70% is very high but that was precisely the point being made in the examination! Candidates should have queried whether a 70% reduction in trade with existing customers was sensible for the business.

Similarly, many candidates had not read the Advance Information carefully enough and so did not understand the difference in volume between "trucks" and "containers", something which was very important to the calculation in Requirement 3. A little more attention to detail is therefore advisable.

2.8   Meaning of the term "commercial" issues

The examiners explained that most examinations will ask candidates to comment on the strategic, operational and financial issues (or some combination of these) of a project. However, sometimes the examination may simply ask for discussion of the "commercial" issues involved with a project. The examiners stated that the term "commercial" is simply an umbrella term which covers strategic, operational and financial issues.

We would add that, looking at the TT markscheme carefully, the term "issues" means both positive and negative impacts. We enjoyed quite a lively discussion with our tuition course students ahead of the November 2016 examination in which many students argued that the term "issues" necessarily has a negative connotation (as in the usage, originally from US English, "She has got issues"). Our reply at the time was that this is a fairly modern and almost slang usage of the term "issues" and so we would expect the examiners to avoid such a usage and instead look at both positive and negative impacts. Perhaps it is just a sign of our increasing age but we do not use the term "issues" in a purely negative way and the examiners are older than us so it is even less likely that they will do so! Therefore, we advise you to look at both positive and negative impacts if you see this term in your examination. (Please note that there was no explicit discussion of the term "issues" during the 2017 Tutor Conference which followed the November 2016 sitting – we are only mentioning the point here since it overlaps with the discussion of the "commercial issues" concept: the term "commercial" was discussed in detail at the 2017 Tutor Conference.)

2.9   Level of knowledge of the Advance Information

The examiners stated that if a candidate had to spend any more than a couple of minutes turning the pages of the Advance Information during the examination itself, then this would be a very bad sign – it would show that they have not really learned the business inside-out. The examiners noted that many candidates do not put sufficient time into learning the Advance Information because they think that they can check any facts on the day – however, this is not possible given the time constraints in the examination.

161

2.10   Achieving 5 or more NA grades does not result in automatic failure of the examination

An NA grade is obtained in cases where a candidate does not match **any** of the points on the markscheme in relation to a specific markscheme Box. The examiners confirmed once again that, contrary to what many candidates seem to be told by their tuition provider, the number of NA grades achieved across the examination is not taken into account in determining whether a candidate has passed or failed. The examiners noted that if a candidate was achieving 5 or more NA grades, then this would make it more difficult to pass the examination as there would obviously be fewer remaining Boxes in which to score a passing grade, but it would not necessarily result in an automatic failure.

2.11   Vague references to Brexit

The examiners confirmed that simply referring to the "uncertainty" caused by Brexit would not attract credit as this point is too vague or easy to make. Candidates should instead spell out some company-specific impacts of Brexit if they wish to score a mark. (July 2018 edition update: Brexit was not discussed at the 2018 Tutor Conference.)

2.12   Marking of Conclusions and Recommendations

Marks will be awarded for recommendations wherever these are written into the report but points in the Conclusions Boxes on the markscheme (Boxes 1.10, 2.10 and 3.10) must be specifically written under a heading entitled "Conclusions".

Points which are included in the Conclusions section for the first time (in other words, points which have not been mentioned in the candidate's main report answer) **will not be given a mark as a Conclusion**. Candidates should not use the Conclusion section as an opportunity to add in points that they forgot to mention earlier in the answer – instead, just repeat what you have already said, supporting this with figures where that is possible. Please bear this in mind when writing your own report.

Although marks will be given for Recommendations wherever these are written, the examiners emphasised that it is still better to include a list of Recommendations under a specific heading at the end of the report section as this will guarantee that the marker interprets what you have said as a Recommendation – if the point is just generally mixed into your discussion, then it could become a subjective matter as to whether it is just a statement or, alternatively, a Recommendation so it is advisable to avoid this risk by simply including the points under a heading such as "Recommendations".

2.13   Some final general points

When reading through markschemes, candidates need to be aware that if a word or figure is written in bold text then they must match this word or figure exactly, or include a word with the equivalent meaning, in order to obtain the mark.

If a percentage figure is stated in bold text then the examiners will allow rounding differences if these make a difference of up to 0.1 percentage points but any larger differences from the right 1dp answer would not attract credit.

If a word or figure is included in round brackets on the markscheme, then it is not necessary to match the figure or word exactly – the points in round brackets are simply illustrative suggestions that the marker could look out for rather than a complete list of what will be given credit, nor a statement of exact wording which must be matched (unless the wording is in bold, but even in that case a close synonym will be accepted).

If there is a colon in the point in the markscheme then the mark will only be given if the candidate's answer matches the relevant context. The candidate can make the point included after the colon without referring to the specific words before the colon, provided that this makes sense in the context of the words before the colon. For example, if the mark says "Industry: 2% decline in soft drink sales in 2014 and 2015" then a candidate does not specifically have to use the word "Industry" provided that the 2% figure that is used is clearly a reference to the whole industry or the wider market, based on the other words that the candidate **does** use.

The Appendices and Main Report (AMR) marks at the end of the markscheme are given by default to candidates and will only be taken away if the candidate does something wrong.

Candidates should not use the term "Requirement 1" or similar as this refers to an examination task and is not something that would be seen in a real-world client report.

Candidates do not need to include page numbers in the Appendices – they will not lose the mark for page numbering if the main report has page numbers but the Appendices do not.

Candidates are permitted to use a page numbering format of 1.1, 1.2, 1.3 when numbering the first 3 pages of Requirement 1, for example. Candidates do not have to number the pages of the script 1, 2, 3, and so on.

Candidates should not use exclamation marks in their reports as these would not be seen in a professional piece of accounting advisory work.

Candidates must be careful not to make any unethical statements as even 1 unethical remark will lose the mark available for tactful and ethical remarks in the AMR Overall Paper section of the markscheme.

Candidates should not use the term "Professional Scepticism" as a heading – scepticism is a professional skill and not a specific section heading in a real world report so this should be avoided.

163

2.14 New ICAEW Case Study Learning Materials

The examiners noted that the Case Study ICAEW Learning Materials had been significantly rewritten and updated for the 2017 edition, creating the most substantial update to the Case Study Learning Materials for several years. We have therefore provided a summary of some of the most important points of these new materials in Appendix 4 of this book. The 2018 edition of the Case Study Learning Materials represent a much more minor update with almost no changes at all being made so we have focused on the 2017 edition in Appendix 4.

3 Tips from the 2016 ICAEW Tutor Conference

We were very pleased to attend the Case Study workshop on the final day of the 2016 ICAEW Tutor Conference. As usual, the Conference provided invaluable insights into the way the examiners are looking to test students as well as into any recent nuances in the way the examination will be set and marked. We will include points in the order that they were made in the workshop rather than in their order of importance: please review all comments in full as part of your preparations for your examination.

Please note that, as is normal at the Tutor Conference, the illustrative examples given by the examiners related to the most recent Case Study that had been sat at the time of the Conference: in this case it was the CC (November 2015) Case Study. Therefore, where necessary we have included the examiners' examples from this Case Study but the principles should also apply more generally.

3.1 Appendices & Main Report Boxes

As discussed elsewhere in this book, at the end of the markscheme there are 4 Boxes termed "Overall Paper" by ICAEW. These Boxes do not assess the overall **quality** of your attempt (that is done by the other 36 Boxes) – rather, these Boxes assess the overall **presentation**, **structure** and **organisation** of your Appendices and report (hence we call the Boxes the "Appendices & Main Report" or AMR Boxes: to us, the term "Overall Paper" does not seem reflective of what these Boxes look at). Here are some useful examiner comments but please also see Appendix 1 and chapter 4 for more details on these Boxes.

Headings

In order to obtain the mark for "sufficient appropriate headings", you should not write the words "Requirement 1" (for example) at the start of your answer to the first requirement. This is because the examiners stated that a real-world report would not contain such language.

Provided that you have at least 1 subheading per Requirement, you will obtain the "sufficient appropriate headings" mark. We have given you a set of subheadings in our Planning & Reminder Sheets for each Requirement in order to keep you focused on points that are more likely to score on the markscheme. Provided you are using these suggestions, you will have no problems obtaining this mark.

164

Paragraph length

The mark for "appropriate use of paragraph/sentences" will still be obtained if paragraphs are only a single sentence each: in fact, the examiners strongly encourage a short and simple writing style. However, there should be no bullet points except in the Recommendations sections. This is in line with our points made elsewhere in this book (particularly in chapter 3 on the correct writing style for Case Study) where we have stressed the importance of making your point quickly and moving on, so that you make as many different points as possible in the time, rather than just focusing on a narrow set of ideas.

We are aware of some other tuition providers who are misinforming students that paragraphs must be more than 1 sentence to be capable of scoring a mark and also of a mistaken view that Recommendations must be detailed and justified in full to be awarded a mark. Hopefully, this direct confirmation from the examiners that single sentence paragraphs are acceptable and that bullets can be used for Recommendations should reassure you to use a simple approach to your writing.

Page numbering

A single mark is available in one of the "Overall Paper" Boxes for correctly numbering your pages. As discussed in chapter 13 of this book, towards the end of the examination you will see other candidates frantically trying to number all their pages to obtain this mark. As we explain in that same chapter, there are actually better uses of your scarce time than this. We therefore do not think page numbering is as important as some students seem to think. Even so, here is the 2016 Tutor Conference advice from the examiners.

The examiners confirmed that provided that the candidate has made a genuine attempt to number their pages then if the candidate misses 1 page out by mistake, the page numbering mark will still be awarded. It is not necessary to number the pages of your Appendices, meaning that you can save a few seconds here.

Although the examiners do not particularly like the approach, you will **not** be penalised if you arrange your page numbering on the basis of 1.1, 1.2, 1.3, and so on, rather than numbering the pages in a "normal" way such as 1, 2, 3, and so on. As you will not know how long your Executive Summary (always presented at the start of your report) will be before you start writing Requirement 1, it is not possible to start the page numbering of Requirement 1 on, say, page 7 and therefore many candidates prefer to start their numbering as 1.1 as they start Requirement 1 and then number that Requirement as they go along. This will mean that the main Requirements can be accurately numbered even before earlier sections are written. It was therefore good to have it confirmed that the examiners will not penalise this approach.

Formal language

To obtain this mark in the relevant "AMR" Box, you should not make use of the terms "I", "we" or similar wording as the examiners feel that a formal report would not use these words. Instead, you should say "it is recommended" rather than "I recommend", for example.

The examiners also indicated that if you refer to individuals by their first name only then this is again an approach which would not be seen in a formal report and so would be penalised.

Tactful/ethical comments

Please note that **even 1 comment which is not tactful or ethical** will result in this mark being lost. Therefore make sure you are always writing in an ethical way and certainly do not say anything such as (an actual example from the CC (November 2015) examination mentioned by the examiners) "CC should try to hide the breach of interest covenant for as long as possible".

Reasonable spelling/grammar

The examiners understand that candidates are working at speed and so a few errors in relation to spelling or grammar will not be penalised. However, if more than 5-6 such errors are made, then this mark will be lost.

The examiners noted that there is currently a problem with many scripts not being legible: in this case the "AMR" mark for "legible writing" would obviously be lost. In addition, it was pointed out that the more illegible the script, the greater the likelihood of also losing the mark for reasonable spelling/grammar as the marker would not be able to check whether the spelling is accurate if the words cannot be read.

Use of abbreviations

The examiners commented that abbreviations such as GP (for "gross profit") or AB (an abbreviation for "AceBod" from the Bod (July 2015) examination) are perfectly acceptable and will not be penalised.

The examiners also advised candidates against wasting time writing out a legend or "Key" towards the start of the examination in which all the abbreviations are defined. This is simply not needed.

Marking of a plan

We are aware that some tuition providers advise students to hand in their plan on the basis that a few marks may be given, particularly in "marginal" cases. Please note that the examiners indicated that plans will **not** be marked in any way and that there is therefore no point in including your plan in your submitted script – your points must be fully written up to be assessed.

Conclusions

Conclusions should be put under a separate heading or included in a separate paragraph which is very clearly a set of conclusions. This is the only instance in which the markers will be "fussy" about exactly **where** you make a point – in the case of all other marks, markers have been instructed to give credit regardless of where the point is made on the markscheme. For example, you could in theory have a Recommendation in your SOC section or a SOC point in your Ethics section and still obtain a mark. This would not be the case with Conclusions.

Although you may obtain your Conclusions marks with a separate paragraph of conclusions even if this is not headed up as "Conclusions", we think that there is no point in risking these easy marks by saving one word and not writing a "Conclusions" heading so we would recommend that you always use a heading and place all Conclusions points in this section.

3.2   The nature of the Executive Summary

As discussed below, at the time of the February 2016 Tutor Conference, the examiners were considering removing the Executive Summary with effect from 2017. This was because the Executive Summary had apparently become a little too easy, since it is very close to the Conclusions points in each Requirement, as explained earlier in this book.

Although it was confirmed a couple of months after the Tutor Conference that the Executive Summary will now not be removed, the examiners did say at the Tutor Conference that they have definitely and consciously tried to make the Executive Summary harder in recent exams by requiring students to make a specific point to obtain the mark: where previously it may have been possible to put **any** Recommendation or project decision (proceed or not proceed) into the Executive Summary and be rewarded, increasingly the examiners will now expect students to match a specific point in some (but not all cases) to obtain the marks. In some ways, this reflects a move back towards the old (pre-2012) method of testing the Executive Summary where specific Conclusions and Recommendations were required.

As examples of this approach, consider the following points from the CC (November 2015) examination:

> In the Executive Summary for Requirement 1, candidates had to specifically recommend that it would be "Prudent to recognise 100% impairment" – no other recommendation on the ET would score a mark

> In the Executive Summary for Requirement 1, candidates had to offer a specific recommendation in relation to interest cover

> Other than the above recommendations on the ET and interest cover, no other commercial recommendations gained a mark

> In the Executive Summary for Requirement 2, candidates had to offer a specific recommendation regarding the proposed partner QR3 – no other recommendations gained credit

> In the Executive Summary for Requirement 3, candidates had to offer specific recommendations on the ethical matters rather than the usual mark being awarded for "concludes on ethics" – however, note that there was then a further "open" mark for making any other Commercial Recommendation as well

We are not entirely pleased to see this approach being taken as in business there is rarely "a" correct answer. For example, to obtain one of the Requirement 2 Executive Summary marks in the Bod (July 2015) Case Study, students had to conclude to go ahead with a project because it related to the company's biggest client but we are aware of many students who decided that it was now time for the business to diversify and look at other options, rather than being "pressured" into a poor deal by its biggest client. Both approaches seem valid to us but only one was rewarded.

This will not happen with every single mark and many will still be open – for example, in Bod (July 2015), the candidate could reach any conclusion regarding Requirement 3 in the Executive Summary

167

and obtain a mark and the 2016 and 2017 examinations also saw a more flexible and open approach where any decision would be acceptable. Even so, we would recommend that you try as hard as possible to get some of the more open marks so that you are not depending on "luck" to match a specific point for those marks where only certain answers are acceptable.

To get the more specific points where only certain answers are acceptable, have a think about the project or position – is there anything absolutely fundamental that you think the client would definitely have to know or do?

We have also noticed that Requirement 1 in the Executive Summary does now seem to require a specific conclusion on the ET to be reached to obtain a mark. The first point is therefore to make sure that you do say something reasonably detailed on the ET in your Executive Summary – then try to ensure that you check whether there is a conclusion to which you are being directed or which seems to be "inevitable" based on the scenario. For example, in CC (November 2015) students had to conclude that it was prudent to recognise a 100% impairment rate for certain bikes – taking a prudent approach would be the most ethical and least contentious way of accounting for the issue and so is likely to be the route that ICAEW would want its almost qualified Chartered Accountants to have learned to take. This was therefore the "right" answer that you had to include to obtain the mark. Therefore, perhaps you should pose yourself the question: "What would ICAEW do?".

It was also noted by the examiners that those students who (exceptionally) have access to a computer to type out their answer (as a result of a medical condition) have tended to copy and paste their Conclusions to create their Executive Summary, with minimal additional work. Although the examiners disapprove of this approach, they confirmed that there would be no penalisation of candidates in this scenario.

It was stated that it is partly for this reason that ICAEW had been considering whether to remove the Executive Summary from Case, with effect from 2017 onwards: the examiners would like to see a section that requires more value to be added. The fact that this **change** has been considered (but will not now be implemented: the Executive Summary will remain in future sittings) of course implies something about the way the examination is **currently** structured – namely, you will not be penalised if your Executive Summary is worded in a very similar manner to your Conclusions (hence the examiners have (unsuccessfully) tried to change the format of the examination). This is what we have termed the "pull through" of your Conclusions into your Executive Summary (see chapter 7 on this principle). Therefore, provided that your Conclusions are appropriate, you should have a good chance of scoring well in the Executive Summary without doing anything too different.

Please see our Planning & Reminder Sheets for reminders on how to attack the Conclusions section to each Requirement, and therefore how to include points that will also be appropriate in the Executive Summary.

3.3   Use of Market Background or Project Background paragraphs

It was confirmed again that just because a student uses a separate section at the start of their answer called something like "Market Background" or "Project Background" does not mean that the points will be ignored by the examiner, as is still being falsely claimed by a certain competing UK tuition provider. (July 2018 edition update: in an effort to make it clearer as to what you should do in these sections, we have now retitled them as "Context of Performance" and "Strategic and Operational Context", respectively, but our advice on what should be contained in these sections is unchanged. See chapters 8, 9, 10 and 16 for more discussion of what to do in your CoP and SOC sections.)

The examiners simply pointed out that the points within this section should be written in an appropriate way to have the best chance of scoring the marks. In particular, students should not just "bash down" everything they know about the market in a "scattergun" approach: if students do so then they may be given credit in the first column of the markscheme (Box X.2) but they may be giving up the opportunity to gain a mark in the third column of the markscheme for "Applying Judgement".

Instead, the points made should be relevant to the specific scenario of the business. We have specifically advised students to ensure that only points which can be meaningfully included in a sentence which includes the name of the Case Study company should be included in this section: this is a test that the point you are making is relevant and has an impact/importance, rather than just being something that you happen to know about the market. (See also chapter 16 on this point.)

We have also specifically advised students to try to provide some kind of impact or evaluation comment within their statement: this is to give students a chance of scoring an "Applying Judgement" mark in case the point is actually in the third column of the markscheme (Boxes X.6 and X.7) rather than in the expected first column (Boxes X.2, and possibly also in Boxes 2.1 and/or 3.1 in some examinations: see chapters 9 and 10 for further discussion). We have therefore never advised students just to include scattered points such as "E-bike sales are high. Web-sales are important to CC. New competitors are entering the market" and we agree with the examiners (see chapter 16) that this should not attract credit.

To generate relevant ideas, the examiners advised students to think slightly outside the scenario and look at the underlying "issue" – for example, in CC Requirement 2, it was relevant to reference the London City Cycle Hire Scheme and also CC's weak cash position. The points were not just about the Manchester City Cycle Hire Scheme proposal in Requirement 2.

In addition to broader context points, candidates should not forget to look for linkages between Requirements. For example, in the case of CC, the Requirement 3 calculation involved analysis of All-Terrain Bikes (ATB) and supply chain considerations – Requirement 1 discussed a possible problem with inventory of ATBs so a brief reference back to Requirement 1 would have been useful.

In relation to the matter of linkages, we would observe that the number of marks for backwards linkages to Requirement 1 appears to have increased at recent examinations, with the November 2017 (R4), July 2017 (PL) and November 2016 (TT) examinations all having credit available for this skill in Box 2.2 and/or Box 3.2.

3.4   Flagging of ETs

It was noted that there were a number of "pointers" in the CC (November 2015) Advance Information which hinted that the focus of the ET would be on an inventory problem: we identified this and included several inventory ETs in our live mock exam pack. The examiners confirmed that there would normally be a strong hint in the Advance Information as to what the extra calculation in Requirement 1 would be and the content of this calculation should never end up being a complete surprise to well-prepared students.

3.5 Alternatives in ETs

Candidates were reminded to consider the different options within an ET, rather than assuming that one approach proposed was completely incorrect and therefore unworthy of consideration.

The example given related to the ET in CC (November 2015) where 2 alternative proposals for the level of an inventory provision were being considered, depending on what could be negotiated. The examiners commented that it was a major failure of exam technique for students to assume that one of these approaches was completely wrong and therefore to do no numerical work in relation to that alternative. Students should look at both alternatives numerically before coming to a decision as to what the right approach should be: they should not reject possibilities out of hand in this way.

It was further emphasised that there may be ethical issues involved in the ET so this would be another reason to consider more than one approach as some approaches may be more ethically dubious than others: considering only one approach and instantly rejecting the other approach would prevent any detailed discussion here.

3.6 More numbers in Requirement 3

The examiners commented that there has been "a steady, incremental change" in which number work has been gradually introduced into Requirement 3 in recent Case Study examinations. This has been part of a conscious effort to change the balance of the examination slightly and it will definitely be maintained in future, according to the examiners. However, candidates do not appear to have picked up on this – **only 2% of candidates produced any form of calculation in the CC Requirement 3**.

Generally, performance in the CC Requirement 3 calculation was poor. According to the examiners, the few candidates who obtained a correct figure should have noted that the possible saving of over £1m seemed a little bit too good to be true – therefore scepticism of the figures will be rewarded in Requirement 3 but please bear in mind that there will definitely not be as much credit for this skill in Requirement 3 as in Requirement 2 as there are not the same number of Boxes available to reward scepticism or querying of assumptions as there are in Requirement 2, given the additional narrative Tasks required in Requirement 3.

3.7 Timing problems in Requirement 3

It was noted, yet again, that performance in Requirement 3 was relatively poor and well below the standard of Requirement 1 and Requirement 2. Despite being mainly narrative in nature, and therefore in theory requiring more writing than the other Requirements, Requirement 3 is normally the shortest section in a candidate's report. This reflects the mismanagement of time and a misunderstanding of the way the examination is marked: **all** Requirements must achieve a passing standard and it is not possible to compensate for a weak end to the report via a strong start to the report.

The examiners again asked tutors to remind students that the single biggest cause of failure in the Case Study examination is to mismanage your time such that you are unable to attempt your final Requirement properly. Please do take this advice and reminder seriously – please consult chapter 13 of this book for a "Plan B" to use in case you do overrun early into the exam.

3.8   Ethics in Requirement 3

The examiners receive feedback from tutor companies after every sitting. In the case of CC, the examiners strongly criticised one comment received (not from us!) stating that there was a "single large ethical issue" behind the financial, operational and strategic perspective of Requirement 3. The examiners stated that this misunderstood the nature of the ethics requirements in Case Study as there will not be one "single large ethical issue" but rather **several** nuanced areas to consider.

Although not mentioned by the examiners, we would note that issues relating to reputation were included in the non-ethics Boxes in CC. This is slightly unusual and could indicate that it is advisable to look for further ethical issues, in case the examiners are now fed up of seeing reputational impact as the only ethical issue discussed by a candidate.

3.9   Studying the Advance Information before the examination

The examiners reiterated that candidates should not worry that they might be "only" looking at obvious areas and should not overthink or overanalyse the Advance Information: the examination is not designed to catch students out and it may test obvious points and scenarios.

As an example, regarding Requirement 1, there were strong indications in the industry background information that growth in the industry was expected, and this was built into the figures for the recent performance of CC. Candidates should not expect to be "tricked" in any way here – if all the Advance Information figures point in a particular direction such as one of continued growth, then almost certainly the Exam Paper will follow this trend, rather than trying to do anything radical. This will hopefully help you in your preparations … but do note that the examiners stopped short of saying that the Exam Paper definitely "will" follow the trend in the Advance Information (to be expected, so that the questions are not revealed in advance and to preserve flexibility when setting the examination).

Candidates were advised to look out for issues/companies/names that come up 2-3 times at various points in the Advance Information. This is a hint that these areas are more examinable. Candidates were advised to spend some time carefully reading through the information and "grouping" points together. We strongly agree with this approach and have advised students that if something comes up more than once then you need to sit up and take notice. As for the idea of spending time "grouping" points together, this is precisely what our Exam Room Pack is all about as we know the importance

171

of identifying the themes and then having all the information on each theme on one page for easy use. Please see **www.acasimplifiedcase.com** for further details of our Exam Room Pack, including a free sample from a recent Case Study examination.

The examiners noted that the cross-referencing in the Advance Information will normally work forwards but not backwards. In other words, when an issue is introduced for the first time then the Advance Information will provide a reference to a later relevant Exhibit – however, within that later Exhibit there will not necessarily be a reference back to the earlier mention of the point. You should bear this in mind when performing your "grouping" of points (or do not worry about it and just buy our Exam Room Pack of course!).

The examiners then made the following important comments, which they specifically asked to be passed on to students (we wonder if your tuition provider has done so?) with the explanation that the "examiners say" the following:

> The candidate must "own" the Case Study and must know the Advance Information inside out – the test here is whether the candidate could stand up and explain the key points in each Exhibit if simply given some basic prompts as to what is within each Exhibit: if so, then they really do know the Advance Information to the standard required

> The candidate's own research should be minimal – the Advance Information is the key

> Candidates should not write out the answer to another question (e.g. a mock) – they must reply to the question set on the day

3.10   Comments on CC Requirement 1

The examiners said it is "foolhardy" **not** to consider prior year revenue growth in Requirement 1. This is in line with our reminder on our Planning & Reminder Sheets to always compare the rate of revenue growth indicated by the new information given in the Exam Paper with the rate of revenue growth indicated in the Advance Information.

Candidates should then extend the analysis to consider profitability and cash.

Candidates should not spend ages analysing figures which have not changed very much – the marks will be for spotting and analysing important changes in the business rather than reviewing every single figure every time.

3.11   Comments on CC Requirement 2

The examiners commented that if the candidate had read and understood the Exhibit relating to the London City Cycle Hire Scheme then Requirement 2 should have been "easy".

However, it was noted that many candidates appeared not to have read the question wording fully as quite a few students did not consider the impact on cash flow, despite the requirement to do so in the question wording. This is in line with our reminders in chapters 9 and 10 to spend time **unpacking** the question wording so that you can understand all the different likely markscheme Boxes, rather than seizing on what is apparently the "main" part of the question in Requirement 2/3 and then only focusing on that.

The examiners noted that the provenance of the data on the London City Cycle Hire Scheme was left deliberately vague, only saying that "independent experts" had been used. This was designed to get students thinking about scepticism points even before they entered the examination hall.

Many candidates did not comment on the impact of rounding – the pro forma calculation rounded the number of drivers needed from 2.6 to 3.0 in a certain part of the calculation. In itself, this does not look like a huge difference but candidates were supposed to spot that when applied to large figures, as in the London City Cycle Hire Scheme, this would increase costs by a material £160k.

Many candidates apparently missed one of the key strategic/financial implications of running a fixed-price contract and stated that CC should be worried about "demand being low". According to the examiners, if the fee for the project is fixed then it would not matter if demand is low – actually, this may be quite good for the supplier as they will not be overstretched. Therefore this point was not rewarded on the markscheme. The more serious problem would be that the scheme was too popular as then the supplier would not be able to recover the likely higher costs caused by being extremely busy. Please bear this in mind for the next time a **fixed price contract** is used in the Case Study.

3.12   Comments on CC Requirement 3

The examiners noted that, to a greater extent than normal, students had a problem structuring their answers to match the requirement. Tutor companies remarked that many students had reported to them after the examination that they were unsure what to do in Requirement 3 whilst ICAEW received more calls (which could not be responded to) than normal from candidates who had asked their invigilator in the examination hall to query with ICAEW how to structure their answers.

The examiners were very puzzled by these comments and so are we – the text of Requirement 3 seems perfectly clear and the markscheme was in no way a surprise. Here is the text of the Requirement, followed by our analysis:

"3. An evaluation and assessment of the supply chain issues raised by the possible introduction of a new supplier of bicycles, KKZ, as summarised by Eva Tomasz (**Exhibit 19a**), and by the problem identified by an existing supplier, MB (**Exhibit 19b**).

You should evaluate the financial, operational and strategic issues (including any business trust and ethical issues) arising with both KKZ and MB, as well as the overall implications for Cyclone's supply chain."

173

Analysis

The first line, as usual, simply sets out the background rather than setting a specific Task – however, it should make the candidate aware that the 2 key issues are (1) KKZ, a new supplier and (2) MB, a supplier with an existing problem.

The next sentence then starts to set the question – the financial, operational and strategic issues of KKZ became Issue 1 (as this is the first point mentioned in this first sentence) and then the same issues for MB became Issue 2 (as this is the second point mentioned in the first sentence). It was then noted that you should discuss business trust and ethical issues so these filled the normal 2 Boxes for ethics (Box 3.5 and 3.8). The final part of the sentence then asked for discussion of the overall implications for CC's supply chain – this part was introduced with the words "as well as", indicating that it was an **additional** Task to be considered **in addition** to the KKZ and MB analysis (which, again, were Issues 1 and 2, respectively): candidates should therefore have followed our advice that if something is mentioned in the question wording on the first page of the examination paper then it needs to be given some attention as it will likely be a whole Box.

Having worked through this analysis, candidates should have been able to allocate the following Boxes, based on the question wording:

Box 3.3   Discussion of Issue 1 – KKZ issues

Box 3.4   Discussion of Issue 2 – MB issues

Box 3.5   Ethics – Issue and Impact

Box 3.7   Other Issue – Supply chain

Box 3.8   Ethics – Recommendations

Certain other Boxes are invariable from sitting to sitting: Box 3.1 is always the mini calculation (or description of the project/client in the July 2017 (PL) and November 2016 (TT) examinations), Box 3.2 is always the SOC box, Box 3.9 is always the Conclusions box and Box 3.10 is always the Recommendations Box. This means that only Box 3.6 would remain (after allocating Boxes either based on the question wording (see above) or their invariable and predictable nature). As we have discussed in chapter 10, if you are given no other specific Task then you have to assume that there will be credit for additional points on Issue 1 and Issue 2: in this exam, there was 1 specific Task given (impact on the CC supply chain) so it would follow that there would only be one Box/Task allocated to additional points for both Issue 1 and Issue 2 in this case. This was exactly what happened with Box 3.6.

An additional hint would have been the word "**evaluate**" in the question wording. This would show that further points were needed on the 2 main issues. Having looked at several past paper markschemes we would be cautious here and make an important point – the points in the "evaluation" Box are often not a **further development** of a point in the Issue 1 and Issue 2 Boxes (Boxes 3.3 and 3.4) but rather just further (sometimes harder), **different** points, so you should not think of the "evaluation" as being **development of a point** (despite the fact that the term may mean this in other examination settings). In Case Study, "evaluation" appears to simply mean "**add additional points**".

174

To see this, please compare Boxes 3.3, 3.4 and 3.6 on the CC markscheme – many of the points in Box 3.6 have no connection back to Boxes 3.3 or 3.4 and the few points that have some connection (60% cost, reputation) should probably have been made in the same sentence as the point in Box 3.3 and 3.4 on this issue, if your sentence was a decent length and looked at whether the issue was serious or not (i.e. something you should be doing anyway, even when not aiming for an "evaluation" point). In other Case Study examinations, there are not even these linkages back and the Boxes in the third column contain completely different points to Box 3.3 and 3.4 – please review a few past paper markschemes to confirm this. Therefore the term "evaluate" should be interpreted carefully but it is certainly an indicator to do **more on Issue 1 and 2**.

Again, like the examiners, we are puzzled by the fact that students found the CC Requirement 3 harder to structure than in other examinations. We can only think that perhaps students were "thrown" by the fact that the question did not relate just to a single project (as many examinations do), with all the different "benefits" being Issue 1 and all the different "risks" being Issue 2 in that scenario.

3.13   Getting AJ marks

The examiners noted that the "Applying Judgement" area is the weakest skills area for students generally. This is always the case, regardless of the specific examination. As you know from earlier in this book, we do not really like the term "Applying Judgement" as this does not really tell you what you need to do to get the marks – we would therefore simply refer to the relevant Box/Task content as below:

Box 1.6	Reasons and pattern spotting for financial figure 1 – RP skills
Box 1.7	Reasons and pattern spotting for financial figures 2 & 3 – RP skills
Box 1.8	Narrative on ET
Box 2.6	Discussion of calculation results or Other Issue
Box 2.7	Other Issue (may be ethics)
Box 2.8	Assumptions extension point OR ethics recommendations
Box 3.6	Further Issue 1 points or Other Issue
Box 3.7	Further Issue 2 points or Other Issue
Box 3.8	Ethics – Recommendations

Of these Boxes, we believe Box 1.8, Box 2.8 and Box 3.8 should not be too hard as these are relatively specific in nature. For the other Boxes, it is helpful to consider the examiners' advice of attempting to answer the following 2 questions in order to obtain the "Applying Judgement" marks:

"So what?"

"How did this happen? Why did this happen?"

As we have indicated elsewhere in this book, it is still perfectly possible to pass the examination very well without always obtaining the "Applying Judgement" marks as the fact is that, according to the examiners, this skill is always "done badly" yet plenty of students go on to pass and qualify as Chartered Accountants.

4   Tips from the 2015 ICAEW Tutor Conference

General Remarks (2015 Tutor Conference: similar points made at the 2014 Tutor Conference)

4.1   Standards are improving, particularly in Requirement 1

ICAEW: The examiners noted that the RS (November 2014) Requirement 1 was done extremely well. In general the standard of Requirement 1 answers is exceptionally strong with around 90% of students passing this element in RS. It is the other Requirements which will discriminate between a pass or fail. Whilst the strength of Requirement 1 is good to see, candidates should always be careful to avoid compromising the other parts of their report by spending too long on Requirement 1. The examiners noted that Case Study Appendices are being prepared to a very high standard indeed as candidates know what to expect and are clearly preparing themselves well. Candidates with weak Appendices will definitely struggle with the examination because they will be at a significant disadvantage to the majority of high-performing candidates.

ACA Simplified: It is great to see that the examiners are happy with student attempts at Requirement 1. As we have advised in several places in this book, please do be careful not to spend too long on Requirement 1. Regarding the preparation of Appendices, we have always advised that students should spend a lot of time drilling these elements of their report before the examination and the comments from the examiners here confirm the importance of doing so: if not, you will be at a significant disadvantage in an examination where the marks are moderated and hence your ranking within your cohort of all candidates sitting the examination is important.

4.2   No plans to change the examination

ICAEW: The examiners are happy with the format and style of the examination and they believe that it provides a rigorous and objective method of evaluating your report-writing skills (which can be a subjective area if evaluated under other methodologies). There are no plans to change the examination or marking approach. If such plans were to be made, they would be very clearly indicated to tuition companies well in advance and would also be notified to students via student publications.

ACA Simplified: We hope that this will act as reassurance that the examiners will not be looking to do anything radical in your examination and therefore that our technique and approach will continue to be applicable. Whilst we have taken time to revise this edition of the book to take into account the most recent examination (and therefore have provided the most up to date materials possible by pointing out a number of slight tweaks deliberately being made to the markscheme by the examiners), please do not overlook the fact that, **fundamentally**, the examinations are very similar from session to session: therefore, doing a solid job of the basics will always get you through.

4.3   Positive marking, no ambiguity and keeping things simple

ICAEW: The Case Study examination is not designed to try to catch students out or make them trip up in their work. The markers will try hard to award marks wherever possible, looking at all elements of the report and they have been specifically instructed to apply positive marking rather than trying to be nasty or withhold marks. The examiners will not set questions which are ambiguous or unclear and therefore students should adopt the simplest interpretation and not overcomplicate their work.

ACA Simplified: We are obviously not going to disagree with a philosophy of keeping things straightforward and **simple**! Please bear this in mind if you are someone who can potentially think about things a little too deeply – the markscheme will not reward this as the examiners are simply looking for a straightforward, practical approach, using the least complex interpretation of information and figures.

4.4   Writing style

ICAEW: The correct writing style to use in the examination is to use short sentences and paragraphs of 2-3 sentences each. Candidates should not use bullet points except in the Recommendations section of each Requirement and in their Recommendations in the Executive Summary: bullet points are acceptable in these (but only these) elements of the report. [July 2018 edition update: as discussed earlier in this chapter, we specifically confirmed with the examiners at the 2018 Tutor Conference that it is acceptable for Ethics Recommendations to be presented in bullet point format so we recommend that you also make the most of this opportunity to save time without dropping marks.]

ACA Simplified: This confirms the advice that we have already provided in chapter 3 of this book.

4.5   Knowledge of the Advance Information is key

ICAEW: Students must know the Advance Information in depth: otherwise they will not be able to respond quickly to the Exam Paper requests nor to spot the connections between what is happening in the Exam Paper and the existing trends in the Advance Information.

ACA Simplified: We strongly agree that knowledge of the Advance Information is very important. This is why all of our classroom tuition takes place **after** the Advance Information has been released since this allows students to have 6 weeks to immerse themselves in their own Case Study, rather than wasting time studying past papers and only turning towards the live Case Study in the final few days of tuition. It is also why we provide 5 full mock exams based on the Advance Information. We also provide our Exam Room Pack to further enhance your knowledge of the Advance Information.

177

Please see our website at **www.acasimplifiedcase.com** for further information on these resources.

4.6   Format of the examination paper Exhibits: no tricks

ICAEW: The Exhibits will continue to be presented in the same order as the Requirements and candidates are welcome to read only the first 2 main Exhibits (i.e. after the Exhibit which sets out the Requirements) for Requirement 1 and then immediately attempt Requirement 1 itself. The next Exhibit will then relate to Requirement 2, and so on. The presentation of the Exhibits is not designed to catch students out nor to require the whole Exam Paper to be read before starting work.

ACA Simplified: It is good to have this confirmed. However, please see the next comment.

4.7   Correct order to attempt the Requirements

ICAEW: Candidates can attempt the Requirements in any order they wish but the recommended order is the same as that presented in the Exam Paper i.e. Requirement 1, then Requirement 2 and then Requirement 3. This is because Requirement 3 could use some information contained in the Exhibit relating to Requirement 1 or may relate to something that candidates should have recognised from completing the first Requirement.

ACA Simplified: In RS (November 2014), Box 3.1 rewarded some basic calculations based on the information in the Exam Paper regarding a new project opportunity. Further marks were then available for contrasting the results with figures from the Requirement 1 information e.g. the average revenue per delivery in the new project in Requirement 3 was well below the average for 2014 in the Requirement 1 information. This supports the view that Requirement 1 needs to be completed first. As noted earlier in this chapter, we have noticed that there has been an increase in the number of marks available for backwards linkages to Requirement 1 in the later Requirements so this perspective is now worth adopting to a greater extent than previously, when some markschemes did not have any credit at all for this skill.

4.8   Headings (1)

ICAEW: Use of the heading "Professional Scepticism" is not really desirable as it does not reflect a real client report: if candidates do use this heading, then markers will still mark the points but candidates are at risk of losing a mark in the AMR Boxes (officially termed the "Overall Paper" Boxes by ICAEW) at the end of the markscheme for use of "sufficient, appropriate headings".

Candidates should always put their Conclusions under a separate heading as this is required on the markscheme: Conclusions should be placed at the end of the relevant report section. Candidates are advised to put their Recommendations under a separate heading but this is not strictly required. There are no headings which could be used that will result in the marker ignoring a section.

The markers will look at all Recommendations: there is no maximum limit to the number of Recommendations that candidates may include but clearly there will be a trade-off in terms of time versus marks.

ACA Simplified: These comments were made in response to a query from one of our tutor team. Our Planning & Reminder Sheets do not use a "Professional Scepticism" heading and include separate Conclusions and Commercial Recommendations headings to respect the examiner advice here. We were pleased to confirm with ICAEW that use of a "Market Background" or "Project Background" section heading (July 2018 edition update: we now recommend use of the terms "Context of Performance" and "Strategic and Operational Context", respectively) will not lose candidates any marks, despite continuing criticism from tutors at another large provider regarding this advice (see page 263 for more on this matter). We are also pleased to see that there is no limit on the number of Commercial Recommendations that can be offered: we sometimes encounter students on our taught courses who have been told by other providers that the examiners will only mark the first 4 Recommendations but this is not true. At the same time, do not go too crazy and list too many points as you are, after all, playing "Recommendations Roulette" in this section.

4.9   Headings (2)

ICAEW: On the same matter of the correct section headings to use, it is advisable for candidates to carefully read the wording of the Requirement on the first page of the Exam Paper, using this to determine the structure of their answer. Candidates should look out for the specific requests made in the Exam Paper and should avoid answering a pre-prepared question. There should be a clear report section with an appropriate heading for each issue that the candidate is asked to consider in the question.

ACA Simplified: We obviously strongly agree with this advice to respond to the question set. This is why our Planning & Reminder Sheets and our explanations of how to write good Requirement 2 and Requirement 3 report sections (chapters 9 and 10) all indicate that students should replace our "Other Issues" generic heading with a section on the specific tasks set by the client, once these are known ("Other Issues" is just a reminder and the best we can do ahead of the examination). We have observed that all examinations from 2014 onwards have given clear guidance to students on what additional matters to consider, if this is required (sometimes the Requirement wording will not specify any "Other Issues" so always read the question wording for your specific examination carefully).

Having agreed on the importance of responding to the specific question set, we continue to believe that the other report section headings specified in our Planning & Reminder Sheets are always valid, whatever the question set: for example, in Requirement 3, it is always worth considering the SOC, the first 2 issues (often risks and benefits but again always check the question paper), ethics, Conclusions and Commercial Recommendations. Similarly, in Requirement 2, the markscheme will always have marks for the SOC, calculation results, querying of assumptions, scepticism regarding the information or methodology, Conclusions and Commercial Recommendations. We believe that the advice from the examiners was primarily aimed at the other specific issues (Boxes X.6 and X.7) which need to be addressed in addition to these standard sections.

4.10   Executive Summary Recommendations – just 1 recommendation is sufficient

ICAEW: Provided that students have at least 1 Recommendation at the end of their Executive Summary section regarding each Requirement, they will be awarded the open mark for "making commercial recommendations" (if available). Bullet points are acceptable.

ACA Simplified: As discussed elsewhere in this chapter and in chapter 7, the examiners are making some changes to the Executive Summary and this means that there may not now always be a mark for a general recommendation. Instead, in recent markschemes (and in the Requirement 1 Executive Summary in particular), candidates have had to match specific Recommendations (often regarding the ET) in order to obtain credit so making just 1 Recommendation in your Requirement 1 Executive Summary is not recommended: therefore, our Planning & Reminder Sheets advise that you make plenty of bullet point recommendations (including 4 on the ET) in your Requirement 1 Executive Summary section. However, in the Requirement 2 and 3 parts of the Executive Summary markscheme it is rare to find a specific Recommendation required so a more open approach is applied: accordingly, you do not need to have so many Recommendations in these parts of your Executive Summary.

4.11   Interpreting the markscheme

ICAEW: Candidates should apply the following rules when interpreting the markscheme:

Bold text – this indicates something which **must** be included as an exact match to be awarded the mark. An important example from Bod (July 2015) would be in the Conclusions to Requirement 1 where a figure to pair up with each comment is required (and is indicated by a "**with figure**" statement in bold in brackets after each mark in the markscheme). As Case Study is an accountancy examination, candidates should expect to include figures in their Conclusions.

Slash – this indicates alternative ways of getting a mark. For example, in the RS (November 2014) markscheme for the Requirement 1 Executive Summary, a mark was available for "explanation of Haulage/Warehouse growth": this means that candidates could explain either Haulage **or** Warehousing growth to obtain the mark.

Use of "eg" – this indicates some possible example ways of obtaining a mark but the markers will take a positive approach and award a mark for any reasonable example of the relevant type of point. However, this only applies if there is an "eg" before the point(s): in all other cases, points must match the markscheme.

Candidates should understand that they do not have to have the **exact** wording or figure used, unless this is indicated in bold text. The markers have been instructed to mark positively and will award the mark wherever possible.

ACA Simplified: It is useful to have this terminology fully confirmed. Please note the warning regarding Conclusions – the examiners expect you to produce figures to support your Conclusions and this is now something that is explicitly stated on the markscheme, for all examinations from 2014 onwards. Note that the figures do not need to be correct to get the marks for Conclusions, provided that your Conclusions quote the same figures as were stated in your main report section.

4.12 The awarding of more than 5 NAs does not result in a straight fail of the examination

ICAEW: If a candidate is awarded more than 5 NA grades then this does not mean that they will automatically fail the examination. However, it makes it difficult to pass because being awarded this many NA grades indicates quite a few weaknesses from the candidate and there will obviously not be as many Boxes remaining to pass.

ACA Simplified: This comment was made in response to a query from one of our tutor team. We are aware that a large number of students are being told by other tuition providers that if they are given more than 5 NA grades then that is it – they automatically fail. Many of the students who attend our retake classes after failing with another provider are under this impression. It is good to have it confirmed that there is no hard and fast rule here. We are not completely in agreement that achieving more than 5 NAs means that the candidate has to be weak – the points in the "Applying Judgement" column (Boxes X.6, X.7 and X.8) are somewhat difficult to predict and it is possible just to be very unlucky in these 9 Boxes (3 such Boxes x 3 Requirements). However, perhaps being unlucky more than 5 times out of 9 is quite unlikely if the candidate is a good candidate.

Ethics (2015 Tutor Conference: similar points made at the 2014 Tutor Conference)

4.13 Keep it simple

ICAEW: Candidates should avoid referring to technical ethical standards such as assurance standards or specific Ethical Codes and should also avoid reference to calling the ICAEW Ethics Helpline. In Case Study, all the examiners want to see is some brief comment on why an ethical issue has arisen (dishonesty, breach of confidentiality) and what the client needs to do. The marks are not for reciting the ICAEW Code of Ethics or going beyond this simple, "common sense" approach.

ACA Simplified: Again, we are not going to disagree with a philosophy of keeping things **simple**! A review of any Case markscheme should already have made students aware that the examiners are only looking for basic, common sense points rather than technical standards but it is good to have this confirmed.

4.14 How many ethics Boxes will there be?

ICAEW: The amount of ethics will depend on the nature of the scenario. There is no pre-agreed amount and candidates must use judgement to look at the number of issues in the Exam Paper before deciding how much to write.

ACA Simplified: This comment was made in response to a query from one of our tutor team. We can fully understand why ICAEW would not categorically state the number of issues. As indicated elsewhere in this book, we believe that there will generally be at least 2 issues in each Requirement where ethics is tested but there will often be more. The amount of ethics in the Case Study markscheme definitely seemed to increase significantly in 2014 and, indeed, moved into Requirement 2 in the RS exam (November 2014), something continued in Bod (July 2015) which had 6 different ethical issues in Requirement 3. All recent examinations other than Bux (July 2016) have had 2 Boxes for ethics in Requirement 3 (and also if tested in Requirement 2).

Requirement 2 calculations

4.15   Keep it simple

ICAEW: The types of calculation set in Requirement 2 will not be complex and the calculations are not designed to catch students out or play any "tricks": the calculations are simply there as a brief check on the candidate's ability to absorb and work with information and to then understand how the Case Study business is affected.

ACA Simplified: Based on our review of the 2014 and later examinations, the calculations do appear to have become easier and hence they are rewarded less than before on the markscheme. This is a good thing, provided that you do not waste time with over-complications and also provided that you can spot enough narrative issues to discuss. Please see chapters 9 and 11 for further advice. Rather than worrying that you are not going to be able to pass based on the calculations, we would put more preparation time into chapters 9 and 11 so that you understand what kind of narrative points to consider. Our Planning & Reminder Sheets in chapter 6 will also provide further useful reminders and tips.

4.16   Calculations flagged in the Advance Information

ICAEW: If the examiners require students to perform an unusual calculation which is bespoke to the client, then this will be clearly flagged in the Advance Information with a pro forma and explanation of how the figures are put together. Otherwise, if there is no such indication, then candidates should expect to perform a relatively simple, common sense financial analysis which involves only a few lines of calculations. If any technical content is required then it will relate to the basic skills seen in the Management Information or Financial Management papers: that is, assessment of the breakeven point, payback period, basic estimates of accounting profit or cash flow analysis. Again, the examiners are not interested in catching students out via any technical complexity.

ACA Simplified: This comment was made in response to a query from one of our tutor team. The RS (November 2014) calculation is perhaps the best example of this kind of "common sense" approach as it involved a calculation that really could not be predicted from the Advance Information. Similarly, although ZM (July 2014) had an entire Exhibit relating to the expected calculation, it contained no pro forma and hence the ultimate calculation required was definitely towards the easier end of what could have been tested based just on that Exhibit. This contrasts with the 2013 examinations and FS (November 2012) where the calculation was based more on a client-specific costing method which was very clearly flagged in the Advance Information. In the July 2012 (LL) examination, the position was similar to ZM in the sense that the Advance Information contained a detailed Exhibit which hinted at the calculation but which did not set out a specific pro forma or example: on exam day, the calculation was again a very straightforward example of what could have been created, based on the Advance Information Exhibit. In Bod (July 2015), CC (November 2015), Bux (July 2016) and TT (November 2016), Requirement 2 tested a client-specific calculation methodology which was clearly flagged in the Advance Information. Similarly, Bod contained industry-specific KPIs which were tested in the real exam. The PL (July 2017) Case Study was perhaps the most open of all recent examinations with the Requirement 2 calculation being very hard to predict but, perhaps as a result, the calculations ultimately required in the examination were relatively simple and far from being the most complicated that could have been set. R4 (November 2017) saw a return to a "flagged" form of calculation.

As such, the examiners' statement on this issue is very much in line with what we have seen in the examinations from 2012 onwards.

4.17   Sensitivity analysis: when will this be required?

ICAEW: If it is clear that one input is driving the output or the input appears to be causing an inaccurate output because the assumption regarding the input is wrong, then this should be a hint to candidates that they should vary this key input and see what happens.

ACA Simplified: This comment was made in response to a query from one of our tutor team. We can understand why the examiners left this issue as a judgemental one for students, rather than stating explicitly when such an analysis will be required. In the 2012 and 2013 examinations, the pattern seemed to be that if there was only 1 clear calculation to perform then candidates would need to find some numbers to fill in the second Box awarded for calculation work: sensitivity was apparently what the examiners wanted to see for this second Box. However, that pattern broke down with the RS (November 2014) Requirement 2 as this contained a very simple single calculation but did not reward sensitivity: no examinations since RS (November 2014) (other than TT (November 2016)) have had a Requirement 2 Box for sensitivity. Similarly, in ZM (July 2014), there was no full Box for sensitivity despite a relatively simple calculation, although in this Case Study exam, there were at least a few diamonds in other Boxes for sensitivity figures and related narrative points. Therefore, it does not appear likely that much, if any, credit will be given for sensitivity analysis in Case Study.

Given the move away from awarding many marks for the calculations and towards additional narrative tasks in Requirement 2, we would advise students to first review the Exam Paper question wording for any additional **narrative** task and make a decision as to how much sensitivity analysis to do based on whether there is such a Task or not. We did try to pin down exactly when sensitivity will be required but this was left open by the ICAEW response and understandably so.

183

5 Tips from the 2013 ICAEW Tutor Conference

General (2013 Tutor Conference)

5.1 Preparation

ICAEW: Candidates must read Examiners' Reports and sample scripts from prior sittings. These are "**the best way**" of preparing for the exam by seeing what previous candidates have done well or badly.

Candidates should also learn the Advance Information properly – they should be able to summarise the Advance Information and know the financial story in detail.

ACA Simplified: We agree very strongly with the need to look at past paper markschemes – you must look for the **patterns** in prior marking. Since Case has its own unique marking scheme (unlike any other exam, whether ACA or otherwise) it follows that you should put more time than normal into understanding what will get the marks.

However, we advise you to concentrate your work on the July 2012 or later Case Studies – papers before 2012 were marked with a slightly different markscheme which gave some credit for development of ideas. The current markscheme requires you to make a **larger number of shorter points**, introduces changes such as the ET and amends the marking of the Executive Summary. As you now have available 12 real July 2012-or-later past papers, as well as our optional mock exam pack of 5 papers based on the July 2018 Advance Information, you should be able to avoid any pre-2012 papers completely (hence also avoiding problems relating to the old markscheme approach). [July 2018 edition update: as discussed earlier in this chapter, the Case Study examiners have suggested that a review of the last 4 past papers (i.e. from July 2016 to November 2017) should be sufficient to understand how the markscheme has evolved in recent sittings.]

With respect to the advice to learn the Advance Information and financial story well, we strongly agree.

5.2 Aim of each Requirement

ICAEW: A simplified summary for each Requirement is:

Requirement 1 – look at what the business has been doing

Requirement 2 – look at what the business might be about to do – an immediate decision

Requirement 3 – look at what the business might possibly do – a longer term decision

ACA Simplified: This is a very useful summary and it can be helpful to remind yourself of the absolutely key aim of each Requirement: this may focus you towards points that will actually be on the markscheme.

5.3 Introductory paragraphs

ICAEW: Candidates should not paraphrase the Requirements at the start of their answers through introductory paragraphs.

ACA Simplified: It is helpful to have this clarified – you can thus save yourself a bit of time. Although there is no point in starting with a paraphrasing of the requirements/question, we recommend to our taught course students that they start with a "Background" paragraph which makes an explicit attempt to gain the marks in Tasks 1.2, 2.1, 2.2, 3.1 and 3.2 (Context of Performance and Strategic and Operational Context) – although it is possible that you may make these points in your main discussion, we feel that it is good practice to have a dedicated section which specifically aims at this Task just in case you do not make enough relevant points "mixed into" your main answer (given that you must get your 3 points in each of Boxes 1.2, 2.1, 2.2, 3.1 and 3.2).

Such an introductory section does not "paraphrase the requirements" but rather starts to answer the question and so it will respect the ICAEW advice above.

5.4 Time allocation

ICAEW: The biggest cause of a failure is bad use of time, often resulting in a poor Requirement 3. This is because students spend too long on Requirement 1 and/or think that Requirement 3 is "the easy one".

ACA Simplified: All ACA exams are time pressured so it is not surprising to see this comment. We also understand that it is very tempting to do a lot of work in the relatively safe realm of financial analysis in Requirement 1. Try to be disciplined – calculate the figures required in your Appendix 1, provide a plausible explanation for each key figure, include some pattern-spotting points, add some background market information, address the ET – then move on!

5.5 Pre-prepared answers

ICAEW: Some candidates appear simply to have memorised analysis from tutor workshops before the exam and so end up answering a question discussed in revision sessions rather than the question in the Exam Paper. This will affect the grade.

ACA Simplified: Take note of this and make sure you are using our own live mock exams to practise **technique** rather than as a **source of points to recycle** in your exam answer – always tailor your exam answer to the question set on the day and do not write about any questions that you have already practised and/or that you hoped/wanted to be on the Exam Paper.

5.6 Addressing Ethics Issues

ICAEW: The candidate does not need to put all Ethics issues into a separate section or cluster them together in the report. Ethics issues arise throughout the Requirements and throughout the markscheme.

ACA Simplified: Although this statement confirms that for the purposes of obtaining the marks you do not need to put all the ethics issues in a particular Requirement together, you may nevertheless wish to do so for practical reasons as this will force you to develop enough points to gain the 1 or 2 Boxes on ethics which could be available. (July 2018 edition update: as discussed earlier in this chapter, the examiners have confirmed that it is acceptable to use bullet points when providing Ethics Recommendations so make the most of this opportunity to save time without losing any marks.)

The statement that ethics issues arise "throughout" the Requirements is arguably not too accurate for examinations before RS (November 2014) – ethics was only really rewarded in Requirement 3. However, RS contained a Box for ethical issues in Requirement 2 and ethics has been tested in most Requirement 2s since then, so there is definitely evidence that students should no longer regard ethics as a "Requirement 3 issue". It should be noted that PL (July 2017) rewarded ethics in all 3 Requirements, showing that ethics can occur even in Requirement 1.

5.7 Planning technique

ICAEW: The Examiners recommend that candidates plan a Requirement and then write it up before moving onto planning and writing up the next Requirement. The best approach will vary by candidate but "the Examiners would advise candidates to tackle each Requirement separately, as it is unlikely that candidates could successfully plan for all Requirements upfront"[53].

Candidates should, however, make sure they read all the Exhibits and Requirements at the start so that they can understand the general position of the business and not duplicate information.

ACA Simplified: If you have attended another tuition provider and been told categorically not to write any of your report answer until 2 hours into the exam, this advice may come as a surprise but we completely agree with ICAEW's advice.

In our view, the ICAEW approach is much more sensible because there is too much to do if you try to plan all at once at the start. Furthermore, if you plan as you go, you will have a better idea of what you have said in the plan when you write up – if you plan everything at once at the start and then write up in order (Requirement 1, 2 then 3) then the chances are you will not remember what you had planned to say for Requirement 3 or even Requirement 2 – hence you will waste time re-reading the points on your plan.

---

[53] This statement was made by ICAEW in response to the statement of a tutor at another provider that "As a tutor, we advise our candidates to spend the first 2 hours reading, planning and sorting their Appendix, followed by writing for the next 2 hours". We are aware of a large number of students who have been not only taught this 2+2 approach but also that **they will not be able to pass the examination if they depart from it**. We advise you to experiment with your own method and to take note of the different advice from ICAEW here.

5.8 Where to state assumptions

ICAEW: Basic assumptions used in calculations should appear with those calculations – usually in the Appendix. The questioning or explanation of complex or dubious assumptions should be included in the main report but will still get credit if stated in the Appendix. For all aspects of stating or questioning assumptions, candidates should ideally write in full sentences and use appropriate headings to make them obvious.

ACA Simplified: Based on the fact that the marks available are for the questioning of assumptions, we would simply refer to these once, in your main report, rather than also listing these in your Appendix.

5.9 Questioning assumptions

ICAEW: Many candidates do not realise that they are supposed to question assumptions. "A questioning approach is the right one to have."

ACA Simplified: Please see chapter 12 of this book for guidance on how to adopt a "questioning approach" in a way that is likely to attract credit.

5.10 Stating Conclusions (versus Recommendations)

ICAEW: Candidates should repeat Conclusions again under a separate heading at the end of each Requirement. It is not enough for the conclusion to be in the main text. Comments made as conclusions will only be marked as such if recorded under a Conclusions heading.

Recommendations do not have to be under a heading but will be easier to spot if they are.

ACA Simplified: Note this point on separate presentation of Conclusions well – **it is an exception to the normal rule that markers will look anywhere in the script for a point**. ICAEW expect there to be a separate Conclusions section under a heading, as in a real report. Here, do not be afraid of simply repeating points already made in your main report section when writing your Conclusions section (and then repeating those points for a second time in the Executive Summary).

This point is good news – you can be rewarded twice (or 3 times if you take the Executive Summary into account) for the same point (once in the main text, once in your Conclusions and then again in the Executive Summary) provided that you express it in the right way within the Requirement itself i.e. once in your main discussion and then again under a **separate "Conclusions" heading** (and then again in the relevant Executive Summary section).

5.11 Recommendations can be bullet points

ICAEW: Bullet point Recommendations are acceptable, provided that everything is clear and relevant. Candidates are encouraged to use a broad range of areas rather than a narrow set of issues. If Recommendations are not on the markscheme then the candidate will not score a mark.

ACA Simplified: Make sure you bear this tip in mind because it suggests that the examiners want to see a good **range** of ideas and this is why they are happy to allow bullet form. Deep development or explanation is not required.

We would recommend that you look at recent past paper markschemes to help understand some of the common Recommendations that are likely to score marks. You can also refer to the Planning & Reminder Sheets contained in chapter 6 of this book. We recommend that you make the most of the permission to use bullet points by including plenty of short points to give yourself the maximum chance of scoring a mark. In Requirement 1, remember to provide plenty of Recommendations regarding the ET whilst in Requirements 2 and 3, remember that, across your answer as a whole, you must give both commercial Recommendations and also ethics Recommendations (assuming that ethics is tested). Our Planning & Reminder Sheets suggest including Ethics Recommendations sub-headings at appropriate places to ensure that you do indeed provide enough examples of both types of Recommendation.

5.12 Will the markscheme change in future sittings?

ICAEW: No, the breakdown will be the same for the foreseeable future: "It is practical and we believe the weighting is correct," stated the examiners. The last time the markscheme changed significantly, a VITAL magazine article was written so changes will be communicated well in advance to students and tuition providers.

ACA Simplified: Make the most of this comment by looking for the patterns we have discussed – ICAEW have assured candidates that the markscheme will be similar each year. Hence our detailed analysis in this book will also remain valid.

5.13 Range versus depth

ICAEW: To score well in Case we recommend a range of answers, particularly when it comes to Recommendations, with the proviso that a "scattergun" approach is not advisable.

ACA Simplified: This has been reflected in the new markschemes from July 2012 onwards with the abolition of marks for the development of ideas and you are advised to bear this in mind when looking at past papers, having past papers marked or listening to tutor advice – **papers for 2011 and earlier are no longer reliable**. (July 2018 edition update: as discussed earlier in this chapter, the Case Study examiners have suggested that the last 4 past papers (July 2016 to November 2017) would provide sufficient examples of up-to-date markschemes.)

5.14   Legibility

ICAEW: Many scripts are hard to read. Markers will do their best to read scripts but if they cannot, candidates will lose out on marks. Candidates should write more slowly as it is possible to produce a high quality script in only 20 pages.

ACA Simplified: We obviously agree that you should make your work legible. However, we are not sure that a 20 page target is a good one.

Let us assume 3 pages for your Appendices, 1 page for your cover (including disclaimer) and 3 pages for your Executive Summary – that leaves 13 pages or 4.33 pages per Requirement. We do not believe that this is enough. With full knowledge of the points on the markscheme, the examiners may be able to construct a model answer in 20 pages by writing only points which are on the markscheme but since candidates are unlikely to score with everything they say, it is only prudent to aim to write significantly more points. This requires greater writing speed but we think it is safer to write too much than too little – if a point is on your script it **might** score; if you have not written a point it definitely **will not** score.

Section-Specific Advice (2013 Tutor Conference)

5.15   Executive Summary

ICAEW: The Executive Summary should be a stand-alone document. It should not tell us anything which is not already stated elsewhere in the report. Candidates should not rewrite their whole report – the skill is to identify the key issues.

ACA Simplified: This is helpful advice. We have analysed the marking of the Executive Summary in detail to try to show you what will always be rewarded. In our view, through to 2014, the Executive Summary was easier than it used to be because you no longer had to match only specified Conclusions and Recommendations on the markscheme as you did in the past – as long as you conclude and recommend in **some** way on the key areas you will get the marks.

However, please refer to the start of this chapter for some recent advice from the examiners regarding the Executive Summary.

5.16   Requirement 1

ICAEW: In FS (November 2012), many candidates spent too long on the financial analysis, with a knock-on effect on Requirement 3.

ACA Simplified: As stated above, just stick to the basics of what you are being asked. It was very surprising to see that FS (November 2012) did not ask for any discussion at all of secondary revenue streams but if the client does not want that analysis, do not include it just because you rehearsed it.

189

5.17   Requirement 2

ICAEW: We will not set a question which simply allows the candidate to put the same numbers in for both years of a multi-year calculation.

ACA Simplified: Subject to our advice to concentrate on the narrative aspects of Requirement 2 rather than worrying too much about the calculation (there are a lot more marks for discussion than for the results and you can pick up many of these regardless of whether your calculations are anywhere near correct), if you find yourself with no difference between your 2 results then have another **quick** look at the data. But do not spend too much time on the numbers.

5.18   Requirement 3

ICAEW: Candidates often provide risks/benefits/opportunities/threats which could apply to any business at all, rather than issues relevant to the specific business in the question. This is unlikely to attract credit.

ACA Simplified: This is the usual ICAEW complaint against stock or "boilerplate" answers – listen carefully to this warning and use the Exam Paper as much as possible. At the same time, there are certainly some recurring themes which you would be advised to learn well (see, for example, chapter 11 on how to develop practical points which are likely to be in the Boxes). Hence it can sometimes be correct to mention points that have been given credit in past Case Study markschemes.

Chapter 15   Tips from Our Tuition Courses

Learning Points

After reading this chapter, you must be able to:

1. understand our answers to certain frequently asked questions from taught course students
2. understand some additional tips and tricks developed during our tuition sessions

---

In this chapter, we will provide some useful tips and tricks from our recent classroom tuition courses. Many of the points were first raised or developed during our tuition sessions ahead of the July 2015 sitting as that sitting was, at the time, our largest intake to date and a big increase on 2014 after 2 of our students won ICAEW prizes (including a global prize) in 2014. Similar points have arisen at subsequent sittings, suggesting to us that students are generally concerned about some of the same issues each time. We have therefore collated the points made at various sittings to create this chapter.

1   The "more than 5 NAs" myth

Firstly, we can clear up a point which many students have been told by their tuition provider: if a student achieves more than 5 NAs (i.e. more than 5 Boxes with no points which match the markscheme) then that student fails the examination regardless of their performance in the rest of the examination.

This is incorrect. We spoke directly with the ICAEW Case Study examiners at the 2015, 2016, 2017 and 2018 Tutor Conferences regarding this issue because we are so frequently asked about it by students who are very worried that if they leave out a certain section and are unlucky in other Boxes then they will automatically be failed: this creates additional stress and worry. We were informed on all occasions by the examiners that there is **no hard and fast rule regarding the number of NAs obtained**: a student will **not** be "straight-failed" just from the number of NAs alone as this is not a metric used in the marking. **Therefore please do not worry about this issue.**

The examiners said that if a student were to achieve more than 5 NAs then this would obviously make it harder to pass the examination because it would mean that quite a few Boxes were not gaining a passing grade. However, again, the **number** of NAs is **not**, in itself, considered in the marking process.

2   Use of a "Market background" section heading is against ICAEW examiner guidance

A number of our July 2015 students had been told this in their first attempt at another provider and we are aware that the statement is still being made by the same provider (despite notification to the provider of their error by ICAEW and by us) at the time of writing (May 2018). As indicated in other places in this book, we are aware that our planning sheets and approach are being criticised by this

191

large provider on the alleged basis that the ICAEW examiners have issued guidance stating that use of a "Market Background" section heading will result in that section being marked as zero by the marker. This statement is **false**: we have confirmed with ICAEW (and ICAEW markers) that there is no such rule and that no such guidance has ever been issued. See chapter 16 for some ways in which the examiners have in fact explicitly stated that using such a section can be a good way of earning marks, if done in the right way. We also note that one of the November 2017 student scripts reviewed at the Case Study Workshop at the 2018 ICAEW Tutor Conference contained a "Market Background" section and marks were clearly awarded by trained ICAEW markers – tutors were shown a copy of the actual marking of this script performed by ICAEW at the November 2017 sitting and it was very clear to see marks being given in full for points within a "Market Background" section.

To be clear: we recommend including a dedicated section on the Context of Performance (CoP, applicable to Requirement 1) or Strategic and Operational Context (SOC, Requirement 2) at the start of each Requirement because we have noticed that without this section, students often forget to adopt a "background" perspective at all and instead quite naturally move straight into discussing the project itself – creating a **dedicated** section will **force you** to think about market patterns, key Advance Information statistics, linkages back to the Requirement 1 picture, the press articles and so on in a way that is unlikely if you go straight into the specific Requirement analysis.

At the same time, you will be rewarded for your background points wherever you state them in your answer (with the exception of marks in the Conclusions Boxes (Boxes 1.9, 2.9 and 3.9) which must be presented under a section heading "Conclusions") so we are not saying that you must **only** include such points at the start of your answer nor that you **have to use** this heading if you prefer to "mix in" your points with the rest of the answer.

All we ask is that you **definitely consider this perspective** (however that may work best for you in practice) and we just think that the best way is to **dedicate** a section to this perspective. As we have seen elsewhere in this book, 2 recent examinations (TT (November 2016) and PL (July 2017)) have allocated more marks for background contextual factors through inclusion of marks in Boxes 2.1 and 3.1 so this perspective is now potentially even more important than in the past.

We have also noted in several other places in this book that even though this section is **presented** first it does not necessarily have to be **written** first and you may benefit from doing other parts of the question and coming back to the CoP/SOC section once you have "**warmed up**" to the scenario. We have also advised this approach because it will ensure that you are **not repeating** points in both the CoP/SOC and then also in your main discussion as there is **no benefit in repeating a point**: you will again be rewarded no matter where the point is mentioned in your discussion and therefore we are recommending a dedicated section for reasons of **technique** rather than for **marking** reasons.

As an update to our technique for the July 2018 edition of this book, we have amended our previous section headings to the background sections ("Market Background" for Requirement 1 and "Project Background" for Requirements 2 and 3) as we believe that our newly-suggested "Context of Performance" (Requirement 1) and "Strategic and Operational Context" (Requirements 2 and 3) section headings should help students focus on points that are more likely to attract credit. However, for the avoidance of doubt, **we wish to be very clear that we are not changing our general advice regarding the content and technique for these sections in any way from other recent editions of this book** – our suggestion is merely a form of change in wording, to help students understand

192

what to do in these sections. Please bear this point in mind if your other provider attempts to falsely state that we have somehow changed our technique because use of a "Background" section is not allowed under ICAEW rules. This is categorically not the case and we continue to refer false statements of this kind to ICAEW.

3   I struggle to generate "Background" points. What should I do?

Our first advice would be not to panic too much: **Requirement 1 and Requirement 3 can be passed easily without passing Boxes 1.2 and 3.1/3.2**, respectively. We include detailed explanation of how to do your "Background" sections because we find that students typically neglect this area because they perhaps have not been informed that the relevant marks even exist on the markscheme. Therefore, it seems worthwhile pointing out the availability of this kind of mark but, at the same time, you could be unlucky with your background points selected because there are obviously a huge number of points that you could pick: we therefore find that even some of our top-performing taught course students can sometimes be unlucky and not pass the "Background" Boxes … but they still easily pass their mock examinations and, more importantly, the final examination without any problems.

Things are slightly different with Requirement 2 because this is, in our opinion, **a slightly harder Requirement** in general terms. Therefore the "Background" Boxes could be a very helpful way of getting nearer to the precious 5 Boxes that you need. At the same time, there appears to be a trend away from numerical Boxes in Requirement 2 as the examiners move more towards practical and strategic narrative analysis, making Requirement 2 easier to pass as it is generally easier to get narrative marks than to get numerical marks (which require fully correct calculations). This then means that the SOC Boxes 2.1 (if not allocated to inputs) and 2.2 become slightly less important as the other narrative Boxes in Requirement 2 are probably easier. (Although note that TT (November 2016) and PL (July 2017) had 2 calculations to perform in Requirement 2. R4 (November 2017) had only 1 calculation to perform so there was plenty of credit for narrative points.)

So try not to worry about this section as it is **unlikely to make or break your examination**. However, in the interests of completeness and to reassure you, here is our recommended way of generating background points which are more likely to score marks:

Requirement 1 ("Context of Performance" (CoP) section)

We recommend that you always start with an Advance Information point (look for market growth forecasts in particular in the Advance Information but also consider qualitative trends) on the **specific market** in the Case Study. Remember, as always in the CoP section, to link the point back to the client company by using the Case Study company's name in each sentence.

After this, think of the very **broadest market-specific** points in the Advance Information, including the press articles. In Requirement 1, take a broad approach and think back over any specific **statistics** mentioned.

Requirement 2 and Requirement 3 ("Strategic and Operational Context" (SOC) section)

We believe that a very similar approach can be followed for both Requirements here. The points must be **project-relevant** rather than relating to the market as a whole. There is clearly a fine balancing act to consider here because you do want points that are project-specific but not so specific that you end up answering the question itself (i.e. addressing later Boxes in the markscheme) in the SOC (you would still be awarded marks for this but it makes it less likely that you will get the SOC marks that you were actually aiming for in this part of your report!).

If you have a company with multiple revenue streams (this is quite common in Case Study) then the first thing to do is identify **which stream(s)** is(are) potentially involved in the project. Think about anything you know from the Advance Information which connects to these streams. The **press articles** will often be helpful here: look for background points that are more specific to that stream. Also think about the **customers**, **competitors** and **locations** specifically mentioned in the Exam Paper (the "proper nouns check"): what do we already know about them from the Advance Information? Some further questions to consider (depending of course on what is contained in your own specific set of Advance Information) might include:

1. What **kind of project** are we looking at? How does this **fit** with our plans?

2. Which **market(s)** will be affected?

3. Think about any previous bad/good experiences or successes/failures in relation to **similar projects/scenarios**, whether for our client or for companies in the press articles.

In both Requirement 2 and Requirement 3, **ethics** will be a key issue. At least one of the ethical issues will come from the press articles so think about any **similarities and differences** between what is happening in the Exam Paper and existing, known issues mentioned in the press articles within the Advance Information (whilst later in your answer raising a **scepticism** point on the fact that the information is only based on **press articles** which need confirming).

As noted elsewhere in this book, we have noticed that there are an increasing number of marks in the SOC Boxes for **linkages** back to the Requirement 1 picture for the relevant stream (and possibly for the business as a whole for matters such as the cash position). Please therefore carefully review our advice in chapters 9 and 10 on what to consider for your linkages marks.

As already indicated, we advise you to ensure that a reference to your client company is included in all SOC sentences. This is, firstly, to ensure that you can pick up the mark as the markers may not award a mark for simply stating "Demand for children's books is growing" without any connection to the Case Study company's performance. Secondly, we advise that you make an explicit link to the Case Study company because mentioning the potential **impact** on the company could lead you to pick up marks if a point that you thought was part of the SOC is in fact one of the "Applying Judgement" points in Boxes 1.6, 1.7, 2.6, 2.7, 3.6 or 3.7: if you do not make the **connection** to the client company, this will not be possible as these types of points are in Boxes relating to analysing the **impact** of the project on the specific client company so if you have not spelled out the impact (and have instead said something vague about the industry such as "Demand for children's books is growing") then you cannot obtain a mark on those later X/6 or X.7 Boxes.

See chapter 16 for further discussion of how to write your CoP and SOC sections.

4 I struggle with the Requirement 1 ET. What should I do?

First of all, as discussed already, the worst thing you can do here is spend **too long** on the ET – it is a maximum of 2 Boxes in a Requirement which is passed by 90% of students so you do not want to screw up the timing of your whole examination by spending too much of your time on this relatively unimportant area.

In a typical ET, Box 1.5 will award marks for **correct calculations** and Box 1.8 will be allocated to **narrative and strategic analysis**. We very much doubt that 90% of candidates who pass the Requirement will be getting the calculation correct (this certainly does not happen in our mock exams on our taught courses) so try not to worry, particularly as **many of the points in Box 1.8 will not actually depend on having exactly correct calculations**: these marks will be more **practical** and **strategic** in nature so they can be obtained just by forming the **correct overall view** on the matter – think about some "Big Picture" points that do not depend on having the correct numerical results.

Please see the points below for some hints on what to do for the narrative marks (applying our **PSS** framework for the ET):

Practical (P) points

Consider capacity, staffing, timing and cash flows

Strategic (S) points

Consider the long run impact, the impact on other clients, the impact on reputation and impact on current plans

Scepticism (S) points

Query the figures quoted (and the source), query the size of the suggested impact (whether positive or negative), look for any simplifications or missing inputs and consider whether the situation is definitely going to happen or not.

Based on the above, you should aim for around **6-7** practical, strategic and scepticism points which are, once again, **independent of having the correct figures**.

Some good standard points to include, based on reviewing past markschemes, are as follows:

1. Consider **negotiating** the matter or taking some other kind of action that may **prevent** a potential problem actually occurring

2. Suggest a **review** of **other** areas of the business in the case of a problem (e.g. if some stock for one stream is impaired, does this mean we have a **wider** impairment issue?)

3. How **important** is this client to the business and what are the potential impacts on **reported profit and cash flows**?

We do not recommend that you leave out the ET entirely as this may affect the marks for your Requirement 1 Appendix in the Appendices & Main Report Boxes at the end of the markscheme by making your Appendix 1 incomplete. Also you need at least **some** ET Conclusions, Commercial Recommendations and Executive Summary points. In a real emergency where you do not attempt the ET calculation, please therefore at least create an **estimated** figure which you can use in your Conclusions to Requirement 1 and in the Executive Summary to ensure that you do not miss out on these very easy or "open" marks.

Remember to always include **at least 4 ET recommendations** (and points which are different to your PSS points: see above) in your Commercial Recommendations section at the end of Requirement 1: there always seem to be a couple of ET recommendations on the markscheme in either Box 1.8 or Box 1.10 and any kind of clue or hint as to what is required within "Recommendations Roulette" is very welcome! **Negotiating**, **confirming the impact** and **investigating whether there are wider implications** are likely to be points with a decent chance of scoring a mark. There were 4 different ET recommendations in Box 1.10 in one recent examination (PL (July 2017)) so it really is worth being thorough in this respect.

You should also use the ET to help guide you in relation to possible CoP points for your report section 1.A: there is likely to be some kind of **connection** to spot.

5   I always overrun in Requirement 1. What should I do?

According to the examiners, the single biggest cause of failing the Case Study examination is spending too long on the relatively easy and "comfortable" accounts analysis in Requirement 1. This frequently asked question therefore addresses a very real danger and it is important to think about how to avoid the related problems.

Our first piece of advice is to **consider doing Requirement 1 last** – this will ensure that you can complete Requirements 2 and 3 properly and to a good standard. You will then not be able to overrun in Requirement 1 because the clock will impose a definite deadline for you – if you attempt Requirement 1 first then it is always tempting to "steal" a bit of time from the later Requirements by overrunning but this cannot happen if Requirement 1 is attempted last because your script will be collected in when you have had your remaining time!

We appreciate that this is an unusual approach so **we strongly advise you to practise this method well before the examination day** to see if it works for you personally, either via past papers or (in our opinion a better way) by means of our pack of live mock exams based on the July 2018 Advance Information.

The method of attempting Requirement 1 last also has a potential drawback in that there are **increasingly** marks in Requirement 2 and Requirement 3 for spotting linkages based on the financial "story" set out in Requirement 1: there have been marks for looking at matters such as the company's cash position, the growth rate of the relevant revenue stream, the gross profit margin of the relevant

196

revenue stream, and so on. **Doing Requirement 1 last would potentially mean giving up on these marks**.

However, in cost-benefit terms it may be better just to sacrifice these points if that means using an approach (attempting Requirement 1 last) that will **ensure that you finish the paper** – if you do not finish your report then you will almost certainly fail the examination, meaning that you will not really see any benefit from picking up those linkage marks anyway!

Our second piece of advice is to bear in mind that around **90% of candidates pass Requirement 1** … whereas only 75% pass the examination as a whole. Requirement 1 is therefore not in itself the most difficult element (even allowing for the fact that some of the passes within the 90% will have been by candidates who spent too long on Requirement 1 – perhaps they would not have passed Requirement 1 if they had stuck to the allotted time …). You do not therefore have to do anything **superhuman or amazing** to pass: just stick to the basics and the "Big Picture" points.

Relatedly, our third piece of advice is not to worry so much about finding a conclusive **reason** to explain every single movement in Appendix 1. We are very aware that many candidates have been trained by other providers to give a **reason** for every movement or change, presumably in the hope of gaining the "Applying Judgement" marks in Boxes 1.6 and 1.7. Whilst reasons do feature in these Boxes, so do **patterns** such as comparing this year's revenue growth to last year or comparing results to any benchmarks in the Advance Information (such as a target level of cash or a target gross profit margin): Boxes 1.6 and 1.7 are **not just about reasons** and it therefore follows that you do need to look for other types of points, some of which are **easier** than reasons. **Try to avoid this exclusive obsession with reasons in Requirement 1**. Also remember that, very often, the mark will be given for any reasonable reason so it is not worth spending too long thinking about "the" or the "best" reason to include in your answer.

Our final piece of advice is to work on your own **clinical and succinct way of referring to the numbers through a "pro forma" Requirement 1 sentence that can just be applied repeatedly to revenue, GP, OP and so on**. Once you have worked out a very quick yet thorough way of referring to the key figures then simply **re-use this same sentence structure again and again in your answer**: do not be tempted to vary the sentence structure just to make the text more varied and interesting (as you should in a normal essay-based marking approach) – it is better to stick to the same standard paragraph structure every time to ensure you do not forget to do something.

We recommend **2 sentences per paragraph**, with the first sentence including the movement in £k or % terms, a descriptive word such as "significantly", "marginally" or "impressively" and a suggested **cause** or **reason** for the change. The second sentence should then look at any **patterns** implied. This should give you excellent coverage of both the second and third columns in the markscheme (Boxes 1.3, 1.4, 1.6 and 1.7).

As an example, the first sentence in your standard paragraph might look like the following (points in square brackets are adjusted as required, whilst keeping the basic sentence wording the same every time):

"[Revenue/GP/OP] [increased/decreased] [significantly/marginally] by £Xk (X%) due to [add reason]."

Simply repeat this structure to ensure that you do not drop any easy marks by forgetting to include one of the elements required whilst also saving valuable thinking time compared to trying to develop a different wording each time you look at each figure: Case Study is not a poetry or fine-writing examination so there is no benefit in trying to mix your wording up and if you do so then there is a risk that you will forget to include something basic.

6   The calculation in Requirement 2 is unexpectedly difficult. Any advice?

Our first piece of advice would be **not to panic**: the Requirement 2 calculations will be a maximum of 2 out of 10 Boxes and we have seen (see the various Forewords to previous editions of this book reproduced in Appendix 3) that in Requirement 2 **the examination is moving further and further in the direction of practical, narrative advice** rather than "number-crunching". Therefore you can easily pass Requirement 2 with some poor numerical work … provided that you stay calm.

You should note that the marks for correct calculations are awarded in Box 2.3 and potentially also in Box 2.4 (if 2 calculations are required) but beyond this **there are no further Case Study marks that depend on having the correct numerical results**! There are, for example, no strategic or practical points that are linked to the numbers so having an incorrect answer has no implications at all for the rest of your answer – you do need to include **some figures** in your Conclusions to Requirement 2 and also in your Executive Summary but remember that these figures **do not need to be correct** to gain the marks. Time and again we see students who waste as much as a **whole page of writing** on discussing their calculation results but this is not a sensible use of time because there are not actually all that many marks for such points and your calculation results may well be wrong anyway! You instead need to move on to consider the other narrative elements requested … and that means moving onto areas which are potentially much easier anyway.

Finally, we would recommend that you **look for any "easy wins"** in the calculations: there will normally be a few elements that are **much easier than others**, particularly for calculations that have been strongly hinted at in the Advance Information, perhaps via an example pro-forma calculation set out by the client. You are welcome to attempt these points first to get some marks and you can then make **a judgement as to whether to persist with the harder parts**, based on how much time is remaining. Bear in mind, however, that with just 4 diamonds per Box for each calculation, you are **unlikely to pass the relevant Box only from workings** (unlike in other ACA exams where your workings may be sufficient to gain enough marks to pass, even without a correct "final" answer).

Once again, passing Requirement 2 is therefore almost certainly going to depend on having good **narrative** points in your discussion.

7   What do I do with the Requirement 3 figures? Do I need an Appendix 3?

Prior to RS (November 2014), Requirement 3 was traditionally the "non-numbers" Requirement and therefore candidates have traditionally expected to perform narrative strategic analysis only. In RS, things changed slightly with the inclusion of a set of basic figures in Requirement 3: the information was nowhere near as detailed as in a Requirement 2 model but it was enough to perform a similar set of calculations to what had already been done in the Advance Information, thus providing some marks for Advance Information linkages if you spotted that a comparison with the Advance Information results was possible. The following examination (Bod (July 2015)) had a single diamond in Box 3.1 for a calculation but with no requirement to reach any specified result (unlike in RS). However, in examinations from November 2015 onwards, calculations were required for **all Box 3.1 marks** (Box 3.3 in the case of PL (July 2017) and R4 (November 2017)) – the examiners have confirmed (see chapter 14) that a more numerical approach to Requirement 3 is likely to remain in place for future examinations.

Our basic rule is: if there are **no** numbers in Requirement 3 (unlikely) then definitely raise a **scepticism** point querying the lack of financial information; if there **are** numbers in Requirement 3 then definitely **use the numbers** as they must be there for a reason but still make a scepticism point on a lack of **detailed** figures or mention some key figures that are still missing (given that the information provided is basic). However, note that there is no longer a dedicated Box for scepticism in Requirements 2 or 3 (see chapter 12).

There have never been any specific marks in the Appendices & Main Report (AMR) Boxes for an Appendix 3, suggesting that the examiners do not require a full Appendix and therefore are not expecting complex calculations. However, in order to keep your work neat and avoid any errors due to trying to squeeze things in too quickly, we still recommend that you do include an Appendix 3 in practice.

8 How do I know how many Boxes have been allocated to ethics in Requirement 2 and Requirement 3?

As with many aspects of the Case Study markscheme, often whilst sitting the examination you will not "**know**" in any kind of absolute, philosophical sense how the Boxes will be allocated on the markscheme: even as experienced tutors, we still need to wait for the official ICAEW markscheme to be completely certain. However, we can say that **all examinations since 2014 other than Bux (July 2016) have allocated 2 Boxes to ethics in Requirement 3**.

We are also aware of how important ICAEW feel the matter of ethics is to your professional training and Case Study is the **last opportunity to test this skill for most candidates**. Therefore we would generally assume that there will be **2 Boxes** for ethics so do not economise on your ethical discussion – in fact, do it relatively early in your answer as your report section 3.D (i.e. before you run out of time towards the end of your answer).

As indicated in chapter 10, this has an important implication for the extent of your scepticism discussion in Requirement 3: **if 2 Boxes are needed for discussion of ethics, then Box 3.8 cannot be dedicated to sceptical remarks**. Therefore **tone down your scepticism** just as you should **boost up** your ethics discussion.

As for Requirement 2, the number of Boxes allocated to ethics can vary. The last 3 examinations (TT (November 2016), PL (July 2017) and R4 (November 2017)) have all had 2 Boxes but previous examinations only had 1. So whilst assuming 2 Boxes for ethics is probably now a reasonable starting point, we would recommend that you look at how many other things you have been asked to do in the question wording before deciding on how many Boxes are likely to be allocated to this area.

9 I sometimes cannot see any "Other Issues" in Requirement 3 in past papers or your mocks. What am I doing wrong?

You may not be doing anything wrong at all – sometimes Boxes 3.6 and 3.7 will not be **separate issues** but rather a set of **further points** on the same Issue 1 and Issue 2 that are considered in Boxes 3.3 and 3.4: often these will be **risks** and **benefits**, or the risks and benefits of **2 different projects**, respectively. In other words, in some examinations, there are no "Other Issues" to consider.

Sometimes we are asked if this means that you need to **further develop** points made earlier in your answer on Issue 1 and Issue 2 (in Boxes 3.3 and 3.4), on the basis of Boxes 3.6 and 3.7 being "Applying Judgement" Boxes and therefore a **harder** skill. Similarly, the standard 4 Column Planning Grid (with which we do not agree) would suggest that you need to work across the page, adding development of each idea to get the "Applying Judgement" marks in the third column.

Whilst we understand this logic, looking at the markschemes for the relevant examinations, it seems that often the points in Box 3.6 and 3.7 are **not** further developments of earlier points but instead just **additional** points in the same general areas (i.e. further risks and benefits, for example), rather than detailed evaluation of the same risks and benefits which score in Boxes 3.3 and 3.4. This means that it really is very important that you include enough different points to have a good chance of accumulating sufficient marks in the relevant Boxes: otherwise there is a risk that you might end up only getting 1 or 2 marks in each of Boxes 3.3, 3.4, 3.6 and 3.7 and passing none of them, due to an unlucky "distribution" of your points. Please see chapter 1 on the importance of "distributing" your points appropriately to maximise the chances of success.

In other examinations there may be some further **different** "Other Issues" to look at so in our mocks we try to vary this a little and this could be why some students feel uncertain that they may have missed something in some past papers or mocks.

The key is always to read the question wording very carefully – as explained above, in Requirement 3, Issue 1 and Issue 2 will be the first 2 areas mentioned in the first sentence of the Requirement 3 question wording. If you then read the rest of the wording and genuinely cannot see any further specific issues to consider, it may be that Boxes 3.6 and 3.7 are just for **further** Issue 1 and Issue 2 points and so you should add to your analysis in report sections 3.B and 3.C to ensure that this is detailed enough. Equally, there might be a request for an Other Issue stated right at the end of the question wording for Requirement 3 so do make sure that you double check that you have not missed something.

10 I never seem to gain the Applying Judgement marks. What should I do?

First of all, we would emphasise that you should not worry about this problem – **it is perfectly possible to pass the whole examination without getting any points in Boxes X.6 and X.7 in**

each Requirement. These are always the hardest and least predictable Boxes in any of the Requirements (with the exception of Requirement 1 where we know that Boxes 1.6 and 1.7 will tend to include points on **reasons** and **patterns** … although we do not know **which** reasons and patterns will be rewarded, of course!). Time and again, at every taught course, we are asked this question by students and our reply is that if this is your main remaining concern regarding the examination (i.e. you are generally getting the marks in all the other Boxes) then you are in a **strong position** because it means that there are 8 other Boxes that you are generally passing in each Requirement and you only need 5 to pass ...

At the same time, in the interests of completeness and giving you the best opportunity to attempt all Boxes (although **watch your timing** if you are aiming for everything …), here are some tips on how to obtain these marks, in each Requirement:

Requirement 1

As noted above, in Requirement 1 the marks in Boxes 1.6 and 1.7 relate to **reasons** and **patterns** connected to the main financial figures reviewed, per the client request. Stick to the most obvious points and definitely consider comparing revenue growth with the equivalent figure for the prior year and use any margins or benchmarks included in the Advance Information (in relation to the "prior year" from the perspective of the updated information given in the Exam Paper): in particular, look for percentages or metrics already quoted by the client in the Advance Information as these are the points that most students will compare back to.

Requirement 2

In Requirement 2, as noted in chapter 9, there has been a movement away from numerical work and towards narrative answers: the examiner has tended to set a greater number of specific tasks for you to do on the first page of the Exam Paper. A careful review of the question wording should help you work out the focus of Boxes 2.6 and 2.7. Once the focus is known, we highly recommend that you use our **core "practical" areas** derived in chapter 11 to direct your attention towards relevant areas. The issues do seem to coalesce around these 8 areas so use these as a starting point.

Then remember that the examiner wants to see evidence of your **knowledge of the Advance Information and Exam Paper** so look out for any possible opportunities to display this knowledge.

In some examinations, one of the Tasks within Box 2.6 or 2.7 may be described in a slightly vague way ("evaluate the wider commercial implications of …") whilst the other Task might be stated quite clearly ("discuss the cash flow implications of …"). In such a situation, it obviously makes sense to start with the Task that is spelled out in a less vague manner as there will be less chance of simply being unlucky with your points (as can happen when it is not completely clear what the question is driving at).

Finally, you may find it helpful to quickly review these Boxes in recent **past papers** (using the markschemes you have printed off per our advice in chapter 17) to keep yourself focused on the right areas.

Requirement 3

As explained in point 11 above, there will be times when Boxes 3.6 and 3.7 are simply a set of **further risks and benefits to consider** and the sign here is that there will **not** be any further specified issues to look at. In this case, there will be a relatively arbitrary allocation of (for example) risks and benefits between Boxes 3.3, 3.4, 3.6 and 3.7. Passing Boxes 3.6 and 3.7 will then basically come down to generating a **lot** of points on Issues 1 and 2.

In other questions, you may be given some more specific guidance as to what to do in Box 3.6 and 3.7. In that case, we would remind you to **read the Exam Paper instructions very carefully** and, as with Requirement 2, to use our list of core "practical" areas derived in chapter 11 as the starting point for your analysis.

As in the case of Requirement 2 as discussed above, in some examinations, one of the Tasks within Box 3.6 or 3.7 may be described in a slightly vague way ("evaluate the wider commercial implications of …") whilst the other Task might be stated quite clearly ("discuss the cash flow implications of …"). In such a situation, we would again advise starting with the Task that is relatively clearer as you will then have less chance of simply being unlucky with the points made.

11 Where do I put my ethics Recommendations?

For the purposes of **being awarded marks**, our short answer to this frequently asked question is simple: it does not matter! ICAEW have confirmed (see chapter 14) that Recommendations will be given credit no matter where they are stated (although a dedicated Recommendations heading is preferred by the examiners so keep them happy!).

For the purposes of **examination technique**, however, we recommend that you **exclude your ethics recommendations from the Commercial Recommendations section at the end of each Requirement**. This is because our review of recent past paper markschemes shows that the Commercial Recommendations in Box 2.10 and 3.10 generally appear **not to include ethical points** (in Requirement 2, however, sometimes ethical points may be included in Box 2.10): instead, Boxes 2.10 and 3.10 are more "commercial" or practical in nature. There is therefore a risk that if you fill your dedicated Commercial Recommendations section with ethics recommendations you will still get marks for ethical recommendations (usually in Box 2.8 or 3.8 on ethics) … **but you will not have made enough of the other type of "commercial" recommendation which compose the bulk of the points in Box 2.10 or 3.10**.

Following our IIR ethical analysis framework, you should in any case be commenting on how to mitigate any ethical problems as your third point on Recommendations (II**R**) in our ethics framework when you create your bullet point list of Ethics Recommendations in report sections 2.D and 3.D (assuming that ethics is tested in Requirements 2 and 3): there is no need to repeat these points in your Commercial Recommendations section at the end of the Requirement, thus leaving space to get in **different and non-ethics** types of Recommendation as suggested here.

Following this approach will ensure you make the **maximum number of different ethical and commercial points** (rather than either repeating your ethics recommendations or taking up your list

202

at the end of the Requirement with ethics recommendations which will not be in Box 2.10 or 3.10, at the expense of including any of the commercial recommendations which **do** end up being in Box 2.10 or 3.10) – making as many **different** points as possible really is the key to passing Case.

12   I have been told to spend 2 hours planning but I never finish a paper. Help!

We could not disagree more strongly with the advice to **always** spend 2 hours planning: we think this is unrealistic as it does not give you enough time to write up your ideas properly and given the restrictive nature of the Case Study marking approach, you really do need to **get as many points down in the time available** to give yourself the best chance in the marking "lottery".

We know that this suggestion to spend half your time planning is very common at other tuition providers and when we studied for the Case Study examination ourselves, we were told that if we did not spend this amount of time planning then we would definitely fail the examination. We are aware that the approach advocated in this book is often criticised by these same providers as a result.

After studying the patterns in the markscheme and therefore realising that there are always 40 specific Tasks to do, no matter what the Case Study business is and no matter how the questions are phrased, we think that it is better simply to **write directly to those Tasks** rather than to spend time planning in a general way. Once you have had enough mock exam practice (including via our live mock exams) and once you know what is needed in each Box every time (having absorbed the lessons of this book, as reinforced by our Planning & Reminder Sheets), we think that there will be certain sections of your report which you **do not need to plan at all** – just **write them up directly into your answer sheets** rather than wasting time writing them in a plan and then writing them **again** in your answer. Some examples of these sections include:

Context of Performance (CoP, Requirement 1) and Strategic and Operational Context (SOC, Requirements 2 and 3) sections

Think of some general trends in the market (for Requirement 1) or project-specific points (for Requirements 2 and 3), based on the Advance Information. In Requirements 2 and 3 you should also include some linkages back to the performance of the particular revenue stream, and the company's cash balance, from your Requirement 1 analysis. Following our advice to **write** this section last rather than first (even though it is **presented** first), you should already know what points you want to say so planning is not needed.

Movements in your Requirement 1 figures

It is pointless to write your figures on a planning sheet and then write them on your answer. Just write them straight up as the first sentence in your standard Requirement 1 paragraph pro-forma structure (see advice in the footnote on page 33 and our example skeleton sentence provided on page 197). Perhaps leave space for your second sentence on patterns as this may require more thought.

Assumptions and Scepticism

As indicated on our Planning & Reminder Sheets, the points here are fairly similar each time and so once you have done some practice you should be able to read the Exam Paper and know what you are looking for. You could perhaps write an "A" or an "S" next to each relevant point as you read the question paper and then just write these up directly rather than "planning" them in the sense of writing them on a piece of paper other than your answer sheets for no real reason – you do not know what points will be rewarded so you need to make as many points as you can and therefore you cannot afford to waste time writing things out twice.

Issue 1 and Issue 2 in Requirement 3

These 2 different issues (often benefits and risks, respectively) are normally based heavily on the **Exam Paper**. Therefore, just as with Assumptions and Scepticism (see above), we really see nothing wrong with writing a "B" or "R" for "benefits" and "risks" as necessary next to each point as you read through the Exam Paper. This can then serve as your "planning" and you can then immediately write up the point straight into your answer.

Conclusions

Simply follow the reminders on our Planning & Reminder Sheets and slot in your standard points. These are very easy marks as the marking is "**open**" and you do not therefore have to match a specific figure or point on the markscheme – you just need some kind of conclusion on revenue, for example, with some kind of figure to support it (whether right or wrong) so there is no need to "plan" or overthink your Conclusions.

Recommendations

There is always going to be a **luck** element here so you are better off **writing down as many ideas as you can**, rather than wasting time planning and picking your "best" points – who knows if those points will be on the markscheme? You might just be unlucky, wasting time picking the "best" points and then finding that some of your other ideas were on the markscheme after all!

In chapters 8 to 10, we have also recommended that you write up your Commercial Recommendations **as you work through a question**, rather than leaving this to the end. This will increase the relevance of your points and will save time as you will not have to sit there at the end of the Requirement having to think of ideas. If you follow this advice then there is again no need to "plan" the Commercial Recommendations – just write them straight into your answer as you go along.

Overall, we think that the emphasis of some other tuition providers on "planning" often amounts simply to writing points out twice (once on the planning sheet and once in your answer) when there is no real benefit from doing this. **Planning is needed when something is complex** and a large number of points or variables have to be carefully organised into an appropriate logical order to give a good "flow" to the writing but most of your Case points should be **basic, simple ideas** which do not need detailed reflection or consideration: if these happen to be written up in a somewhat random order as they come into your head then so be it – the Case Study markers are not trying to assess your writing elegance but are instead simply performing a "**matching**" exercise (see chapter 1) on each separate point that you make so it does not really matter to them how the points are made. Indeed, planning could lead you into spending too long developing complicated points that do not figure on the markscheme.

In contrast, we believe that reducing your planning through practice and proper learning of the lessons in this book could be one of the most important contributions to helping you pass the examination. We are aware of a number of Case Study ICAEW prize winners, including our own students, who barely planned at all, giving them over 3 hours to write (allowing for the numerical Appendices) and this will allow you to write a lot more ideas down in the time, maximising your chances in the marking "lottery".

13   My exam paper will provide the management accounts for the year ended 30 June 2018 (or 31 May 2018). The Advance Information has figures for the 3 prior years. How am I supposed to analyse all this information in the examination?

Our answer to this is simple: **you do not really actually need to use any of the information for the years before the latest year in the Advance Information** (i.e. the "prior year" from the point of view of the Exam Paper information and so the year ended 30 June 2017 (or 31 May 2017) in this example). We have not seen many marks at all on past markschemes for points regarding the years before the "prior year", in line with the examiners' comments (see page 160).

Additionally, we would remind you that Case Study is heavily focused on **Income Statement** figures: Statement of Financial Position figures other than cash are rarely mentioned at all in the markscheme. This may also help you manage your time when learning the Advance Information: you should concentrate on the Income Statement.

Therefore, we would **effectively ignore the years before the "prior year"**, with just a few exceptions:

1. Comparing this year's revenue growth with last year's revenue growth

This point is very often rewarded in either Box 1.2 on what we term the "Context of Performance" or Box 1.6 on revenue. As we are looking at growth rates, we do need to dip into the **year before the prior year** to find last year's revenue growth rate. For example, if your Exam Paper gives you updated management accounts figures for the year ended 30 June 2018 then the years will work out as follows:

Revenue growth rate this year: 30 June 2018 (Exam Paper year) versus 30 June 2017 (prior year)

Revenue growth rate last year: 30 June 2017 (prior year) versus 30 June 2016 (year before the prior year)

As we have said, ordinarily, we would not advise you to do **anything** with the figures for the year ended 30 June 2016 (or earlier) but in the case of revenue **growth rate** comparisons you do need to go this far back (although the percentage change is often given to you anyway directly in the Advance Information – see next point).

2. Any specific figures relating to prior years which do not need to be calculated from the management accounts (i.e. figures which are given "on a plate" in the Advance Information narrative)

In selecting your points for discussion, you need to be choosing the most obvious points that most students are going to mention: the markscheme does not give any extra reward for anything too complex or heroic – in fact, the markscheme penalises such points because no credit can be given for points which are not on the markscheme and hence you will have lost time with no reward.

If the Advance Information gives a specific statistic "on a plate" – in other words, it **does not require any calculations** because it is already calculated and mentioned in the Advance Information narrative[54] – then this is **highly likely** to be on the markscheme because most people will be picking it up … whereas points that require calculations may not be (since different candidates will do different calculations). Therefore it may be worth mentioning "pre-prior year" datapoints if they are **specifically given to you "on a plate"** … but definitely **not** if **calculations** (even if very easy) are required to determine a pre-prior year datapoint.

3. Cashflow

Cashflow is always important to a business so it is worth chucking in a couple of points on the trend here: this will not take long at all and does not require any ratios or complex calculations, just quotation of SFP figures already given.

For some businesses, the cash **balance** may be more important than the cash**flow** – for example, if there is an overdraft limit in place. Use your judgement but stating something in the general area of cash is probably always a sensible idea in Case Study (and definitely worth including in your Executive Summary).

4. Bottom line profitability if there has been a change in the pattern

If a company has been profitable for several years but will now be making a loss, then this may be something to comment on briefly (and vice-versa if the company is now making the first profits for some time: usually, however, the Case Study business is profitable). For such a **fundamental** pattern, we believe there is a chance that the longer term trend may need to be spotted.

In the Bod examination (July 2015), there was a slight variation on this point with candidates having to spot that contribution was negative (unusually and out of line with the prior years). In TT (November 2016), a mark was available for noting that the company was moving close to breakeven at the operating profit level (in contrast to stronger performance in prior years). In PL (July 2017), candidates had to suggest that making an operating loss would be unsustainable: prior years had not seen such

---

[54] A good example here would be revenue growth between the latest year in the Advance Information (the "prior year" when writing your examination since you will be given an even more recent set of figures in the Exam Paper) and the preceding year: this is almost always provided as a percentage movement for you in the narrative. As students do not need to calculate anything here, this statistic is frequently mentioned in their reports and, as such, almost always ends up being in either Box 1.2 or Box 1.6 on the Requirement 1 markscheme.

an outcome. As such, looking for these "inflection points" from profit to loss (or vice versa) can be a worthwhile exercise.

5. Company-specific statistics (e.g. KPIs)

This point is really a reflection of point 2 above since we have already said that "unusual" and very client-specific figures which are specifically given to you on a plate should be used: KPIs will be of this type, by definition.

Other than the above points, then, as mentioned, be **very careful of going back beyond the "prior" year** (from the point of view of the Exam Paper year end). This includes if your tuition provider has encouraged you to spend a day analysing ratios and other factors before the prior year: these are quite simply not rewarded on the markscheme and you are not only wasting tuition time in calculating these in the first place but you will also be wasting precious writing time if you use them in your examination answer.

14   I have heard that the more students I tell about how useful *Cracking Case*™ is, the more luck I will have in the examination

We have not confirmed this suggestion scientifically but we would not be upset if readers would continue to put it to the test.

Chapter 16   CoP and SOC Sections: Some Clarifications

Several years ago, we spotted that many of the students coming to us for a retake (not as a result of failing with us previously) were not achieving a good score in the markscheme Boxes allocated to "business issues and wider context". These Boxes are Boxes 1.2, 2.2 and 3.2 on the markscheme (and **also** Boxes 2.1 and 3.1 in TT (November 2016) and PL (July 2017)).

We therefore suggested that students should start each part of a Requirement with a "Market Background" or "Project Background" section, targeting these marks. (July 2018 edition update: we now suggest using the terms "Context of Performance" (Requirement 1) and "Strategic and Operational Context" (Requirements 2 and 3) as we believe that these terms provide better guidance on what to do: see chapters 8, 9 and 10 for more details.) Little did we know the controversy this would create and sitting here a few years later with another large tuition provider regularly misquoting our advice, and even misinforming students that the examiners have said that such a section will be ignored by the markers, it is important to clarify exactly what we have suggested you should be aiming to achieve here.

We would also like to spend some time analysing relevant recent examiner comments on this matter to prevent any further misinterpretation of what we are suggesting.

We wish to be clear that the change in terminology which we are implementing for the first time in this July 2018 edition of *Cracking Case™* does not mean that we are in any way changing our advice on our underlying technique for these sections: we simply believe that the terms "Context of Performance" (CoP, Requirement 1) and "Strategic and Operational Context" (SOC, Requirements 2 and 3) will provide better guidance to candidates than our previous terms "Market Background" and "Project Background" because we have noticed that some students have been making points which are too broad to have a chance of scoring credit. Our change in terminology does not in any way indicate that we accept the false statements made by another large tuition provider that ICAEW will "zero mark" any form of separate context section of this kind (see further discussion below).

1   Not a dumping ground

It is important to emphasise that we have not suggested (nor do we now suggest) that you should simply dump down any points that you happen to know about the wider market at the start of your answer, writing a section such as (based on CC (November 2015)):

"E-bike sales are strong. Manchester is a popular cycling city. City Cycle Hire Schemes are in use throughout the world. Some manufacturers have been copying bike designs. The government wishes to encourage use of bicycles."

This kind of section clearly does nothing to help the client company to address the project or problems faced. **Please do not use your Context of Performance (Requirement 1) or Strategic and Operational Context (Requirements 2 and 3) sections as a "dumping ground" in this way**: you need to word your points differently and we will explain how to do so below.

If you wish to make your "wider context" points "mixed into" the main body of your answer rather than having a separate section then we have absolutely no problem with this, **provided that you remember to do so**. Our advice to create a separate section is only provided because we have noticed a **tendency** for students **to forget to adopt this perspective when they are writing the rest of their answer**: this could be due to time pressure or simply the understandable fact that once you start to focus on the details of recent financial performance (Requirement 1) or a specific project proposal (Requirements 2 and 3), it can be hard to remember to "step back" and look at the broader context.

Our recommendation to create a separate section is therefore based purely on observation of a tendency within student answers and our recognition of what it is like to do the examination – it is not provided as an absolute recommendation that **must** always be followed, if you are happy to use a different approach that has the necessary "wider context" perspective somewhere in your answer.

2   The relevance and impact test

There will be many things happening in the "wider context" of the market in your examination. Some of these will be too "wide" to be relevant and are therefore unlikely to score marks. Other points **will** be relevant. How do you know which is which?

The only way to be **certain** which is which is to be the examiner. Failing that, we recommend that you apply the following test:

> **Can I write a sentence that starts with the name of the Case Study company and indicates how the "wider context" point relates to something with significance for that company in the specific scenario provided?**

If the point **does** pass this test, then it may be something relevant and worth using in a CoP or SOC section.

If the point **does not** pass this test, then it probably does not have any direct linkage to the Exam Paper scenario or the impact on the client company and so you should leave it out.

As an example from the CC (November 2015) examination, the examiners noted that many candidates referred to "e-bike sales" in their Market or Project Background sections (as indicated above, prior to this July 2018 edition of *Cracking Case*™, we used the terms "Market Background" (Requirement 1) and "Project Background" (Requirements 2 and 3) for these sections) – this was because of a detailed press article on e-bikes in the Advance Information. However, as no part of the Case Study had anything to do with e-bike sales, then there was no point referring to this point.

A second reason to apply the above test is that if the point passes the test and does say something about the possible **impact** on the client company, then you may benefit from the possibility that your point could **alternatively** score in Boxes X.6 and X.7 which normally relate to reasons and patterns (Requirement 1) or strategic and operational impact (Requirements 2 and 3) – as points are placed in only one Box, if a point is not in the CoP or SOC Box then if you have **applied** or **evaluated** the point sufficiently you may be able to pick up a mark in a different Box for evaluation. Effectively, if written properly, your CoP or SOC section turns into a further attempt to gain evaluation marks in the tricky X.6 and X.7 sections.

On the other hand, if you say something that is not analysed in any detail ("dumped in") then you are unlikely to make the necessary connection to the reason/pattern (Requirement 1) or strategic and operational impact (Requirements 2 and 3) since scoring an Applying Judgement mark requires more application to the Case Study business than a mere statement. This is another reason why a "dumping in" approach is not recommended: it will not give you any chance of alternatively scoring in Boxes X.6 and X.7.

We do regularly see students on our taught courses unintentionally scoring a mark in the Applying Judgement Boxes (Boxes X.6 or X.7 in each Requirement) with points that were actually intended to score CoP or SOC marks – this is only possible because those students have included the **relevance of the issue to the business** in their CoP or SOC section.

Put another way, if written appropriately then a separate context section is effectively giving you a chance to score in 2 different parts of the markscheme. Although you will never be awarded a mark in 2 different Boxes for the same point, the correct writing style in your context section will increase your chances of scoring a mark **somewhere** on the markscheme.

3   The correct CoP/SOC section writing style: not "isolated" points

We have already established that you need to do a bit more than simply "dump in" a point to score marks in the CoP or SOC Boxes (and also to give yourself a "second chance" opportunity of possibly scoring in Boxes X.6 or X.7). We have thus asked you above to develop your point a bit more to avoid any "dumping in".

As always with Case Study, the clock is the biggest challenge so how much "development" are we looking to see? Not a huge amount and you should certainly not be writing pages and pages for your background section.

We would recommend that you always start each background sentence with the **client company name** – this should force the rest of the sentence to say something that is relevant (and thus potentially something that could also be in the Applying Judgement Boxes as a "back up") because it will force you to make some kind of impact or linkage statement (as opposed to just saying that "E-bikes are popular", or whatever).

Secondly, we would recommend that you clearly explain not just the possible impact of the "wider context" issue on the company but also that you try to refer to the **significance** of that impact (will it be a major problem/benefit or not?). Generally, you should be concentrating on points that have a **significant** relevance after all.

With the considerable benefit of having a real markscheme in front of us at the time of writing, here are some suggestions for succinct, relevant and non-"dumped in" background sentences in the example of the CC (November 2015) examination.

Requirement 1 examples

"CC's revenue has benefited from the recent popularity of cycling, allowing CC to boost sales despite an increase in competition."

"CC is facing a squeeze on margins as competitors launch price matching schemes and customers use internet comparison sites, potentially explaining CC's lower rate of revenue growth this year."

Requirement 3 example

"CC should be aware that MB's apparent copying of bike designs has a precedent with an incident involving Pacey & Speedo leading to a large compensation claim and a significant impact on future sales, **issues which could affect CC's reputation.**" (emphasis added for tuition purposes: see next paragraph)

This last example would in fact score 3 marks: 1 mark in Box 3.2 for recognising the similarity with an Advance Information precedent ("wider context" mark) and 2 marks in Box 3.6 (Applying Judgement on the impact on CC, both (1) monetarily and (2) in terms of reputation), **but only provided that you make it absolutely clear that the previous precedent** ("wider context") **could have a similar, serious impact** ("Applying Judgement") **on CC**, by means of the final few words which we have highlighted above in bold text – if you did not add these final few words then you might only score 1 mark in Box 3.2 for noting the Pacey & Speedo precedent: indicating the **impact** on CC is what would then turn this into "Applying Judgement" points in Box 3.6. This would be an excellent return of 2 further marks merely for adding 5 further words into your "context" section.

We hope this explains a bit further the importance of making the reason/pattern linkage point.

4   Examiner comments: July 2015 markscheme

As you may have noticed from looking at past paper markschemes, each Case Study past paper markscheme grid is actually provided at the end of a long document which first provides a very detailed examiner review of the Advance Information and tendencies among students who sat the examination. As the markscheme grid is provided at the end of the document, many students (and tutors, it seems …) neglect to read the examiner comments in the useful first part of the document.

The examiner comments provide a very valuable insight into how the examiners are thinking about the examination. In the July 2015 markscheme, some useful comments about the use of a separate "Background" section were made and we reproduce and comment on these here.

Comment 1 – relationship to "Applying Judgement" marks

"A number of candidates used the technique of beginning the answer to each requirement with a "background" section; **while this was successful in garnering some credit** under Assimilating & Using Information, the facts were not then brought forward into the discussion, **removing the opportunity for Applying Judgement marks**."

Translating the term "Assimilating & Using Information" into our terminology, the examiners are here confirming that **points in a "Background" section will have the opportunity to gain marks in Box X.2 in a Requirement** (this is the "wider context" Box under the first or "Assimilating & Using Information" column). The examiners then indicate that some of the points made by students in this section could actually have been **extended** into Applying Judgement points.

This is in line with what we have advised you to do when you make your "context" remarks: you should **develop** these in such a way that your points could potentially score as reasons/patterns (Requirement 1) or impact (Requirements 2 and 3) points and this can be achieved by ensuring that the points are not short nor "separate" from the impact of the business (i.e. not "dumped in").

As we have suggested above, always start your sentences with the name of the client business to ensure that you are providing a statement with some kind of impact.

Comment 2 – the risk of an isolated section

"Some candidates include a separate "market background" section at the start of each requirement. **This can be a good technique that introduces the answer and earns A&UI marks**, but often it is done in isolation and then forgotten about, depriving the candidate of grades towards the right of the key for evaluating the issues arising in context (see AJ below)"

Again, here the examiners are confirming that using a separate section is perfectly valid and will achieve its **primary** target of the marks in the X.2 Boxes (Assimilating & Using Information) in each Requirement. The point is just that if the "Background" remarks are not written in quite the right way then there will not be an opportunity to achieve a **secondary** target of marks in the "Applying Judgement" Boxes.

This is entirely in line with our recommended way of writing the CoP or SOC sentences where we have advised you not just to write short or "isolated" comments. Yet even if you were to do so, you may well achieve the primary target anyway.

Comment 3 – forgetting points

"In Box 1 [here meaning the first Box for Applying Judgement in Requirement 1], there were 3 bullets available for referring to market changes – bad news for those candidates who had mentioned these in an introductory "background" section and then forgot about them (see above)"

Once again, it is important not to misinterpret this examiner statement. The examiners are not saying that students who have an introductory "context" section therefore categorically cannot score "Applying Judgement" marks just because they used an introductory approach. Rather, the examiners are stating that it is a bad idea to have points in an introductory section and then "forget about them", **meaning that no evaluation is offered**.

If you follow our recommended approach of evaluating the statements made **within** your introductory section, as well as our related advice to always start your introductory sentences with a reference to your client company to keep you focused on impactful comments, then you should not fall into the trap noted here.

212

The point is again that using an introductory section approach is not, **in itself**, a bad technique – it is just important to write in the right way. The same could be said of any section – if you are not going to write up your Recommendations in the right way, for example, then that section will not be done well. The examiner statements are not against using a separate "context" section per se – they are rather reminders to try to write in a certain way. We have no disagreement with this.

In any case, many of the comments in this July 2015 markscheme indicate that, even if you do not follow our advice to evaluate the points, students will often score in the **primary** target of the X.2 Boxes, even with points which are not particularly well integrated with reasons/patterns (Requirement 1) or impact (Requirements 2 and 3) perspectives.

Overall, then, we do not take any of the above comments as an argument against writing a properly constructed introductory "context" section.

We have not noted any further reference to the issue of separate "background" or "context" sections in any examiner reports after July 2015 so we do not provide any further notes in this sub-section. If such a section is not permitted, then, given our increasing market share since 2015, it is surprising to see no further comments on this technique in any recent report. Such a lack of reference to the matter is of course not at all surprising if one accepts that there is nothing wrong with our suggested technique under ICAEW rules.

5   Examiner comments: example student scripts

As you are hopefully aware, after every examination sitting, ICAEW upload to the ICAEW student website a typed out version of one top quartile script and one failing script, selected from the real attempts of students at that sitting. In each example, the examiners work through the script in detail and provide a large amount of useful technique advice. We strongly recommend that you take the time to look through a few of these example scripts and their related feedback before your own examination: no other ACA examination provides this level of feedback on actual scripts so make use of it!

In this section, we will not review **all** the various tips provided (that should be a task for your own preparation time) – our focus is instead on the matter of the Market or Project Background sections (July 2018 update: we now use the terms "Context of Performance" (Requirement 1) and "Strategic and Operational Context" (Requirements 2 and 3) to refer to this section) and what the examiners think of this method. As will be obvious from the comments below, there is absolutely no sense in which the examiners have indicated that this approach is not permitted under examination rules, as has been claimed by another large UK tuition provider (this is clearly contradicted by the fact that the examiners have many positive comments to make: see elsewhere in this chapter) – rather the question is how to write these sections in the most effective way.

If we have highlighted some text in bold in this section then this is our own added emphasis to show how the comment relates to the PoC or SOC issue – this use of bold text was not included in the original examiner report.

Please note that discussion of use of a "Background" section does not arise in every script uploaded by ICAEW so we can only refer to 3 specific scripts below.

July 2014 failing script

Whilst this candidate unfortunately did not pass the examination, the examiners were relatively positive about the "Background" sections included – the candidate certainly did not fail the examination **because** these sections were included but for other reasons. Here are some relevant comments:

"Throughout, there are multiple references to the wider business environment, indicating a candidate that was well prepared for a requirement on microchipping. **The section opens with a powerful "background" section** setting out the context within which the discussion is set."

"As with Requirement 2, **the opening "background" section sets out succinctly the context for this proposal**. In general, the candidate shows good familiarity with the Advance Information, though (as for virtually the whole cohort) there is no reference to the Risk Register."

From the above comments, it is clear that it is acceptable to include an opening "Background" section and this is actually considered to improve the quality of the answer.

July 2015 top quartile script

Here the examiners commented that one of the strengths of the script reviewed is that the wider context remarks were included as part of the general discussion. It was stated that "a feature of many weaker scripts" is that candidates include "an introductory "background" section **that is then ignored**".

We have no doubt that the competing tuition provider will seize upon this statement as justification for saying that a "Background" section should not be used. However, notice the text "**that is then ignored**" – here the examiners are making the point that the issues raised in a Background section need to relate to the scenario and should not be separate from it nor standalone points that are distinct from anything which follows. As we have explained above, when writing appropriate Background sentences, you should be aiming at some "Applying Judgement" points anyway and so will be making some connections into points that students who do not use a Background section will be making in their wider discussion (assuming, of course, that they **remember** to do so).

Therefore, the point is not that if a student uses a Background section that they must be a weak student. The point is that the issues raised in the Background section should have at least some connection to the wider discussion of the issue or project rather than being isolated – as we have suggested, this could be achieved by ensuring that you do not have points which are "dumped in" but rather have some elements of evaluation in there already at the start of the answer – this will remove the risk involved in what the examiners refer to as being "ignored later" i.e. a potential missed opportunity to gain an "Applying Judgement" mark.

214

November 2015 top quartile script

"This section of the report starts with a market background summary statement that 'There has been a lot of web competition in the cycling industry. Web sales are fundamental to CC's operations (85%).' **If these 2 sentences had been reversed and, with some appropriate editing, the issue of competition for web sales had been emphasised, that would have been a defining statement of the analysis of Cyclone**."

As we have suggested above, you should aim to start your Background sentences with the name of the client to ensure that what you say in the rest of the sentence(s) relates back to the client as the focus. Here is the examiner confirming that if this is done it would be an excellent and "defining statement" of the Case Study business.

"The candidate starts this topic with a section entitled "Project Background" but this is **too wide to be rewarded and needs to be tied into Cyclone's position** in order for it to be relevant."

At first sight, this kind of remark makes it look as though a Project Background is not a good idea. However, let us now quote the points made by the candidate:

"City cycle hire schemes have been successful in many cities such as Paris and Montréal.

There has been a major resurgence in cycling due to traffic delays.

Success of such a project requires a good supply of bikes and adequate docking facilities.

Placement near train stations could lead to a very high demand at peak times. People who cannot return their bikes are charged for and have recently been frustrated in London.

Students will be a large user group of such a scheme in Manchester.

Brompton bikes already have a stand at Piccadilly so Cyclone can learn more about the performance of such a scheme."

With the exception of the final statement (which is in any case an attempt at an "Own Research" mark, something which was rewarded on markschemes prior to R4 (November 2017): see the Foreword to this edition of *Cracking Case*™ for further details on an important change regarding "Own Research" marks), none of these sentences include any reference to CC and therefore clearly breach our guidance to ensure that you start your sentences with a reference to the client company to ensure that the sentence is relevant to the scenario. In other words, here the candidate appears to have engaged in "dumping in" of points. **This is not what we have recommended.**

6 Timing: Should I Bother With a CoP or SOC Section?

Having clearly established that there is no suggestion by the examiners that you will be breaking any examination rule by including a separate context or background section to your report Requirements, it remains to consider the usual challenge of timing.

The approach advocated in this book is designed to give you an opportunity to understand how to achieve **all** the various different marks available on the markscheme (although see chapter 13 for our Plan B to use in situations when things do not go perfectly on exam day …). Our technique is designed to be a "best case" (no pun intended!) approach.

From our taught courses, we know that it is certainly possible, from both a physical and mental perspective, to complete the examination in full within 4 hours whilst attempting all the sections in our Planning & Reminder Sheets to a good standard.

At the same time, we recognise that there may be some students who find it difficult to complete the examination in the time available if they attempt **all** the different Tasks possible. This could be for various reasons, including the fact that you may mess up your timing early into the exam. It is for this reason that we provide our "Plan B" in chapter 13 of this book.

In the grand scheme of things, there are probably easier marks to obtain than the CoP and SOC marks – despite all our suggestions and techniques, there is still definitely an ineradicable "luck" element in terms of whether your points will match what is within Box X.2 in each Requirement (and also in Boxes 2.1 and 3.1 in TT (November 2016) and PL (July 2017)). We have also noticed from our taught course that some students almost create a timing problem for themselves by spending far too long on their context section: for example, writing a full page of ideas and ending up scoring nothing!

If you find that you consistently cannot complete the examination paper whilst attempting a context section in each Requirement, we would actually advise you to drop the writing of your context section – there are easier and more predictable marks out there. It is certainly very possible to pass the examination without these separate context sections and we have only suggested that you use this approach to give you an opportunity to attack all the Tasks on the markscheme.

Therefore, rather than spending a long time thinking about context points and then actually not gaining anything for your investment of this time, **if you have timing problems you should perhaps leave these sections out completely**.

As explained in chapters 8 to 10, we in fact suggest that whilst you should **present** your context sections at the start of your answer, you should not necessarily actually **write** such sections first in your answer – this is partly so that you can have a bit of time to "warm up" to the scenario and get into what is happening (helping you to generate context points more easily) and partly so that you can ensure that you do not say something in your introductory sections which you just end up repeating later into your answer: by writing your main answer first you can then return and introduce **different** points into your context section, thus writing the greatest total range of points across your answer as a whole and hence giving yourself a greater chance of matching the points on the markscheme.

However, a third reason not to attempt your context sections first (even though they are presented first in each section of your report answer) is that it allows you to make a judgement call regarding your timing – if time is tight and you think there are some easier sections to do in your answer, you can just leave the context section out entirely (i.e. never actually come back to do it) whereas if you always **start** with your context section then you will have already invested and lost that time and you

216

will never get it back, nor have the opportunity to strategically drop this section if that would have been the best option on exam day.

In other words, to engage in some very brief revision of the Financial Management Professional Level paper (do not use this concept in Case Study as it is far too technical!), you will have an "abandonment option" if you do not attempt the context section first.

7   Conclusion

Overall, it is clear that using a CoP or SOC section is perfectly acceptable to the examiners, provided that it is handled in a sensible way. We hope that this chapter clarifies what you should (and should not) do when writing these sections of your report. We have also reviewed some circumstances in which you may decide to "mix in" your "wider context" points or, alternatively, to drop these sections completely.

We do not mind exactly how you address the "wider context" **as long as you remember to do so**. This fundamentally is what our suggestion to have a separate section is there to do but as we have already said, if you feel comfortable making the relevant points "mixed in" as you go along, then feel free to do so.

And finally, please do not listen to anyone who says that if you use an introductory context section then the marker will simply ignore the section – as confirmed by the examiner comments reviewed in this chapter, and also by the example officially-graded marking grid for a November 2017 candidate used during the Case Study Workshop at the 2018 ICAEW Tutor Conference[55], such a statement is simply not true.

---

[55] In the Case Study Workshop at the 2018 ICAEW Tutor Conference, the examiners provided an example script from a real November 2017 candidate who used a "Market Background" section to her Requirement 1 answer. It was clear from the example marking grid (a copy of the grid completed by a fully-trained ICAEW Case Study marker) that marks were awarded in an entirely normal way for the points made in the candidate's "Market Background" section. When the script itself was discussed at the Workshop, at no point did the ICAEW Case Study examiners make any reference to an "impermissible" "Market Background" section: this part of the report was discussed in exactly the same way as the rest of the candidate's answer and no criticisms of the use of a Market Background section were made. If, as alleged by the competing provider, it were the case that "Market Background" sections are ignored by the ICAEW markers because they breach examination regulations, we would have expected something to have been said in relation to the exam script by the examiners ... but no related comments were made at the 2018 Tutor Conference.

Chapter 17   Practicalities of the Exam Day

Learning Points

After reading this chapter, you must be able to:

1. understand various practical issues in relation to the sitting of the exam
2. develop personally effective strategies to deal with these issues
3. undertake our recommended steps to prepare your exam room folder

---

1   Getting used to the lack of desk space

By this stage in your ACA career, you should be familiar with the cramped desk facilities at your local examination hall. We found that whilst the lack of desk space is a bit annoying in other ACA exams, it can become a genuine problem in the Case exam as you are likely to need access to the following as you work:

- answer pad, which contains loose-leaf sheets (see below) which could get lost or placed in the wrong order
- Advance Information
- our Exam Room Pack condensed version of the Advance Information (if purchased)
- Exam Paper
- our Planning & Reminder Sheets (see chapter 6), personalised to your requirements
- pre-prepared notes and lists (perhaps even including a tabbed up version of this book)

There is very little space available on your desk for all of these resources.

It is therefore a good idea to prepare by getting used to working on a cramped desk whilst completing some Case Study past papers or mocks. Take some low tack masking tape and mark out an area of approximately 60cm x 40cm on your regular desk (hopefully your actual desk will be slightly larger but we suggest these dimensions on a prudent basis). Then do all your practice using this area only.

2   Saving some desk space and making use of the Advance Information easier

The Advance Information will be sent to you by ICAEW as loose-leaf, double-sided A4 paper. This is fine but quite bulky. Being double-sided also means that you may waste time flicking over to find the correct side of the page for the information that you want.

As a more efficient alternative, download the Advance Information PDF from the ICAEW website. Then print off the Advance Information at 2 pages per sheet but **single sided**. Since **everything** will then be printed on the top side of the page you will not waste any time turning pages over to find the detail you want. Depending on how your memory works, you may also find that, after sufficient reading, you seem to know that certain information is on the right or lefthand panel of your single-sided sheets: this will again be beneficial to your speed.

You should also try to **separately** print the narrative and numerical information as explained in our next tip.

3 Separate out the narrative and numerical information

Once Requirement 1 is complete, you will mainly be using the narrative information, even in the Requirement 2 and 3 calculations – the management accounts will not be needed. Similarly, you will not really need any financial modelling or strategic information (Requirements 2 and 3, respectively) whilst completing Requirement 1.

You are therefore advised to use the Advance Information PDF from the ICAEW website to print off as 2 **separate** packs of paper (1) management accounts information (2) remainder of the Advance Information. Then when you have done Requirement 1 you can discard the management accounts information and concentrate on your remaining information.

This makes it easier to work with the remaining information, which will also appear much less intimidating as there will be fewer pages of paper floating around (and, having followed our prior tip, all your information will be on the top side of the page and therefore easily accessible).

Tips 2 and 3 should ensure you spend less time turning pages to find the information you need for each Requirement. Once Requirement 1 is done, for example, you can just put the statutory and management accounts information on the floor and out of the way.

However, to ensure that you make maximum gains from these tips, make sure you do plenty of mock practice in which you use the different packs of paper which you are expecting to use on exam day so that you become very familiar with where to find everything under time pressure.

4 Practising use of loose-leaf sheets

Unlike the other ACA papers, all Case Study answers must be written on loose-leaf sheets. An example can be downloaded as a PDF from our dedicated Case Study-specific website **www.acasimplifiedcase.com** (see the Free Downloads section).

You are recommended to print off a large number of these example answer sheets and exclusively use them when writing practice scripts. This will allow you to get used to the limited space available on the answer sheets – although the paper size is A4, the writing area is not, due to large margins for the marker's use.

Note that in the real examination you will be provided with a tear-off pad of answer sheets. The answer sheets are only printed on one side so we recommend that you print off your practice examples **single-sided** to maximise the realism of your practice attempts.

Practising use of these sheets will build your sense of how much can be written on a page and will help you to create an organised, well laid out report (particularly in terms of your Appendices – see also section 6 below).

5 Risk of not handing in

Make sure you develop a process to manage your completed sheets, particularly if you are tackling the Requirements out of order. If a sheet is not handed in, you will get no marks. Therefore, be careful of putting completed sheets on the floor, underneath notes or within a folder. In the past, we have had students come to us for a retake course who have told us that they did not hand in their Appendices as these were placed in the wrong pile and somehow ended up being taken home by the candidate rather than being handed in. Not ideal and unlikely to lead to many marks being achieved for your hard work in writing those pages!

The best approach is probably to attach each completed sheet to a treasury tag and keep this set of pages face down on your desk or on your lap. That way, at the end of the exam, all your completed sheets will be in one place – you can always rearrange the order during the 5 minutes permitted for organisation of materials after the end of the examination (subject to the fact that you cannot write anything (including page numbers) during this 5 minute period).

6 Prepare as much as possible of your Requirement 1 Appendix in advance

It is also a good idea to start drilling your Requirement 1 Appendices on real ICAEW-style answer sheets (see above) – this can be helpful to building your understanding of how you will format your Appendix 1 in the real examination (for example, you can start to think about how many columns you can fit in for each calculation/Income Statement figure). Remember that you are allowed to format your Appendices in landscape format if you wish: the marker will receive your actual physical script rather than a scanned version (scanning is used regarding all other ACA papers) so there will not be any inconvenience caused and the markers would in any case prefer to be able to read your Appendices, rather than having everything squashed into a portrait format.

Given that many "prior year" (i.e. Advance Information) figures such as profit margins or KPI results can be calculated in advance, you should create a draft Requirement 1 Appendix with the prior year figures and calculations filled in on the correct column and row of the page, leaving space to slot in the current year figures given in the Exam Paper.

You are not allowed to hand in work written before the exam day but if you have carefully formatted your Advance Information (i.e. prior year) figures, you can simply copy these across very quickly into the exact same place on your real answer sheet in the exam itself – because you will have prepared these, and will have prepared them on the identical answer pad paper mentioned in section 4 above, you will know how much space to leave to slot in the current year figures whilst presenting a very neat Appendix. With luck, **all** the prior year figures you need will be on your pre-prepared sheets, meaning that you do not have to go around hunting in the Advance Information at all and you can be completely confident that you have picked up the correct figures. Once you have rapidly copied across the

220

figures, then you can start using the Exam Paper information safe in the knowledge that you have pulled the correct baseline figures across.

This approach will ensure that you quickly and correctly state the prior year figures and that you end up with very neat Appendices with no crossing out or squeezing in of figures.

Ensure that you use a different coloured pen to that of your actual examination answer for your pre-prepared prior year figures as this will avoid the danger of you handing in a pre-prepared sheet, which is not allowed. Given that your answer must be in black pen, set out your pre-prepared prior year figure draft Appendix 1 in a colour other than black so you do not confuse your sheets.

Note 1

If you follow this approach, you will complete the Requirement 1 calculations well ahead of schedule as all your prior year calculations and formatting choices have already been made. You should then be able to get the Requirement 1 Appendix done in a maximum of 20 minutes (10 minutes less than is typically recommended by some other tuition providers). This is a very good thing but **please try to avoid the temptation to use the time saved to start doing more calculations** – chances are you will be analysing in too much detail, wasting time on the Appendix and then wasting time in the written sections as you will be tempted to include and discuss these additional calculations. Therefore make sure you stick to what is being asked.

Note 2

The question paper may not ask you for one of the pre-prepared prior year figures – for example, somewhat unexpectedly, FS (November 2012) did not ask for any information on various secondary revenue streams whilst Palate (July 2013), ZM (July 2014) and Bod (July 2015) all focused on just **one** of the client's various revenue streams.

Therefore make sure you stick to what is asked – **do not put things in just because you got them ready in your pre-prepared prior year draft Appendix or because you think they are particularly clever things to say. Be prepared to drop certain pre-prepared calculations if they do not seem relevant.**

Note 3

ICAEW apply a random colour to the edge of the answer pad on exam day so it is not possible to hand in pre-prepared work and this would be cheating anyway. Do not be tempted to try anything in this respect. Instead, using the tips mentioned here, plan out your exact format and "prior year" figures from the Advance Information and copy these quickly across onto your exam day answer paper as soon as the exam starts. Yes, copying across will take time, but less time than if you have to first find **and calculate** the prior year figures in the Advance Information and with the advantage that you have assurance you are pulling through the correct figures: hence this is likely to be quicker than calculating the prior year figures for the first time on the day. Copying across from sheets which are identical in format to the paper on which you will write your examination answers will also ensure that you are placing everything into a sensible place/column on the page, rather than having to squeeze things in or, even worse from a time management perspective, crossing things out and starting again due to a lack of space on the page to complete your write up properly.

7   Prepare your pro-forma cover sheet and terms of reference/disclaimer in advance

There is a single mark in the Appendices & Main Report (AMR) Boxes for inclusion of an appropriate disclaimer at the start of the report. In cases where you are working as an external adviser (most examinations involve this scenario), you should include a brief Bannerman-style disclaimer paragraph and state that the report is being written by your employer firm (not by you personally nor by your partner).

In the rarer case where you work for the Case Study company itself in an internal role, you are awarded a mark for **not** including a disclaimer (yes, a mark for not doing something – take it!) and for stating that the report is being written by your manager. For example, in Bux (July 2016), your Case Study character was employed in an internal role at the company so you were required to write your manager's name (Zephaniah Bishoo) as the author on the cover page to get the relevant mark: simply omitting a disclaimer was not enough.

Some students like to calm their nerves at the start of the examination by writing the cover sheet (including disclaimer) before doing anything else in the exam, just to get something which it is impossible to do incorrectly down on their exam script. If you do this, try to avoid the temptation to write too much, thinking that you still have 4 hours to go – someone's rushed cover page written with a minute to go will probably gain no fewer marks than a highly involved disclaimer which was drafted at the start when there were still 4 full hours to go.

Please note that a table of contents or listing of sections is **not** necessary and achieves no marks.

The minimum possible (and therefore quickest) cover sheet is therefore probably constructed as follows (include only the text in bold as the non-bold text is just for explanatory purposes – text in square brackets should be replaced as appropriate):

> **Draft [External] Report to the Board of [company name] by [name of accountancy firm** (NOT your character name) OR **name of your manager if an internal report], [date of exam]**
>
> [If an external report then add:] **Liability is only accepted to the Board of [company name] and information has not been verified.**

During the preparations for the July 2016 examination (Bux), which was the most recent occasion on which an internal report was tested, we received a large number of enquiry emails regarding whether the report should be written in the form "**We** have experienced revenue growth of …" or "**Bux** has experienced revenue growth of …". Apparently, these students had been informed by their tuition provider that this was a material matter and therefore our mock examinations (which used "Bux" throughout) were being criticised.

We could not see any mark for this on the markscheme and queried the matter at the 2017 ICAEW Tutor Conference. The examiners stated that they were not concerned whether "we" or "Bux" was used and students would not be marked down on this matter as they do not consider it important. Please bear this in mind if your own examination involves an internal report.

8   What notes should I take in?

It is tempting to bring in as many resources as you can and you may see some candidates with boxes of large lever arch files apparently overflowing with notes, tabs and mindblowing ideas. Do not be intimidated by this just before the exam.

The risk of bringing in too much is that you will waste a lot of time trying to find the information you need. You will then need to find space on your desk to accommodate all these files and notes. There is also a risk, given the loose-leaf format of your answer, that you might mistakenly mix in an answer sheet with your notes and the more bits of paper you have flying around, the greater this risk.

You should try to keep your notes to an absolute minimum, given that you will not have to do anything technical and will not be rewarded for depth of thinking or original points. You will only really need:

    1. **Planning sheets with past paper markschemes for at least the last 4 sittings**[56] **stapled behind** – this will provide you with both blank Planning & Reminder Sheets on top but also, and perhaps more importantly, an easy access reminder of points which were rewarded in recent real examinations via the full markschemes stapled to the back of your blank planning sheets. This should be more than enough reminders on scepticism, risks, benefits, Conclusions and Recommendations and so on – you should not need any further notes on this, given that the past paper grids will show you what definitely scores marks.

    2. **Pre-prepared Appendix 1** – prepared per the instructions in section 6 above. This will include the "prior year" Advance Information figures and will rehearse the correct format to maximise your use of space on ICAEW's special answer pad paper.

    3. **One page/side of CoP and SOC factors** – any more than this and you will waste time looking for points and will go into too much detail. Keeping everything on one side of paper means you will know exactly where to find it. If possible, it would be better to add these points to the margins of your planning sheets as then you will be more likely to remember them. Remember not to force points in simply because you got them ready before the examination: only include points that contribute to analysis of the examination scenario provided by the Exam Paper.

    4. **Trimmed down, single-sided Advance Information management accounts and other narrative information** – prepared per the instructions at section 2 above. This information will fit more easily on your desk and will be easier to work with – since you know that all information is on the facing page, you do not need to keep flicking between pages.

As a fifth and final document, you may also wish to consider our popular **Exam Room Pack** which simplifies the Advance Information and reorganises and links the material so that points on certain key issues which are scattered around in the Advance Information are placed on the same page for

---

[56] We recommend that you have the markschemes for the last 4 past papers because this will mean that you have 2 examples of papers written by the July Case Study examiner and 2 examples of papers written by the November Case Study examiner. Each examiner has subtly different ways of working so it is helpful to have some examples of both types of approach. Please see chapter 14 for a recent statement by the examiners that the last 4 past papers provide a detailed enough set of examples, and that it is probably not worth going too far back before the last 4 papers as the markscheme emphasis has changed over time.

easy reference. See **www.acasimplifiedcase.com** for more details on our Exam Room Pack, including a free downloadable sample from a recent past paper.

These 4 or 5 documents are all you need. Do not be tempted to overcomplicate things by taking more information into the exam hall than you will need or be able to use in the time available.

9 The Exam Paper Impact Information – use it as much as you can!

As previously stated, there may well be parts (and even entire Exhibits) within the Advance Information which you will not use at all in the end (**do not try to force in pre-prepared points based on the Advance Information if this is not required**).

This will not be the case at all with the Exam Paper Impact Information – **everything on the Exam Paper is there for a reason and potentially relevant**.

Given that you could potentially prepare large parts of your answers in advance using the Advance Information, the examiners need to ensure that you can respond to the **information given on the day**. The markscheme will therefore allocate a **significant** number of marks for issues only mentioned in the Exam Paper: the Advance Information will have a lesser importance.

This is particularly the case in Requirement 2 and Requirement 3 where you need to go through the respective Exam Paper Exhibits on a sentence by sentence basis and ask: **why I am being told this?** Then try to think: **how can I use this to complete Tasks such as scepticism, testing of assumptions, practical issues, risks, benefits etc?**

Whilst we definitely advise that you use the Exam Paper as much as possible it is worth noting that Requirement 1 in RS (November 2014) had almost no information at all on events during the year as the Exam Paper generally related to the ET, meaning that candidates had to know the Advance Information very well to find relevant points to discuss. Some recent examinations such as CC (November 2015) and Bux (July 2016) have contained either no (CC) or minimal (Bux) information on "events during the year": the Exam Paper Exhibit for Requirement 1 again related to the ET only. **You should therefore ensure that you are well prepared for both "styles" of Requirement 1.**

10   Comments from students

> **Student 1 says:** *"A good rule of thumb is to regard everything in the Exam Paper as relevant and likely to be on the markscheme whereas a good 80% of the Advance Information will not be relevant in the end. Think about it – Case is still ultimately an* **exam** *so the examiners are looking to see how you respond to information which you could not have anticipated. Anyone can learn the Advance Information, given the 6 weeks or so you have to look at it, but not everyone can absorb and react to the Exam Paper information in the 10 minutes or so which you have to read it (if possible, try not to read it more than once, meaning you only have 10 minutes to absorb the information – when you have done a lot of practice you will know what you are looking for in each section and can underline it on your first reading). The examiners are interested in this quick response skill, not the deep analysis skills which you may have used to analyse the Advance Information in the plentiful period of time (6 weeks or so) before the exam."*

> **Student 2 says:** *"When you have done a lot of practice, you will realise there is little in the Exam Paper information that is not in some way relevant. However, some parts are more relevant than others, so don't get distracted if it is not immediately obvious where it will be useful".*

Chapter 18   Final Thoughts

Best of luck with your Case Study exam!

As we have made clear throughout this book, Case is marked in a very unusual manner but it is not intrinsically any harder than other ACA papers (indeed, once you understand the markscheme, it can be easier than a technical exam). To get to this stage in your ACA, you must have passed a number of very difficult and technical exams so there is clearly no doubt regarding your ability – what you need to have is a proper understanding of the **unique markscheme** and therefore the **unique technique** which is needed to help you pass your final examination and qualify as a Chartered Accountant.

We hope that you have found this book useful and that it has clarified any areas of uncertainty. However, if you still have any queries, please email us at **getqualified@acasimplified.com** and we will be happy to help further.

Please do keep an eye on our dedicated ACA Simplified Case Study website at **www.acasimplifiedcase.com** as we will be releasing a number of materials once the July 2018 Advance Information has been made available. In addition to this book, our website will offer various other resources to help you get through Case:

1. **PL Mock Exam Pack as a sample and for additional practice** – we have uploaded a free PDF copy of our PL (July 2017) live mock exam pack to serve as a sample of what will be included in our live July 2018 mock exam pack. As the sample contains our complete July 2017 mock pack, it will also provide you with 5 opportunities to practise your Case technique whilst only having to read one set of past paper Advance Information: this is far more time efficient than practising 5 different past papers (and learning 5 different sets of Case Study Advance Information) to obtain the same amount of technique practice. As our sample relates to a July past paper, it provides an opportunity to practise 5 Mocks based on the last set of Advance Information created by the same examiner who will write the July 2018 examination, providing you with useful context, particularly if you also practise the real July 2017 past paper as well as our Mock sample pack (making use of the time you will have put into learning the July 2017 Advance Information). **Available now.**

2. **July 2018 Mock Exam Pack (5 exams)** – we do not yet know what the subject of the July 2018 Advance Information will be. However, we do know that it will be essential to **immerse** yourself in the Advance Information if you wish to pass. We will therefore produce a set of 5 full exams, based on our expectations of likely exam day scenarios. This will be an excellent opportunity to practise technique and time management 5 times, in the context of a set of Advance Information which you really do need to learn well. We have a very good record of anticipating likely exam day scenarios. **Release date 22 June 2018** (or as near to this date as possible). Do not forget to claim your £20 discount on the mocks as a purchaser of this book (see page 6)!

3. **July 2018 Exam Room Pack (ERP)** – following high demand and strong feedback on the notes provided to our tuition course students, we will be preparing a 15-20 page ERP containing all the key information you need in a super quick reference format including: key

figures, explanations and possible patterns to spot for Requirement 1; summary of likely Requirement 2 calculations including assumptions points; and Requirement 3 and ethics notes. Using our experience of tutoring the Case Study examination we will be able to summarise and simplify the Advance Information down into its most important components, saving you time and ensuring that you have all the important information to hand. We will also work hard to collate the various points scattered around the Advance Information onto single, thematic pages of information, providing quick reference to all material on a particular topic. We will work on our ERP during our tuition course phase in order to create the best possible product so we anticipate releasing the ERP **in early July 2018** – as the ERP is a set of condensed notes on matters you should already have learned from your preparation (and our mock exams) we think you can still definitely make very good use of the pack even if it is purchased close to the exam day: by releasing the pack as late as possible we can include all the ideas generated during our tuition phase, improving the quality of the pack. A free copy of an example Exam Room Pack for a past paper is already available as a sample at **www.acasimplifiedcase.com**. Release date **early July 2018**.

4. ***Cracking Case On-Demand*™** – we are delighted to be launching at the July 2018 session an on-demand video course to serve as a companion to this book, allowing us to go into certain matters of examination technique in more detail. We will also make the most of a video tutorial format to review other areas that are quite difficult to explain or demonstrate via a book format. *Cracking Case On-Demand*™ will also include detailed videos tailored to the specific July 2018 Advance Information, allowing us to apply our general technique points explained in this book to the live set of Case Study Advance Information. Please see Appendix 5 for more details regarding this exciting new development in our Case Study offering.

Ten final things to remember to pass the Case Study

We wish you all the best for your Case exam and we hope that this book will make the exam less stressful for you to sit.

Here are 10 final things that we think you should remember in order to pass the exam:

1. Manage your time – you must complete your report to have a chance of passing

2. Everything within the Exam Paper information is there for a reason – work through the information on a line by line basis and use it all!

3. Drill and practise Requirement 1 (both numbers and narrative explanation) several times a day in the run up to the exam

4. Do not stress about the ET in Requirement 1

5. Do not panic about the Requirement 2 calculation – having correct figures is much less important than providing a good number of **narrative points** on business context,

assumptions, assumptions extension, ethical issues (if tested in Requirement 2), any other narrative Tasks asked for in the Exam Paper, Conclusions and Commercial Recommendations

6. Leave enough time for Requirement 3 – this Requirement has a high average number of diamonds per Box so in theory it is easier to get those passing grades (3 points or more in a Box) but only if you leave yourself a decent amount of time – make sure you understand our Plan B for Requirement 3 just in case (see chapter 13)

7. Write your Commercial Recommendations (within each Requirement) and the Executive Summary as you go along, sticking very strictly to the advice given in this book

8. Learn the core themes (see chapter 11) which seem to form the basis of the strategic and operational considerations that are rewarded time and time again on the markscheme

9. Make use of our blank Planning & Reminder Sheets for each Requirement (see chapter 6), with the related markschemes from ICAEW past papers stapled to the back, as per our instructions in chapter 17 – a vital source of reminders of what kinds of point are likely to score – remember to always prioritise the most recent past papers as the markscheme has been evolving over time

10. Learn the 40 Tasks or Boxes as well as you can – learning the set of 40 Tasks or Boxes properly will fix what you need to do in your "**mind's eye**" so that under time pressure you will instinctively stick only to making points which have a good chance of "**matching**" the markscheme and which are "**distributed**" over a sufficiently wide range of Tasks such as to give you a good chance of passing the examination

Most importantly of all …

Good luck!

Best wishes

ACA Simplified

Appendix 1   The 40 Markscheme Boxes – Summary

Task	Content	Skill	Diamonds[57]	Difficulty
	EXECUTIVE SUMMARY			
E.1a	Review Requirement 1 Appendix figures	n/a	4	Easy
E.1b	Evaluation and recommendations on financial performance and ET	n/a	4	Medium
E.2a	Results of Requirement 2 calculations and assumptions	n/a	4	Easy
E.2b	Other Issues, scepticism, proceed or not, recommendations	n/a	4	Easy
E.3a	Results of Requirement 3 calculation and 2 main Issues	n/a	4	Easy
E.3b	Proceed or not, ethics, scepticism, Other Issues, recommendations	n/a	4	Easy
	REQUIREMENT 1			
1.1	Results of Appendix 1 calculations for overall company headlines	A&UI	5	Easy
1.2	Discuss wider context of performance	A&UI	5.5	Medium
1.3	Basics for financial figure 1 – F skill	SP&S	5	Easy
1.4	Basics for financial figures 2 & 3 – F skill	SP&S	5	Easy
1.5	Calculations for ET	SP&S	5.5	Hard
1.6	Reasons and pattern spotting for financial figure 1 – RP skills	AJ	5.5	Medium
1.7	Reasons and pattern spotting for financial figures 2 & 3 – RP skills	AJ	5.5	Medium
1.8	Narrative on ET	AJ	5.5	Easy
1.9	Conclusions **with figures**	C&R	5	Easy
1.10	Commercial Recommendations	C&R	6	Hard
	REQUIREMENT 2			
2.1	Outline contract terms & strategic and operational context OR model inputs	A&UI	4.5	Easy
2.2	Discuss wider context and R1 linkages regarding relevant revenue stream	A&UI	5.5	Medium
2.3	Correct results for calculation 1 with brief discussion	SP&S	4.5	Hard
2.4	Correct results for calculation 2 with brief discussion OR Other Issue	SP&S	4.5	Hard
2.5	Query and evaluate assumptions	SP&S	5	Easy
2.6	Discussion of calculation results or Other Issue	AJ	5.5	Hard
2.7	Other Issue (may be ethics)	AJ	5.5	Hard
2.8	Assumptions extension point OR ethics recommendations	AJ	5.5	Easy
2.9	Conclusions **with figures**	C&R	5	Easy
2.10	Commercial Recommendations	C&R	7	Medium
	REQUIREMENT 3			
3.1	Outline contract terms & strategic and operational context OR calculations	A&UI	5	Medium
3.2	Discuss wider context and R1 linkages regarding relevant revenue stream	A&UI	5.5	Medium
3.3	Discussion of Issue 1	SP&S	6.5	Easy
3.4	Discussion of Issue 2	SP&S	6.5	Easy
3.5	Ethics – Issue and Impact	SP&S	5	Easy
3.6	Further Issue 1 points or Other Issue	AJ	5.5	Hard
3.7	Further Issue 2 points or Other Issue	AJ	5.5	Hard
3.8	Ethics – Recommendations	AJ	5.5	Easy
3.9	Conclusions **with figures**	C&R	5.5	Easy
3.10	Commercial Recommendations	C&R	7	Medium
	APPENDICES & MAIN REPORT			
AMR.1	Appendices R1: Content and style	n/a	4	Easy
AMR.2	Appendices R2: Content and style	n/a	4	Easy
AMR.3	Report: Structure	n/a	4	Easy
AMR.4	Report: Style and language	n/a	4	Easy

---

[57] Average of marks or "diamonds" in each Box for Case Study examinations from July 2012 onwards, rounded to the nearest half diamond (except for the Executive Summary as the examiners have now confirmed that only 4 diamonds will be available: see chapter 14. We have therefore used the figure 4 within the Executive Summary elements of our table above).

229

Appendix 2   The 40 Tasks – Requirement by Requirement

In the summary boxes below, we have used a * symbol to indicate "key" Tasks which are your easiest path towards the 5 Boxes which you need to pass in order to have a chance of passing each Requirement (3 Boxes required to pass the Executive Summary).

Executive Summary – a reminder of the 6 Tasks

E.1a*	Review Requirement 1 Appendix figures
E.1b	Evaluation and recommendations on financial performance and ET
E.2a*	Results of Requirement 2 calculations and assumptions
E.2b	Other Issues, scepticism, proceed or not, recommendations
E.3a*	Results of Requirement 3 calculation and 2 main Issues
E.3b*	Proceed or not, ethics, scepticism, Other Issues, recommendations

Requirement 1 – a reminder of the 10 Tasks

1.1*	Results of Appendix 1 calculations for overall company headlines
1.2	Discuss wider context of performance
1.3*	Basics for financial figure 1 (e.g. revenue (Note)) – F skill
1.4*	Basics for financial figures 2 & 3 (e.g. gross profit and operating profit (Note)) – F skill
1.5	Calculations for ET
1.6	Reasons and pattern spotting for financial figure 1 – RP skills
1.7	Reasons and pattern spotting for financial figures 2 & 3 – RP skills
1.8	Narrative on ET
1.9*	Conclusions **with figures**
1.10	Commercial Recommendations

Note – Our mention of the topics revenue, gross profit and operating profit is based on likelihood and not certainty – you must prepare yourself for testing of other areas and always respond to the question set on the Exam Paper: do not be tempted to write about what you had hoped would be on the Exam Paper.

Requirement 2 – a reminder of the 10 Tasks

2.1*	Outline contract terms & strategic and operational context OR model inputs
2.2	Discuss wider context and make R1 linkages regarding relevant revenue stream
2.3	Correct results for calculation 1 with brief discussion
2.4	Correct results for calculation 2 with brief discussion OR Other Issue
2.5*	Query and evaluate assumptions
2.6	Discussion of calculation results or Other Issue
2.7	Other Issue (may be ethics)
2.8	Assumptions extension point OR ethics recommendations
2.9*	Conclusions **with figures**
2.10	Commercial Recommendations

Requirement 3 – a reminder of the 10 Tasks

3.1	Outline contract terms & strategic and operational context OR calculations
3.2	Discuss wider context and R1 linkages regarding relevant revenue stream
3.3*	Discussion of Issue 1
3.4*	Discussion of Issue 2
3.5*	Ethics – Issue and Impact
3.6	Further Issue 1 points or Other Issue
3.7	Further Issue 2 points or Other Issue
3.8*	Ethics – Recommendations
3.9*	Conclusions **with figures**
3.10	Commercial Recommendations

Always read the question paper carefully to identify the 2 issues required in your specific exam. This is crucial. At the same time, remember that there may be up to 8 other unrelated Boxes to complete and hence it is impossible to pass Requirement 3 by only doing a good job of these 2 issues.

Appendix 3   Forewords to Previous Editions of this Book (July 2015 to November 2017)

Starting with the July 2015 edition of this book, we have provided a Foreword containing a detailed review of key learning points from the examination which had been most recently taken by students at the time of writing each new edition of *Cracking Case™* – the July 2015 edition therefore reviewed the November 2014 examination (RS), the November 2015 edition reviewed the July 2015 examination (Bod), and so on.

We have retained these Forewords for your reference in this Appendix as they provide a useful and very detailed review of each examination from November 2014 onwards – if you review this Appendix carefully then you will obtain very valuable insight into how the markscheme has subtly evolved at recent sittings: these slight nuances in approach are important as you must not base your report on an out-of-date approach.

Whilst we appreciate that it will take some time to read through our detailed reviews, this time **will** be worthwhile as you will acquire a completely up-to-date understanding of what to do in your own examination. As always, and given the evolution of the markscheme over time, please give greater weight to the more recent examinations: at the 2018 ICAEW Tutor Conference, the examiners suggested that the 4 most recent examinations (November 2017, July 2017, November 2016 and July 2016) are the most representative of how the examination is currently assessed (see chapter 14 for more details).

Foreword to the November 2017 Edition and Review of PL (July 2017)

We have retained this Foreword written in September 2017 for your reference as it provides a useful review of the idiosyncrasies of the July 2017 examination, Piccolo. Please note that we have updated the Foreword presented below to allow for the new terminology implemented in the July 2018 edition of this book and have removed content that is no longer applicable. Otherwise, the Foreword is as originally presented in the November 2017 edition of this book.

Welcome to this November 2017 edition of *Cracking Case™* and many thanks for your purchase!

We have thoroughly updated the book for some key learning points in relation to the July 2017 examination. We have noticed a couple of subtle markscheme changes that are similar in both the November 2016 and July 2017 markschemes so the book has been updated for these apparent patterns, which are also discussed in detail in our review of PL below.

As normal, this Foreword includes a brief review of the most recent Case Study examination (July 2017) which had been taken at the time of writing (September 2017). This initial brief review simply aims to highlight some of the key learning points from the most recent examination – we have obviously integrated all these ideas where relevant later in the text as well. Please note that the Foreword does require some knowledge of the terminology that we discuss in greater length later in the rest of this book so we would recommend that you read the rest of the book first and then return to this Foreword as everything will then make a lot more sense.

We hope you will find this updated edition of *Cracking Case™* useful to your preparation for your examination. Don't forget that as a purchaser of this book, you are entitled to a discount of £20 plus VAT (if applicable) on our pack of 5 full mock examinations based on the live November 2017 Advance Information – the mock exam pack is due for release on **6 October 2017**, shortly after the release of the Advance Information itself by ICAEW on **26 September 2017**.

Shortly before this latest edition of *Cracking Case™* went to press, we were delighted to be notified of another ICAEW prize for one of our students: Jordan Raiye placed first in the ICAEW North East region (and also first in KPMG nationally) with a very impressive score of 86% at the July 2017 sitting (just a couple of marks below the global prize-winning score). We were delighted to hear of this achievement, which we hope will give you confidence in the technique set out in this book.

Good luck with your examination and please do let us know how you got on.

All the best,

The ACA Simplified Team   **September 2017**

Review of PL (July 2017)

Despite PL being one of the least predictable recent Case Studies (with Requirement 2 in particular being very hard to predict, given the lack of any pro-forma or hint at the eventual calculation), students coped well with the examination and the global pass rate for PL was higher than normal at around 77%. As usual, we were pleased to significantly exceed this pass rate, with a 98% pass rate overall.

Unlike the July 2016 examination (Bux), which contained a few unusual quirks, the July 2017 examination was very much in line with a typical Case Study markscheme. Our main observations on this examination (which are also fully integrated into our Planning & Reminder Sheets and other discussion in the remainder of this book) would be as follows.

Executive Summary

As discussed later in the book, the ICAEW examiners have stated that they want the Executive Summary to be more than a mere repetition of the points already made in the Conclusions sections of each Requirement (such Conclusions must of course be included in the Executive Summary as well but the Executive Summary should consist of more than simply a regurgitation of these points alone). The examiners have spoken about the importance of noting the "Big Picture" in the Executive Summary so that the reader is informed of the fundamental issues facing the business.

Box E.1 in the PL Executive Summary markscheme therefore contained a "Big Picture" point for noting that PL was making a loss (unusual in recent years, based on the Advance Information which had shown profits for several years) and that this would not be sustainable in the long term. We did advise all our taught course students to look at whether the business was making a loss when writing their Executive Summary, on the basis of a similar point being in the November 2016 Executive Summary markscheme (in that examination, the candidate had to observe that the company was close to a breakeven point at the operating profit level, despite good revenue growth). It was therefore pleasing to see this point on being near a loss-making position on the final PL markscheme.

Rather unusually, the PL Executive Summary markscheme awarded a mark for a CoP comparison (comparing PL's performance against a forecast 5% decline in the market more generally). Normally, CoP points are not rewarded in the Executive Summary. However, it should be noted that this mark could alternatively have been gained for a more "classic" Executive Summary point on financial performance (in this case, comparing performance against budget, with the budget being a key focus of the Advance Information). We would therefore have expected many students still to obtain this mark even if they did not refer to the CoP.

Box E.2 was left fairly open, unlike some examinations where very specific comments are required. Candidates were able to make any reasonable comment on customers/products, operating expenses (all categories were acceptable) and the ET (**any** comment on impact would be accepted, together with **any** recommendation). We were pleased to see this more open approach but would note that November examinations have tended to require more specific points in this Box.

In Box E.3, candidates were specifically required to separate out the 2019 and 2020 results for each calculation (i.e. 4 different figures had to be provided, 2 for each calculation). This required a thorough presentation of the calculation results as a student attempting to save time by just presenting a combined total for both years would lose credit. We have emphasised on our classroom tuition courses that it is best to play it safe and provide separate figures for each of 2 years: this does not, after all, take very long. Our students should therefore have picked up these marks through a thorough approach.

Box E.3 was perhaps also a little strict in relation to assumptions: there were separate marks for querying, firstly, **revenue** assumptions and then, secondly, **fee** assumptions. Normally there would be a more general mark simply for querying any "assumptions". Again, it really does pay to be thorough and respect the Executive Summary.

We were very pleased to see credit in Box E.5 for a reference back to PL's existing strategic objectives as outlined in a specific Exhibit in the Advance Information. We have noted elsewhere in this book that there tends to be quite a bit of credit in Requirement 3 in the recent examinations for comparisons between the Requirement 3 project and a strategic plan or similar document mentioned in the Advance Information: after all, if the client has some specific objectives in place, it follows that advisers should take these into account.

Slightly more unusually, Box E.6 contained a mark for demonstrating scepticism towards the information provided. As set out in detail in chapter 12 of this book, the tendency in recent examinations has been for there to be an ever-decreasing reward for scepticism in Requirement 3: a few years ago, there used to be a dedicated markscheme Box for scepticism in Requirement 3 but now there are simply a few marks scattered around in other Boxes. This reference to scepticism in the Requirement 3 Executive Summary is therefore definitely worth noting.

Requirement 1

Turning now to the main Requirements, probably the most unusual aspect of PL Requirement 1 and its related markscheme is in relation to the ET (see later in this book for a definition of this term). For the first time since the ET was introduced in the July 2012 examination, **there was no requirement to perform any calculations at all**. This meant that Box 1.5 was not allocated to the ET and could instead be allocated to operating profit. We feel that this should have made Requirement 1 substantially easier to pass: not only would time be saved on doing tricky calculations relating to the ET, it is obviously substantially easier to pick up marks for further analysis of the Income Statement (operating profit) than on any unpredictable "think on your feet" calculation. Therefore, the learning point to take away is that if the ET appears not to involve calculations, you should expand the detail of your main financial statement analysis (whilst resisting the common temptation to go overboard on the accounts analysis).

Staying with the topic of the ET, another noteworthy aspect of PL Requirement 1 was the emphasis on the ET in Box 1.10 for Recommendations: no fewer than 4 of the 7 acceptable points related to the ET issue. The ET has always figured quite prominently in Box 1.10 with generally at least 2 of the Recommendations relating to this matter but we have not seen a markscheme with as many as 4 Recommendations on the ET. Perhaps this is a consequence of the lack of calculations, which would otherwise have reduced the reward on the ET to a single Box (Box 1.8): by rewarding ET Recommendations in Box 1.10 for Recommendations, the examiner was perhaps ensuring that the ET could still effectively gain 2 Boxes of credit, if done well.

We have seen that the examiner replaced ET calculations with detailed analysis of operating profit (constituting all of Box 1.5 and much of Box 1.7, which was shared with gross profit comments). Arguably, the operating profit analysis was more difficult to pass than the revenue and gross profit analysis because the operating profit points are more specific in nature and thus less open. This could be a consequence of the operating profit partially replacing the ET, given that the ET is often quite tricky to pass.

We would strongly advise you to bear the above points in mind if the ET in your examination does not have any calculations to perform.

Following the PL examination, we received a higher than normal number of queries from students who were unsure if they had identified the correct ethics issues in the examination. As we will see in more detail below, the ethics issues in PL were slightly unusual in that every issue was committed entirely by a third party and not by Piccolo – Piccolo was essentially blameless in all cases, perhaps causing confusion for students as there are normally a few issues where the client's own actions are questionable (combined with other issues which are clearly the responsibility of third parties). Requirement 1 in PL was no exception here as it was clearly not PL's fault that fake versions of its cookware had been sold. The fact that PL was not directly at fault was actually one of the specific points on the markscheme, together with a standard point on potential reputational and financial damage. Our recommendation as always is not to overcomplicate the ethics issues in Case Study: state the obvious about the matter, together with straightforward advice such as to investigate the facts, take legal advice, protect the company's reputation and reconsider working with any parties involved in the problem … and then move on!

Requirement 2

For the second sitting in a row, Box 2.1 (which always used to be awarded for correct identification of the inputs to the financial model) in PL was allocated to an outline description of the key terms of the proposed contracts: 2 of the marks available in this Box required the candidate to "outline contract terms". The other 2 marks were available for points regarding what was already known about the potential partners in the project (2 celebrity chefs discussed in the Advance Information). As there have now been 2 consecutive examinations with no marks in Box 2.1 regarding the financial model, we would recommend that you include plenty of narrative background of this type instead. Please review the markschemes for the July 2017 and November 2016 examinations to see examples of the types of point to make. (July 2018 edition update: the R4 (November 2017) examination returned to the more traditional type of inputs-based Box 2.1, probably because there was only one calculation to perform, unlike in the July 2017 and November 2016 examinations. Please see chapter 9 for more discussion of this issue.)

The markscheme indicates that there were 4 different ethics issues to consider in Requirement 2. This is pretty high for ethics in Requirement 2, compared to other past papers. As noted regarding Requirement 1 above, it was noteworthy that PL was not in any way responsible for the problems that had arisen and it was perhaps for this reason that students wrote in to us wondering if they had missed something. The learning point is therefore that Case Study ethics problems do not necessarily have to be matters caused by the client company. Instead, the candidate needs to consider the impact of becoming involved in work with other parties who may be doing questionable things. Standard impact or evaluation points would then surely always be to consider the impact on the client company's reputation (the Case Study company always has an outstanding ethical reputation and holds itself to high standards) and to take legal advice and/or respond to reputational damage (the PL markscheme suggests the use of social media to protect the company's position).

Perhaps as a result of the emphasis on ethics (2 Boxes), there was only one Box on Assumptions rather than the 2 Boxes seen in the July 2016 examination. The inclusion of only one Box on Assumptions was consistent with the previous November 2016 examination which also had 2 Boxes for ethics so the learning point seems to be that if there is quite a lot of ethics in Requirement 2 then you are advised to prioritise this over Assumptions. (July 2018 edition update: note that the R4 (November 2017) examination had 2 Boxes for Assumptions and 2 Boxes for ethics so it is possible for the markscheme to be equally weighted here. R4 (November 2017) only had 1 calculation to perform whereas the July 2017 and November 2016 examinations had 2 calculations to do so perhaps the pattern is that if there is only 1 calculation then there may be 2 Assumptions Boxes but if there are 2 calculations then there may only be 1 Assumptions Box. See chapter 9 for more discussion of this point.)

Box 2.8 on recommendations in relation to ethics was noteworthy for the inclusion of the verb "Discuss" in relation to 4 different points. As such, if the student had simply advised PL to discuss each different ethics issue with the relevant party then this would have been all that was necessary to score very well in Box 2.8. This result is in line with our advice elsewhere in this book to keep things simple when it comes to ethics … the examiners are certainly not looking for rocket science!

Requirement 3

Box 3.1 was the most unexpected Box of any Box in the PL markscheme (whether in Requirement 3 or elsewhere). In PL, this Box did not allocate marks for the Requirement 3 calculation but rather to a very similar "contract outline" as was rewarded in Box 2.1 (see above): marks were available for mentioning what was already known about the client (Dougal Hotels), followed by 2 marks for describing the start date (or duration) of the proposed contract and for explaining that the contract involved a full refurbishment of the client's hotels. The marks for the calculation were moved out of Box 3.1 and put into Box 3.3. It is therefore important that you include enough background contextual information in both Requirements 2 and 3.

The PL Requirement 3 also made several cross-references back to information contained in Requirement 1: specifically, there was reference to the company's cash balance (Box 3.2) and the fact that redundancies had been made (Box 3.5). Box 3.2 also referred to the most recent gross profit margin of the relevant stream and client (Dougal): this should have already been calculated to obtain marks in Requirement 1. The number of marks for backwards cross-referencing in Requirement 3 does seem to have increased in recent examinations so please bear this in mind. See chapter 10 of this book for further discussion.

Although Requirement 3 always contains ethics, it was interesting to see reward for the point that one of the issues (disposal of existing tableware to schools) was **in line** with PL's ethical stance. Therefore, it seems that there may now be credit not only for finding ethical **problems** but also indicating that a policy is consistent with the company's ethics (and so is **not** a problem, but actually a good thing): previous examinations only ever awarded ethics marks for finding ethical **problems** in the proposals.

Box 3.6 contained quite a lot of comments in relation to the calculation results. This might have made this Box quite hard to pass if the candidate made mistakes in the calculation but fortunately Box 3.6

also contained plenty of other acceptable points that were nothing to do with the calculation so it would still have been possible to pass the Box with good narrative analysis.

Finally, Box 3.9 on Conclusions was a little easier to pass than normal as there were 5 acceptable points available, an increase on the more usual 4 points.

We hope that this review of the slight nuances in an otherwise pretty standard Case Study examination has been useful. As noted, we have incorporated the relevant points into our advice throughout the remainder of this book to ensure that our technique advice and popular Planning & Reminder Sheets have been fully updated for the latest available information.

Foreword to the July 2017 Edition and Review of True Taste Limited (November 2016)

We have retained this Foreword written in February 2017 for your reference as it provides a useful review of the idiosyncrasies of the November 2016 examination, True Taste. Please note that we have updated the Foreword presented below to allow for the new terminology implemented in the July 2018 edition of this book and have removed content that is no longer applicable. Otherwise, the Foreword is as originally presented in the July 2017 edition of this book.

Welcome to this July 2017 edition of *Cracking Case™* and many thanks for your purchase!

After making only incremental updates to *Cracking Case™* for several recent sittings, we felt that the book was becoming slightly long. This new July 2017 edition therefore represents our first complete rewrite of the book since its initial publication in 2013.

Don't worry! We have not removed anything which is important for you to know about your Case Study examination – we have simply trimmed out the fat, condensed the discussion where possible and reorganised the chapters so that the book flows in a better way.

As always, we include in this Foreword a brief review of the most recent Case Study examination (November 2016) which had been taken at the time of writing (February 2017). This initial brief review is simply to highlight some of the key learning points from the most recent examination – we have obviously integrated all these ideas where relevant later in the text as well.

We hope you will find this fully rewritten edition of *Cracking Case™* useful to your preparation for your examination. Don't forget that as a purchaser of this book, you are entitled to a £20 discount on our pack of 5 full mock examinations based on the live July 2017 Advance Information – the mock exam pack is due for release on **16 June 2017**, shortly after the release of the Advance Information itself by ICAEW on **6 June 2017**.

Good luck with your examination and please do let us know how you got on.

All the best,

The ACA Simplified Team   **February 2017**

Review of True Taste (November 2016)

Overall, the TT examination was very much in line with recent Case Study examinations and was, in our opinion, a relatively "plain vanilla" Case Study with no real surprises or alterations to the markscheme.

Immediately after the examination, our students were slightly concerned regarding the calculations required in Requirement 2. Our students reported that they were not quite sure how to apply the relevant model inputs and therefore they felt that more than one answer was reasonable. The examiners agreed – in a slightly unusual step, the markscheme for TT Requirement 2 awards marks for a range of answers to the 2 financial model calculations: normally in Case Study, there is only "a" single correct answer which you must match exactly in order to obtain credit. The concerns expressed by our students were therefore taken into account in a reasonable way by ICAEW in awarding the marks. Please bear this in mind if you genuinely feel that a range of answers is possible in your own Requirement 2 – if you are right, then the marking will reflect this.

Other than this issue, there is nothing hugely unusual or innovative in the TT markscheme. Even so, we will briefly review each element of the markscheme here in the interests of completeness.

Executive Summary

The TT markscheme is very much in line with recent examinations and the comments of the examiners (see chapter 14) that the Executive Summary will be marked a little more harshly than in the past. The TT markscheme retains only 4 permissible points per markscheme Box, meaning that you must match 3 out of the 4 possibilities available (quite a high strike rate and requiring a good understanding of what is required).

Additionally, and again in line with recent examinations, the TT Executive Summary markscheme for Requirement 1 does require students to reach very specific recommendations in order to be awarded credit: specifically, candidates had to conclude to recognise a full 100% bad debt provision and then comment on the impact of this for operating profit and cash – then, as a second specific mark, candidates had to recommend that TT should speak to its bank or customers regarding the bad debt issue and the impact on cashflow.

Other than this, the TT Executive Summary markscheme applies a relatively open approach such that provided you are concluding on the right areas then you will attract credit regardless of the specific point that you are making. As with other recent examinations, it does seem to be the case that it is only in respect of Requirement 1 that the Executive Summary will require very specific conclusions to be reached in order to attract credit. Therefore, the learning point is that you should spend just a little bit more time in formulating your Requirement 1 Executive Summary section, perhaps adding quite a few specific recommendations to give yourself a good opportunity to match the points on the markscheme.

Our only other observation regarding the TT Executive Summary is that there was a mark in both the Requirement 2 and Requirement 3 elements for stating that the relevant contract or opportunity was "significant" to the business – the word "significant" also came up in a number of other TT markscheme Boxes so the learning point is that you should always look to comment on the relative size or significance of the project in both Requirement 2 and Requirement 3.

Requirement 1

Here the markscheme was very standard indeed.

As already noted, the word "significant" was perhaps the "word of the Case Study" in the case of TT. Therefore, candidates had to observe that the decline in operating profit was "significant" (bringing the company close to a breakeven point at the operating profit level) in order to pick up a mark in the Requirement 1 Conclusions Box.

As with other recent Case Study examinations, the TT Conclusions Box required supporting figures in relation to most of the points made so always ensure you support your narrative with figures.

The Recommendations Box in TT was relatively difficult as there were only 5 acceptable recommendations in this examination – normally we would expect to see 6 possibilities that could be awarded marks. However, within those 5 points, the ideas were pretty standard in nature and concentrated on the usual areas of promoting the stream that was performing well, investigating how to improve performance in the stream that was struggling, recommending further analysis of costing and to review the way costs were being allocated in the management accounts (together with an open mark for any other sensible recommendation) – all very standard recommendations when it comes to Requirement 1.

As the July 2016 examination took place just a month after the historic Brexit vote in June 2016, TT was in fact the first Case Study to award credit for reference to this market background issue. The CoP Box awarded one mark for discussing how Brexit could affect currency issues and TT's general level of trading. As noted at the later Case Study Workshop at the 2017 ICAEW Tutor Conference, candidates will not obtain credit simply for mentioning the word "Brexit" or its twin word "uncertainty": candidates must explain **specifically** how the Case Study business may be affected.

Our only other observation regarding Requirement 1 is that there were several marks available for spotting that the business was close to turning an operating profit into an operating loss and, secondly, that the trade receivables (ET) issue could potentially turn PBT into a loss. This suggests that you should always look out for these possible "inflection points" in which the company moves between a profit-making position and the loss-making position, and vice versa. Presumably the examiners would expect you to comment on these points as they are serious and material for the company.

Requirement 2

Overall, the markscheme for Requirement 2 in TT is fairly standard in nature. This is despite the fact that TT was the first Case Study examination for several years to require the candidate to perform 2 different financial modelling calculations.

We have already mentioned above that another slightly different aspect of the TT Requirement 2 markscheme was that the examiners were happy to award marks for a range of different results to the costing calculation, given that there were different reasonable approaches available. The examiners did not accept any range of answers in relation to revenue as the correct answer here was pretty clear-cut but it is good to know that if there are valid alternative approaches, then these will be acceptable to the examiners.

The only other slightly unusual aspect of the TT Requirement 2 markscheme was that there was no markscheme Box available for correctly identifying the inputs to the financial model (as opposed to correctly calculating the outputs of the financial model, something which is rewarded in other markscheme Boxes, as was the case in TT). All other recent Case Study markschemes have given candidates a relatively easy opportunity to pass a markscheme Box (Box 2.1) simply for building up the model in the correct way – even if their results go completely wrong, the inputs Box would be obtainable as a separate skill. It is possible that the TT examiners felt that because they had already awarded 2 markscheme Boxes for the 2 different financial modelling calculations, adding a third numerical Box in relation to the model inputs would be overkill, leading to too much emphasis on numbers in the markscheme. Therefore, if your examination only has one financial model alternative to calculate, there may well still be a markscheme Box available for gathering together the correct inputs – we certainly hope that there will be, but it remains to be seen. [July 2018 edition update: the R4 (November 2017) examination had only 1 calculation in Requirement 2 and allocated Box 2.1 to inputs so our prediction stated here in February 2017 proved to be correct.]

Like many recent Case Study examinations, TT required analysis of ethical and business trust issues in Requirement 2. You should note that a full markscheme Box was available for recommendations in relation with how to deal with the ethical problems identified – therefore make sure you do get in plenty of mitigation points if ethics is tested in Requirement 2.

Our only other observation regarding the TT Requirement 2 markscheme is that most of the points in the SOC Box depended on the candidate having some appreciation of the financial story in Requirement 1 – the candidate had to recognise that the proposed projects related to a revenue stream that had become increasingly important, per the Requirement 1 figures, and that the problems experienced in another revenue stream (again only evident from the Requirement 1 figures) would mean that the company now had spare capacity for the project proposed in Requirement 2.

In addition to this, there were 2 further marks in the SOC Box in Requirement 2 for referring back to the current level of gross profit margin of the relevant project revenue stream and for mentioning that TT was relatively near to its overdraft limit at the previous year end and therefore may not have significant cash resources to invest in the project.

In our opinion, this represents the most extensive cross-referencing back to Requirement 1 that we have seen in any recent Case Study. Please bear this in mind when answering your own Requirement 2. Although the examiners have stated that candidates are free to complete the Requirements in any order, they have always recommended that candidates complete Requirement 1 first to obtain an overall picture of how the business is performing. Perhaps it is now time to propose that what has previously been a mere suggestion is now highly advisable, given the emphasis on cross-referencing in the TT Requirement 2 SOC Box 2.2.

Other than this, we thought that the TT Requirement 2 markscheme was fairly standard in nature. There were 7 different acceptable recommendations, which was good to see, and the Conclusions Box had 5 opportunities to obtain a scoring mark.

In closing, we would note that one of these points in the Conclusions Box was to refer to the contract as constituting a "significant" amount of revenue – our "word of the Case Study" (**significant**) was used here once again!

Requirement 3

As with the other Requirements, here the TT markscheme was very standard in nature. After the very challenging approach taken in the Bux (July 2016) examination in which candidates had to evaluate no fewer than 3 different strategic opportunities in Requirement 3 (meaning that the Bux markscheme had very few marks for the easier area of ethics as this was somewhat squeezed out of the space on the markscheme), it was good to see the requirement only to analyse a single strategic project in TT.

242

Accordingly, there was more emphasis on ethics in the TT markscheme than in the July 2016 markscheme, making the Requirement as a whole easier to pass.

As in the case of Requirement 2, there was credit available for a cross-reference back to Requirement 1 in the SOC Box in TT Requirement 3. In this case, there was a mark for identifying that the revenue stream relevant to the proposed projects in Requirement 3 was an increasingly significant part of the company's business. This was the only mark available for a cross-reference and therefore this skill obtained less credit than in Requirement 2. Even so, in light of what we have advised above regarding Requirement 2, it is probably sensible to look to do a bit more cross-referencing between Requirements than was advisable in the past when this would attract either a solitary mark or often no marks at all across the examination as a whole. Please bear this in mind when you answer Requirement 2 and Requirement 3 in your own examination.

Our only other observation on the TT Requirement 3 markscheme is that in contrast to other recent Case Study examinations, in TT, candidates were required to achieve perfectly correct results to their financial model in Requirement 3 in order to obtain credit – previous examinations have not been so restrictive in Requirement 3 (whilst still requiring a perfectly correct answer to the financial model in Requirement 2) and the examiners had previously said that Requirement 3 would be marked relatively generously. Based on the strict approach in TT, the learning point seems to be to spend just a little bit more time on your Requirement 3 calculation than we would previously have advised – whilst at the same time remembering that the answer to this calculation is only worth 1 of the 10 markscheme Boxes available for Requirement 3 and therefore will not make or break your Requirement 3 (unless you let it break your attempt by spending far too long on the calculation).

We hope that this review of the slight nuances in an otherwise "vanilla" Case Study examination has been useful. As noted, we have incorporated the relevant points into our advice throughout the remainder of this book to ensure that all advice has been updated for this latest examination.

Foreword to the November 2016 Edition and Review of Bux Limited (July 2016)

We have retained this Foreword written in September 2016 for your reference as it provides a useful review of the idiosyncrasies of the July 2016 examination, Bux. Please note that we have updated the Foreword presented below to allow for the new terminology implemented in the July 2018 edition of this book and have removed content that is no longer applicable. Otherwise, the Foreword is as originally presented in the November 2016 edition of this book.

The Bux Limited (Bux) Case Study was largely in line with our expectations and the predictions reflected in our mock exam pack. The only unusual element of this examination was in Requirement 3 which asked students to assess **3** different project opportunities as opposed to the more normal 1 or 2 projects – this certainly caused some challenges for time management and slightly changed the composition of the markscheme from its usual pattern. Otherwise the examination seemed very much as expected, based on the preceding November 2015 markscheme and the comments made by the examiners at the February 2016 ICAEW Tutor Conference.

Executive Summary

The Bux Executive Summary was in line with the examiners' comments suggesting that the Executive Summary will be marked more strictly as there were only 4 acceptable points per Executive Summary markscheme Box. At the same time, it is noticeable that there were fewer points of a very specific nature that had to be made – Requirement 1 in particular was more "open" in nature than in the 2015 examinations and there was only really one Executive Summary markscheme Box that had very specific points in it (the second Box for Requirement 2). Therefore the Executive Summary was not marked as strictly as could have been the case.

There was pleasingly a return to the position in examinations set before 2015 in which **any** decision (proceed or not proceed) regarding the projects in Requirement 2 and Requirement 3 was acceptable – there was no "right" answer required. This is fair, given the uncertain nature of business.

Requirement 1

As expected, the usual focus on revenue, cost of sales and gross profit was evident in Requirement 1. The examination therefore returned to requiring analysis of 3 Income Statement captions, fewer than in the November 2015 examination.

There was minimal information provided on events during the year, with most of this relating to the ET[58] (see below), but at least students were given more to go on than in the November 2015 examination where no information of this type was provided.

It was noticeable that, for the second July examination in a row, the ET did not require an additional "project or problem-based" calculation – instead there were marks for analysing updated figures

---

[58] See chapter 8 for a definition of our term "ET".

already mentioned in the Advance Information regarding book sales, revenue splits, production costs and royalties: as we predicted in our taught course classes and as we identified in one of our live mocks, the examiners therefore tested whether students had familiarised themselves with a specific set of "non-accounting" figures in the Advance Information. Provided that students had looked at these figures beforehand, this would have been a relatively easy ET since there was no need to forecast anything or think on one's feet … however, if student knowledge of the Advance Information was not strong then time would have been wasted learning about these non-accounting figures for the first time.

Requirement 1 was standard in nature and should not have caused any problems for a well-prepared candidate.

Requirement 2

As was obviously going to be the case from the Advance Information, Requirement 2 required a calculation of the potential royalties to be earned from a new author contract: although there was no explicit pro-forma given in the Advance Information, there were various places where the examiners hinted that this calculation would be tested through worked examples of separate parts of the overall calculation. This supports the advice we have given on our taught courses to always look carefully at any numerical workings where the examiner says "For example" or similar – this clarifies once and for all what the treatment should be and this would not be necessary if the relevant workings were not going to be tested in the real examination.

Frustratingly, the question wording asked students to discuss the "wider commercial" aspects of the opportunity – as always, the term "wider commercial" is very open and could result in students making good points which are not on the list of acceptable points. As advised elsewhere in this book, we would recommend looking at some past paper markschemes where "commercial" aspects have been tested in order to understand what is likely to be rewarded in this very open area.

In this examination, students did have to possess detailed knowledge of the usual Bux approach to book launches: the average promotional spend and even the number of book-signing sessions and television appearances normally organised had to be known and assessed relative to the data given in Requirement 2. Therefore, always work carefully through any specific numbers or figures stated in the Advance Information as these are always going to be easy to introduce as straightforward assumptions and inputs.

Requirement 2 also had some marks for ethical issues with a specific hint that you needed to consider the author's agent, Liza Halstead. It was very clear from the Advance Information that Liza would figure in the examination somewhere so students should have been prepared for this.

The 2 Boxes on Assumptions in this Requirement continued a pattern seen in the previous July 2015 examination – 6 assumptions could be queried as being too high or too low, with a reason, to score the marks in the first Assumptions Box and then a second Box was available for a second comment on those same 6 assumptions: some of these second comments connected to points in the Advance Information whilst others were more commercial in nature. As advised on our taught courses, it is therefore important not simply to state that "royalties appear high": you must expand on **why** they appear high (drawing on the Advance Information) and what the **implication** could be for the business (similar royalties might have to be offered to other authors, so this could become expensive).

Rather unusually, the question wording specifically asked candidates to "reach a reasoned decision as to whether Bux should offer a contract to Emily". Candidates have **always** had to reach a reasoned "proceed or not" decision in both Requirement 2 and Requirement 3 but this was the first occasion where we have seen this specifically written into the question wording. Perhaps the examiners have been finding that students have not been reaching a decision but in this examination there really was no excuse for missing out this element. [July 2018 edition update: the PL (July 2017) and R4 (November 2017) examinations also contained a specific request to reach a final recommendation/decision on the proposal within the wording of Requirement 2. The TT (November 2016) examination did not contain any such language. Although it is also necessary to reach a "proceed or not" decision in Requirement 3, we have not seen any explicit mention of this in the Requirement 3 wording in recent examinations, meaning that Requirements 2 and 3 seem to be worded differently, even though both Requirements do award credit in exactly the same way for a "proceed or not" decision.]

For the second examination in a row, the SOC Box (Box 2.2) focused primarily on points made in the **Exam Paper** rather than in the Advance Information: these points were, as in November 2015 examination, very closely related to the specific project rather than the broader market points seen in the equivalent Box in Requirement 1. This suggests that your SOC section should be made shorter than in Requirement 1 as the markscheme does not reward such wide points and the points that are rewarded should already mainly be mentioned in relation to the risks and benefits of the project. Try to focus on the Exam Paper for most of your points here.

Finally, we would note that, like Requirement 3 (see below), Requirement 2 in this examination did make full use of the space available on the 2 pages in the Exam Paper to include Exhibit information for each Requirement: this was yet another way in which this examination was very time-pressured. Sometimes on our taught courses students object that our mock examinations contain "too much" Exhibit information since we use 2 full pages every time for every Requirement 2 and Requirement 3 that we write – in the case of the Bux examination, this method of preparing for the "worst case" would have worked well and we would always prefer to err on the side of caution and train students to complete challenging mocks rather than write short Exhibit information and thereby create a false impression as to how difficult the real examination might be. In a variation of this point, some students note that our mocks contain more information than the comparable mocks which they are using at another provider so do be careful if you find that you are doing practice Requirements with other providers that only have perhaps a single page or a page and a half of Exhibit information to absorb: the real Exam Paper information can be longer.

Requirement 3

In our view, this was the most unusual (and therefore most difficult) aspect of the examination – no previous Case Study has asked for analysis of 3 different business opportunities and this would have been a challenging task, especially given that students are generally short of time for Requirement 3 even in the best case scenario (just 1 project to look at!). Certainly in the emails received from our taught course students immediately after the examination, Requirement 3 and timing issues were the main worry. As always, then, Requirement 3 in this examination was an opportunity to test time management as much as accountancy skills.

To make room for enough marks on 3 different project possibilities within the markscheme, there was a reduction in the number of Boxes available for ethics – **for the first time ever, there was no Box dedicated to ethics in Requirement 3**. Plenty of ethics points were rewarded in other Boxes (Box 3.6, 3.7 and 3.8 all had some ethics marks available) and students had to give conclusions and recommendations on ethics both in Requirement 3 itself and also in the Executive Summary for Requirement 3 but there was less **specific** reward for ethics than in any previous Case Study examination. Should Requirement 3 return to the more usual 1 or 2 project opportunities then we would expect the dedicated ethics Boxes to be reinstated but if there are 3 different opportunities you should reduce your ethics analysis.

The focus of the analysis was on the usual "triplets" of "financial, operational and strategic issues" so good candidates should have been prepared for the typical points that tend to score under these areas.

As discussed in further detail on page 170, the examiners were very clear at the February 2016 ICAEW Tutor Conference that a calculation will now normally be set in Requirement 3. Therefore, before this examination we ensured that all our taught course students would always use the minimal numerical data provided for this Requirement in the mock exams within our live mock exam pack. It is noteworthy that in the final question wording for the real Bux examination, the examiners also included a reminder by stating "Where appropriate, you should provide brief calculations to support your arguments". It appears, therefore, that the examiners will remind you to attempt these marks – it was noted at the February 2016 Tutor Conference that almost no students used the figures in Requirement 3 at the November 2015 sitting so action appears to have been taken regarding this.

Ethics was, as always, tested in Requirement 3 so this meant that there were ethics marks in both Requirements 2 and 3 in this examination – potentially plenty of relatively straightforward marks available.

The SOC marks in Box 3.2 contained quite a few points from the Advance Information, such as the competitive nature of the market and, in particular, references back to the Bux Core Principles and Key Risks – these were taken from a very specific Advance Information Exhibit which is often included in sets of Advance Information and looks at risk reviews/business strategies: as such, make sure you are familiar with any such Exhibit in your own examination and quote it extensively. It is worth noting that there were several further marks for this cross-referencing in other Boxes such as Boxes 3.6, 3.7 and 3.8 so again look out for this key Exhibit if it is contained in your set of Advance Information.

As noted above, Requirement 3 in this examination did include a full 2 pages of information, as with Requirement 2 – in the case of Requirement 3, the examiners really did exploit all the available space with every single line in the formatting available being used with Exhibit material that did have to be absorbed. On top of the request to analyse 3 different options, reading and using all of this information would have created time management challenges, even for the best of students.

Despite this extensive provision of information in the Exam Paper, it is noticeable just how many Requirement 3 marks required some reference back to a specific Advance Information Exhibit regarding Bux's core principles, objectives and key risks – we have counted 8 different marks which reference this single Exhibit, including in one of the Boxes for SOC points (Box 3.1), and this number is extremely high compared to previous examinations. As such, make sure you are very familiar with the Advance Information, particularly if there is any kind of strategic plan or risk review (the Advance Information has generally always contained such a document but it appears that the emphasis given to this has now increased).

We hope you found this review useful and we wish you all the best with your preparations for your November 2016 examination. We would obviously be happy to welcome you to our taught courses and/or to provide you with our mock exam pack or other November 2016 resources (please see page 6 for further information). Additionally, we hope you will consider making the most of our launch of our new on-demand Case Study tuition resources for the November 2016 sitting, including webinar reviews of the November 2016 Advance Information, advice on examination technique for each Requirement and tutor debriefs of our November 2016 mock examinations.

Please let us know how you got on with the examination and whether you found this book useful to your attempt.

All the best,

The ACA Simplified Team   **September 2016**

Foreword to the July 2016 Edition and Review of CC (November 2015)

We have retained this Foreword written in March 2016 for your reference as it provides a useful review of the idiosyncrasies of the November 2015 examination, CC. Please note that we have updated the Foreword presented below to allow for the new terminology implemented in the July 2018 edition of this book and have removed content that is no longer applicable. Otherwise, the Foreword is as originally presented in the July 2016 edition of this book.

The CC Case Study (November 2015) was somewhat similar to the previous Bod (July 2015) Case Study in the sense that Requirement 1 could have been very complicated indeed, given CC's various different types of bikes sold. As with the Bod examination, fortunately the examiners did not require detailed analysis of all the different types of revenue in Requirement 1.

Overall, CC was very much in line with recent Case Study examinations and there was nothing particularly surprising or novel. It was noteworthy that all the marks in the tricky and variable Box 3.1 were for calculations – this is a higher amount of marks for the Requirement 3 calculation than other Case examinations and is in line with the statement by the examiners (see chapter 14) that Requirement 3 will continue to have more of a numerical element in future.

CC maintained a relatively strict marking of the Executive Summary with only 4 acceptable points per markscheme Box. This is again in line with the statement by the examiners (see chapter 14) that the Executive Summary is deliberately being made more difficult to pass.

The CC Executive Summary also required specific Recommendations in both Requirement 1 and Requirement 2 to obtain the marks whereas Requirement 3 allowed a mark for the more open "other recommendations" as used to be the case in all Requirements in the Executive Summary. As such we can see that the examiners are correct in their statement that they are deliberately making the Executive Summary harder to pass: please see chapter 14 for more on this. We would advise that you recommend in detail on the ET in Requirement 1 because this was worth a mark in the Executive Summary in the last 2 examinations. Based on the CC markscheme, there was basically a mark in the Requirement 1 ES for a recommendation on each of the matters you were asked to analyse: revenue, gross profit, operating profit, interest cover and the ET. **Therefore, make sure that your recommendations relate to the financial figures requested.**

For the first time, in Requirement 1 candidates were required to analyse 4 different financial figures (revenue, gross profit, operating profit and interest cover) rather than the more usual 3 different financial figures (typically, revenue, gross profit and operating profit/cash, with some variance from exam to exam). Although this did affect the way some marks were awarded in Requirement 1 compared to previous examinations, the question wording in the Exam Paper was very clear that these 4 financial figures had to be analysed and therefore candidates should have allowed for this in their allocation of the different markscheme Boxes.

CC also included a few marks for ethics in Requirement 1, something that is not usually the case: however, no ethics marks were included in Requirement 2. Requirement 3 tested ethics, as usual.

As with the previous November examination (RS (November 2015)), CC contained no "events during the year" in the Requirement 1 Exam Paper information except in relation to the ET. This meant that candidates had to rely on knowledge of the Advance Information to explain the changes in revenue, gross profit, operating profit and interest cover.

There was no requirement to analyse ethical matters in Requirement 2 (unlike in the previous 2 examinations) as Requirement 2 focused on the expected analysis of a City Cycle Hire Scheme. Candidates should have been well prepared, both for the calculation and for the assumptions and wider context comments regarding such a Scheme. Despite some criticism from another tuition provider that our mock examinations had focused on "too obvious" a calculation, it was pleasing to see that the real examination did focus on an area which we practised in detail on our taught course and in our pack of 5 mock exams. This reflects the examiners' comments that Requirement 2 is not there to "catch out" candidates or make candidates fail the examination: a financial model is included merely to get the discussion going and this Requirement is not designed to fail students who do not get precisely the correct figure. Therefore, the financial model required will not be complicated and will often be very clearly flagged in the Advance Information, so do not worry if you think you have spotted something "too obvious" when preparing for your own examination – you may well have identified something very relevant.

The ever controversial matter of the technique of using an initial background paragraph continued to evolve slightly: see our new chapter 16 for detailed discussion of this issue, as well as our comments on markscheme Boxes 1.2, 2.2 and 3.2 in the rest of the book. We would observe that in Requirement 2 in particular the markscheme Box that rewards the "wider context" was very narrowly related to CC and the project proposed, rather than to the genuinely "wider context" such as the competitiveness of the market, reactions of competitors or previous instances of similar projects (as was rewarded in the equivalent Box in Requirements 1 and 3 in CC). We would therefore advise you not to think **too** widely in Requirement 2 when attempting to gain these marks as the nature of the points required has changed in recent examinations. Please see our new chapter 16 for a full discussion of this issue.

In Requirement 3, it is interesting to note that issues regarding the reputational impact on the Case Study business of a supplier problem were this time allocated into Boxes other than the Ethics Boxes. In all previous Case Study examinations, we have seen the issue of reputation rewarded as an ethics issue but perhaps the examiners are now fed up of students simply using this point to get through the ethics requirement. You are therefore advised to still mention reputation (it could go back into the Ethics Boxes and if not it appears to score elsewhere in Boxes which are intrinsically harder than the Ethics Boxes – this is a good thing!) but also to look at other ways to get Ethics marks.

Whilst not strictly a completely new issue for this examination, given the "steady, incremental change" involving introduction of calculations into Requirement 3 (see chapter 14 for full details), we do have to bring your attention to the fact that the CC markscheme awarded a full Box (Box 3.1) of marks for the results of calculations in Requirement 3 – yet only 2% of candidates attempted any calculations in Requirement 3, according to the examiners. We are not really sure why this is the case as we have advised now for several editions of this book that if there are figures in Requirement 3 then they are there for a reason and to be used. Similarly our packs of 5 mock examinations based on the live Advance Information have included calculations in Requirement 3. However, it appears that neither readers of this book nor other candidates have not responded to the figures in Requirement 3, if only 2% of candidates are attempting the calculations. **Please learn from this in your own attempt** as calculations in Requirement 3 are here to stay (see chapter 14 for further details).

Other than the above slight nuances, the CC examination was very much in line with expectations, and with previous Case Studies. The number of changes is not as high as the previous 2 examinations and therefore we have not provided as detailed a review as we have of the Bod (July 2015) and RS (November 2014) examinations on the pages that follow. This is also because our update to this edition contains a review of points from the Case Study workshop at the recent ICAEW Tutor Conference held in February 2016 (see chapter 14) – most of the examples given by the examiners relate to CC so the key points are already covered in chapter 14. We would advise you to look at the more detailed reviews of the July 2015 and November 2014 examinations that follow and to build these learning points into your preparations for your own examination.

We wish you all the best with your preparations and your examination. We would obviously be happy to welcome you to our taught courses and/or to provide you with our mock exam pack or other July 2016 resources (please see page 6 for further information). Please let us know how you got on with the examination and whether you found this book useful to your attempt.

All the best,

The ACA Simplified Team   **March 2016**

Foreword to the November 2015 Edition and Review of Bod (July 2015)

We have retained this Foreword written in September 2015 for your reference as it provides a useful review of the idiosyncrasies of the July 2015 examination, Bod. Please note that we have updated the Foreword presented below to allow for the new terminology implemented in the July 2018 edition of this book and have removed content that is no longer applicable. Otherwise, the Foreword is as originally presented in the November 2015 edition of this book.

The Bod Case Study (July 2015) could potentially have been one of the more complicated Case Study examinations, particularly in Requirement 1 (financial performance analysis), given Bod's 4 sub-divisions, inclusion of a separate "contribution" row in the Income Statement and use of 3 different KPIs.

Fortunately, the examiners chose to use a very clear and focused approach in Requirement 1, asking for analysis of only 2 sub-divisions and a single KPI. We are sure that this led to a big sigh of relief from students when they opened the question paper! Accordingly, we maintained our usual high pass rate, achieving the same high 96% rate of success as at the previous November 2014 sitting.

Overall, Bod maintained many elements of the previous RS (November 2014) examination, particularly in terms of the "new" narrative-focused approach in Requirement 2 and Requirement 3 (see below): now that these approaches have been used in 2 consecutive examinations, perhaps it is appropriate to view these as the new norm and to write your report accordingly.

We include a detailed review of Bod on the following pages. Please read this carefully so that you are aware of the most up to date analysis and please use that advice in your preparations and in your November 2015 examination script itself. We **strongly recommend** that you return to the review presented here several times – please do not ignore these pages simply because they are near the start of the book!

We wish you all the best with your preparations and your examination. We would obviously be happy to welcome you to our taught courses and/or to provide you with our mock exam pack or other November 2015 resources (please see page 6 for further information).

Please let us know how you got on with the examination and whether you found this book useful to your attempt.

All the best,

The ACA Simplified Team   **September 2015**

Review of Bod (July 2015)

In our opinion, the most important learning points from the Bod Case Study were as follows:

Executive Summary

The Bod Executive Summary markscheme points were generally as expected but the markscheme was tough with only 4 points per Box available (see below).

As we always emphasise, it is important to support each Requirement 1 Executive Summary statement with a figure: the Bod markscheme maintains the recent emphasis on figures by stating "**with figure**" in bold and in brackets after most Requirement 1 points.

Unlike on some markschemes which ask for "evaluation" points in Box E.1b, the Bod markscheme required "explanation" of changes. The points were for revenue, gross profit and contribution, the 3 areas on which candidates were required to focus by the question wording so this fits with our advice to re-read the question wording before writing the Executive Summary to ensure that you do not stray off the main areas to be discussed.

One very unusual point in the Bod Executive Summary markscheme is the fact that Box E.1b did not have a mark for "commercial recommendations" as normal but rather a mark for a recommendation specifically in relation to the Extra Task or ET (analysis of KPI 3). (Please see chapter 8 of this book on the ET.) This contrasts with all other Case Study papers from July 2012 onwards and also with the similar Box in Bod Executive Summary Requirement 2 and Executive Summary Requirement 3 where the usual (and broader) "commercial recommendations" mark was available. Our advice is therefore to make at least one of your Commercial Recommendations relevant to the ET as this way you will hedge your bets regardless of whether this mark is broad or narrow.

With respect to the calculation in Requirement 2, the Bod Executive Summary markscheme awarded separate diamonds for the reporting of (1) revenue and (2) gross profit and contribution. This shows the importance of thoroughly stating your figures, particularly if there is only a single calculation to perform (if there are 2 calculations then the markscheme would probably award a single diamond for stating both the revenue and gross profit (for example) of calculation 1 and a second diamond for the same data for calculation 2).

A diamond was also available for commenting on the financial impact implied by the calculations: therefore simply stating the numbers with no narrative points would be a bad idea.

Another tough aspect of the Requirement 2 Executive Summary markscheme was that students were required to reach the conclusion that "Bod has little choice but to accept" the proposal. In requiring this specified decision to be reached, the Bod markscheme resembles markschemes from the pre-July 2012 period where candidates had to reach the examiner's own "correct" conclusion to be awarded marks. All examinations from July 2012 onwards have applied "open marking" in the Executive Summary, meaning that as long as you offer a point in the right general area then you will be awarded a mark, regardless of the precise point made. "Open marking" is evident in all other parts of the Bod Executive Summary so it was only this single diamond in Box E.2b that was specific in nature and hopefully therefore we will not see a move back towards the old style of stricter marking: in business, there is not always a clear right or wrong answer (except with the benefit of hindsight).

253

The Requirement 3 Executive Summary markscheme was relatively light on ethical issues with only 1 diamond being available despite a large number of ethical issues arising. This contrasts with an examination such as ZM (July 2014) which had a similar number of ethical issues but which provided more reward in its Executive Summary markscheme. This lack of reward for ethics in the Bod Requirement 3 Executive Summary markscheme was slightly surprising, given ICAEW's emphasis on ethics (as shown by this second examination in row in which ethics was tested in Requirement 2 as well as Requirement 3: see below). The Bod Requirement 3 Executive Summary markscheme instead emphasised the risks and benefits of the project with the whole of Box E.3a relating to this area: a mark was available both for a main benefit and a second benefit and then for a main risk and a second risk. You are therefore advised to spend a reasonable amount of time on Issue 1 and Issue 2 in your Executive Summary. (Please see chapter 10 and our Planning & Reminder Sheets in chapter 6 for more explanation of Issue 1 and Issue 2 in Requirement 3.)

The Bod Executive Summary markscheme has only 4 points in each of the 6 Boxes, a decrease on the RS (November 2014) examination where 2 Boxes still allowed 5 points and also a decrease on prior year papers were it was common to see 5 acceptable points in all Executive Summary Boxes. This means that there is an increasingly narrow range of acceptable points in the Executive Summary so you really must stick closely to what is required.

There were no marks in the Executive Summary for "wider context" remarks unlike in some previous examinations so we suggest that you do not rely on this type of point as one of your scoring marks.

Overall, then, whilst the Bod Executive Summary markscheme was fairly typical in its general nature, there were some subtle ways in which passing the Executive Summary has become more difficult than in the past. As always, do not disrespect the Executive Summary or assume that it is an easy element just because it involves repeating information: you are indeed simply repeating information contained elsewhere in your report ... the trick is to know exactly **what** information to repeat.

Requirement 1

The Bod Requirement 1 was unusual in having no additional separate or "unpreparable" calculation as the ET, instead focusing on analysis of Bod's KPI 3, which could (and should) have been practised in advance as part of the preparations for Requirement 1: normally, this calculation cannot be rehearsed in advance but in the Bod examination candidates should definitely have prepared themselves to calculate the KPIs so this should have made the Bod Requirement 1 substantially easier to pass. Candidates were in fact given very detailed explanation as to what to do for the narrative points on the KPI analysis with instructions to explain the movement in the figure, to explain why it might differ from the latest industry benchmark (including scepticism points) and advising on what could be done to improve performance. In many papers, there is really no way of knowing what narrative points will be rewarded regarding the ET but in Bod the guidance was very clear indeed so this was a great opportunity to pass Requirement 1. The ET was not the feared "break even" calculation that appeared to be suggested by the unusual inclusion of a "contribution" line in the Income Statement.

The amount of detail in the question wording on the ET should have indicated to candidates that the ET was worth 2 Boxes, as had been the case in previous examinations. We would therefore advise you to assume that the ET is worth 2 Boxes in your examination. (See chapter 8 for a detailed discussion of the ET.)

In the Bod Requirement 1 markscheme, Box 1.2 on the CoP was quite unusual: 2 of the points related to the calculations performed for Requirement 1 rather than being points in the background (in the sense of matters to consider as context to the calculation results rather than those results themselves) as had been the case in all other examinations from July 2012 onwards. We have never seen the result of a numerical calculation in Box 1.2 before. There were only really 2 points relating to what we would consider to be the genuine "wider context": the highly competitive nature of the industry and Bod's recent decline in tender success rates despite increased use of marketing events. This contrasts with Requirement 2 and Requirement 3 where the points in Box 2.2 and 3.2 respectively were of the more traditional genuine wider context type.

There was no reward for discussion of the UK recession in Box 1.2, unlike in most prior papers, so it appears that the examiners are now a bit tired of this point and instead want you to look at other more interesting background points.

The Requirement 1 markscheme very heavily emphasised analysis of the client revenue breakdown provided in the Advance Information and as updated by the management accounts information in the Exam Paper: it would have been tricky to pass Requirement 1 without this analysis. We had already advised all taught course students to use this table in their answer, particularly if the Exam Paper focused on only one stream (as it did in practice) because there would then not be much to discuss if the client table was not used. It was unusual to provide so much information on the different clients in the Advance Information so this was a hint that it would be relevant to the examination. Candidates really had no excuse for not using this data table because the Exam Paper specifically requested analysis of the "client table". The lesson is therefore to treat detailed and Case Study-specific numerical data with respect and assume that it will form a substantial part of the marks, particularly if mentioned in the question paper itself: do not treat such data as merely an optional or insignificant element of the analysis.

In terms of the overall financial "Big Picture" (relevant to the marks in Boxes 1.6 and 1.7), the examiners used 2 classic points/contrasts that candidates were supposed to identify (and which have been used in other examinations). Firstly, candidates were supposed to note that revenue performance was good but gross profit and contribution performance was weak. Secondly, candidates were supposed to notice that a change in the revenue mix towards an activity with a lower gross profit margin would pull down Bod's gross profit margin overall. Always be on the lookout for patterns such as these.

Another standard pattern noted in the markscheme was to compare revenue growth to the industry benchmark growth rate or to the prior year growth rate. We told all taught course students to mention these patterns and as expected this point was the first diamond in Box 1.6. (For more discussion of relevant patterns in Requirement 1, please see chapter 8.)

As advised by ICAEW at the February 2015 Tutor Conference, the Conclusions Box for Requirement 1 required a numerical figure to support each narrative conclusion with all 4 points stating "with figures" in brackets, meaning that the mark would only be awarded if a figure was provided. There were only 4 diamonds available in the Conclusions Box 1.9 and it was noteworthy that 2 of these diamonds contained the word "AND" meaning that candidates effectively had to make 2 points for just one diamond. Overall, it would have been very hard to pass this Box without a thorough review of all the figures requested by the first page of the examination paper. This reminds us once again of the importance of regularly going back to the first Exhibit in the examination paper and reconfirming exactly what you have been asked to do.

Requirement 2

The Bod Requirement 2 markscheme resurrected the content of Box 2.1 which was seen in all examinations since July 2012 other than RS (November 2014): namely, the inclusion of a Box simply for identifying the correct inputs needed to build your model, rather than for the correct model results (as was, exceptionally, the case in RS). This is great to see as it means that you can get some credit for elements of the calculation, even if the overall result is not correct. [July 2018 edition update: Box 2.1 in both TT (November 2016) and PL (July 2017) was **not** allocated to inputs, probably because there were 2 Boxes for the calculation results (Boxes 2.3 and 2.4) whereas R4 (November 2017), which only had one calculation (rewarded in Box 2.3), did allocate Box 2.1 to inputs: see discussion in chapter 9 of this book.]

Box 2.2 contained some relatively straightforward points such as identifying that Bod had Favoured Provider status with Wilson and that Bod had previously worked in Leeds for Dollond. There was also mention of the REC code of conduct or the Bod "How We Behave" code. All these points would have been achieved by candidates who follow our advice in chapter 16 to look for the key client or location names in the question (the "proper nouns check": see chapter 15) when deciding what to mention as context. As always in Requirement 2, these points need to be very specific to the project and not broad industry points. Therefore, we would advise you to think of this Box as a Box about the strategic and operational context of the project itself, and not as an opportunity to discuss the industry in general. At the same time, there was still a mention of 1 broader point that went beyond the specific project or Bod (the fact that incidental costs are normally recharged to clients). The advice is therefore to balance your points more heavily towards **project**-specific issues compared to market points.

The most significant (and therefore the most important) change noted in Requirement 2 was with respect to assumptions. In all other recent examinations, Requirement 2 has provided a Box of points for assumptions and then a separate Box for scepticism. (Please see chapter 9 and chapter 12 for further discussion.) In the Bod examination, 2 Boxes were dedicated to assumptions, with the first Box being for the identification of up to 6 specific areas and stating that the actual figure could be different to the estimate but then the second Box awarded marks for identifying that the estimate differed from certain **specific** figures in the Advance Information. This may be because the specified assumptions were listed in bullet point format in Exhibit 16 of the Bod Exam Paper and so were signalled more clearly than normal.

We have always told our taught course students to pick assumptions which can be contrasted with information from the Advance Information on the basis that these would be more likely to figure in the assumed single Box for assumptions but this advice is now even more pertinent since the Bod markscheme expected students to specifically mention and contrast with what was known from the Advance Information. This is a very rare example where Boxes in the third column of the markscheme build on points in the second column, rather than being completely separate Boxes.

In the Bod Exam Paper, the practical issues to be considered were also flagged more than normal with specific bullet points stated, making it easier than usually the case to identify the relevant practical considerations.

Consistent with what we have seen above regarding the Executive Summary, the Conclusions Box 2.9 required students to reach the very specific conclusion that "Bod has little choice but to accept the client's offer" rather than candidates being able to reach any conclusion at all ("open marking") as has been more normal in all other Box 2.9s in other papers. This was a tough approach which, as noted above, hopefully does not mean we are moving back towards the old ways in Case Study. We would advise you to be a bit more careful in your Conclusions from now on and see if there is any reason why a particular decision is clearly "correct" (despite our concerns whether it is possible to know at the time that a particular business decision has been made): in Bod, the client involved in Requirement 2 was Bod's largest client and really very fundamental to the business so the examiner decided that there was no choice but to do as the client demanded.

Overall, then, the Bod Requirement 2 was fair and made the required analysis very clear to students. The return of the inputs Box (Box 2.1) was very welcome. [July 2018 edition update: Box 2.1 in both TT (November 2016) and PL (July 2017) was **not** allocated to inputs, probably because there were 2 Boxes for the calculation results (Boxes 2.3 and 2.4) whereas R4 (November 2017), which only had one calculation (rewarded in Box 2.3), did allocate Box 2.1 to inputs: see discussion in chapter 9 of this book.] There was also only 1 page of information to absorb and analyse so the Bod Requirement 2 was definitely not the hardest Requirement 2 that we have seen. However, please do bear in mind that it is now certainly advisable to query assumptions by reference to knowledge from the Advance Information or the Exam Paper rather than by just making the more generic point that the "actual figure could be different".

Requirement 3

In our opinion, the Bod Requirement 3 does not contain any relevant changes or nuances compared to previous papers and it was the least surprising element of the examination. Looking at the markscheme and the points tested in our mock examinations, as well as our emphasis on the Bod Business Plan and the insurance market in our taught course, this Requirement was very predictable indeed. As always with Requirement 3, the trick is to have enough time remaining to do a proper job, rather than the specific content being difficult in itself.

Unlike in some examinations, there were no "Other Issues" to discuss beyond issue 1 (benefits) and issue 2 (risks). Looking at the markscheme, Box 3.6 is termed an "evaluation" of benefits and Box 3.7 is termed an "evaluation" of risks. This might lead you to conclude that Boxes 3.6 and 3.7 reward the further development of specific benefits and risks points (as in the case of assumptions points in Requirement 2: see above) but on further inspection the points in Boxes 3.6 and 3.7 are just **more** benefits and more risks. You are therefore advised to try to find a large number of points on Issue 1 and Issue 2 if the question wording suggests that there are no "Other Issues" to consider.

In line with the previous examination (RS, November 2014), there was no specific Box for scepticism in Requirement 3 and the points were instead mixed into Boxes 3.6 and 3.7. This is consistent with our advice (see chapters 10 and 12) that if the number of ethical issues in Requirement 3 appears high then you should reduce the number of scepticism points accordingly because ethics (and not scepticism) will form the basis of Box 3.8. This is exactly what happened in Bod which had **6** different ethical issues to consider, the highest we have ever seen! Although this number was very high, the marks followed the usual pattern of identification of an issue (Box 3.5) followed by evaluation and mitigation techniques (Box 3.8).

The tricky Recommendations Box 3.10 contained some fairly standard points such as to negotiate the terms of the contract, to perform market research and to undertake due diligence on the potential partner firm. To see such standard points in an otherwise potentially difficult Box serves to underline the "vanilla" nature of the Bod Requirement 3.

Appendices and Main Report Boxes

These 4 Boxes at the end of the markscheme are designed to ensure that your report is well presented and has the appropriate disclaimer and writing style. In the Bod examination, these Boxes were very standard and almost identical to the previous RS (November 2014) examination which, as we note in our review of RS below, was slightly unusual in requiring correct numerical answers for some of the Appendix 2 marks: this was not required before November 2014 and was not required in Bod either.

For the disclaimer, as in previous papers, candidates need to indicate that the report is provided by the accountancy **firm** of their Case Study character: you should not author the report in the name of your Case Study character him- or herself.

Conclusion on the Bod Exam Paper and Markscheme

Overall, despite some nuances and a slightly tougher marking approach in some areas, the Bod Case Study was very much in line with expectations: some points were highly predictable and were drilled into our students thoroughly during the tuition phase. We believe that our mock exam pack and tuition classes gave excellent preparation for what was ultimately tested so hopefully this will give you confidence that we correctly understand the unusual Case Study examination and therefore that our suite of materials will help you succeed in the November 2015 examination.

Important Notice – Criticism of *Cracking Case*™ Methodology by Another Tuition Provider – Part 2

As was noted in the Foreword to the July 2015 edition of this book (see below), another large UK tuition provider has unfortunately resorted to making false statements regarding the successful approach set out in this book. Specifically, it has again been stated that the ICAEW examiners have released an official statement to students and tuition providers indicating that any points included under a "Market Background" or similar section will be marked as zero by the examiners. **We can confirm that no such statement has ever been made by ICAEW.** As a result of a second instance of the same false statement previously made during the July 2015 examination session, we have reluctantly had to make a further complaint to ICAEW regarding the conduct of the other provider.

We have confirmed in writing with ICAEW, and also with the Case Study examiners during the February 2015 ICAEW Tutor Conference, that use of a background or context section at the start of each report section is permissible under ICAEW rules – contrary to the statements of the other tuition provider, **there is no section heading which will result in a report section being marked as zero by the examiners**. At the Tutor Conference, the examiners indicated that believing that markers would ignore a section simply because of the section heading chosen would be very unfair to students: the markers have been instructed to look at all parts of the script when awarding marks. (July 2018 update: as explained elsewhere in this book, at the 2018 Tutor Conference, one of the example student scripts from a real candidate at the November 2017 sitting was very clearly awarded marks in the official ICAEW marking for a section entitled "Market Background" and the examiners did not state that this candidate had committed some kind of breach of examination rules – no comment at all was made about the use of this section heading even though other aspects of the script were criticised by the examiners.)

We are very disappointed by the approach taken by this other provider. Accordingly, we have referred the matter to ICAEW. If you find that any similar statements are being made in your tuition sessions, please notify us on a confidential basis at **getqualified@acasimplified.com**. We have confirmed with ICAEW that it is a breach of Partner in Learning rules to allocate tuition time to criticising the methods and publications of other providers and we are making our best efforts to bring an end to this unprofessional behaviour.

Please be assured that the approach outlined in this book is fully compatible with ICAEW rules and this is reflected in our very high pass rates and recent ICAEW prizes.

Foreword to the July 2015 Edition and Review of RS (November 2014)

We have retained this Foreword written in February 2015 for your reference as it provides a useful review of the idiosyncrasies of the November 2014 examination, RS. Please note that we have updated the Foreword presented below to allow for the new terminology implemented in the July 2018 edition of this book and have removed content that is no longer applicable. Otherwise, the Foreword is as originally presented in the July 2015 edition of this book.

Overall, we enjoyed teaching the RS Case Study as it concerned a significantly larger business than other recent examinations and the potential exam day scenarios were harder to predict than normal (with the possible exception of Requirement 1). We were very pleased to achieve a pass rate of 96% in the examination, significantly outpacing the ICAEW average of approximately 75% and representing an excellent performance from a student cohort primarily made up of retake students who had previously failed with another provider.

We hope that the pass rate achieved gives you assurance that our methodology continues to be an effective way of tackling this unusual examination.

Shortly before finalising the text of this book, we were delighted to be informed of another ICAEW Case Study prize won by our students in 2014 (in addition to our global prize-winning student at the July 2014 sitting). Our taught course student David Watson placed first in his region (East Midlands) across both sittings of the Case Study in 2014, having previously failed his first attempt after attending another provider. We hope that this success story will act as inspiration and reassurance for any readers of this book who are unfortunately having to retake the examination: what better way to put the stress and frustration of failing the exam behind you than to win an ICAEW prize in your retake attempt?

We include a detailed review of the most recent Case Study examination (RS) on the following pages. Please read this carefully so that you have the most up to date analysis and then use the advice in your preparations and July 2015 examination script.

We wish you all the best with your preparations and your examination. We would obviously be happy to welcome you to our taught courses and/or to provide you with our mock exam pack or other July 2015 resources (please see page 6 for further information).

Please let us know how you got on with the examination and whether you found this book useful to your attempt.

All the best,

The ACA Simplified Team   **February 2015**

Review of RS (November 2014)

In our view, RS was generally in line with previous Case Study examinations but it contained a couple of innovations which candidates should be aware of: these changes may hint at the future perspective and approach of the examiners. Despite these changes, our methodology appears to have been successful as we achieved a 96% pass rate for our tuition course students.

The unusual aspects of RS were as follows:

Executive Summary

In the Executive Summary markscheme, 4 of the available 6 Boxes (opportunities to score a competency grade) contained only 4 acceptable points rather than the more normal 5 acceptable points per Box seen in examinations from November 2012 onwards. (The July 2012 examination LL also contained only 4 acceptable points per Box, although in this case in 5 of the 6 available Boxes.)

The fewer the number of acceptable points, the harder it becomes to pass a Box since a unique aspect of the Case Study marking approach is that if a candidate makes a point which is not within the list of acceptable points, no credit can be given.

In this sense, the RS Executive Summary was harder to pass than a typical Executive Summary and you are therefore advised to look carefully at the list of points considered acceptable in case the July 2015 ES is also "tightly" marked.

Requirement 1

For the first time, the Requirement 1 Exhibits in the examination paper contained no "review of the year"-style comments from the client. This meant that candidates were forced to rely on points from the Advance Information to explain the year on year changes in the management accounts figures. The only narrative information provided in the Requirement 1 Exhibit related to the additional calculation required rather than to the management accounts.

We have always advised students to use the Exam Paper or Impact Information as much as possible, and in priority to any knowledge of the Advance Information, on the basis that as the Exam Paper information is shorter, there should be less chance of being unlucky by mentioning a point which is not on the markscheme since there is a relatively narrow set of points to discuss: in contrast, as the Advance Information is over 40 pages in length there is always a chance that you may be unlucky with the point chosen. Obviously, you will have to amend this advice if there is no Exam Paper information to use in a Requirement, as happened in RS.

A second innovation was that candidates were asked to review the whole of the Income Statement. In previous examinations, the analysis has always tended to focus on revenue, gross profit and operating profit but no further down the Income Statement than this. The comments required on finance charges and PBT at the bottom of the Income Statement were not complicated (the change in finance charges reflected a reduction in finance lease purchases, something flagged in the Advance Information, whilst candidates were only required to mention that PBT was very low and close to a breakeven level, rather than anything complicated) but the fact that candidates were required to review the whole Income Statement did cause some uncertainty.

The markscheme for the Conclusion section of Requirement 1 required a comment **with figures** for all available marks, reflecting a change that started with the July 2014 markscheme. As such, you are advised to always include figures in your Conclusions section as narrative alone is no longer enough.

Requirement 2 and Appendix 2

The primary innovation here was the inclusion of ethical issues within this Requirement. In previous examinations, ethical issues were only rewarded in Requirement 3. In RS, however, there were marks in 2 different Boxes in Requirement 2 for ethical considerations and it would have been difficult to pass these 2 Boxes without a good amount of ethical discussion.

As a result of this emphasis on ethical issues, there were accordingly fewer marks for the results of your financial modelling. In fact, only 1 Box provided marks for these results and marks for correct results were (unusually) awarded in the "Overall Paper" Boxes at the end of the markscheme where the marker evaluates your Appendix 2 format and presentation.

This is the lowest emphasis on the results of your calculations which we have seen in any Case Study in the post-2011 period. It reflects a trend towards emphasis on narrative analysis which was also evident in the previous Case Study (ZM) which had an additional narrative/strategy task to complete in the supposedly "numerical" Requirement 2.

Overall, we believe that this is good news because it means that even if your calculations go wrong you should still have a very good chance of passing Requirement 2. On our taught courses, Requirement 2 has always been the Requirement which worries students the most and on which they scored the lowest marks when sitting our mock exam pack. At the same time, it will be important to identify all the narrative issues that you are being asked to discuss as otherwise you may be throwing away entire Boxes of marks.

Requirement 3

In our opinion, the markscheme for RS Requirement 3 is a very standard or "vanilla" markscheme with no real innovations or unusual aspects.

Our only observation would be that Box 3.1 was entirely devoted to quoting the figures given in the Requirement 3 Exhibit or very basic calculations based thereon: this Exhibit contained a lot more numerical information than is normal for the supposedly "narrative-based" Requirement 3.

In previous editions of this book, we have advised students to use any numbers given in Requirement 3 as much as possible (on the basis that the examiners must have given you the figures for a reason) but not to perform calculations as this will use up too much time and potentially not be rewarded anyway: in other words, with respect to numerical information, the approach should be "comment but do not calculate". However, in RS there were some marks available for very basic calculations such as finding the percentage increase in volume or calculating the number of extra deliveries required, given a percentage figure. Therefore, we would amend our advice to "comment and only calculate the very basics, using numbers already given".

RS contained 2 full Boxes for ethical issues, in the same way as the previous paper (ZM), so we again advise you that ICAEW are putting more emphasis on ethics than in previous years, as reflected by the innovative inclusion of ethical issues in Requirement 2 (see above).

Overall Paper Boxes

The markscheme has always included 4 Boxes at the end of the markscheme in which the marker evaluates the format and presentation of your report and its appendices, as well as the language used in your report.

The innovation in RS was that some of the marks in these final 4 Boxes were awarded for correct results to your financial model in Requirement 2: previously, the marks were more open and simply rewarded the inclusion of **a** result (even if completely wrong), rather than **the** correct result. However, please do not panic that your entire script will depend on correct calculations: there are still more than enough marks within these 4 Boxes for other aspects of your report and you should achieve these by writing neatly, with correct headings and using ethical and tactful language.

Conclusion

As you can see from the extensive discussion above, RS does contain some interesting innovations of which you should be aware ahead of the July 2015 examination session.

We hope this review has been useful. Best of luck with your attempt at the July 2015 Case Study!

Important Notice – Criticism of *Cracking Case*™ Methodology by Another Tuition Provider

During the November 2014 examination session, we were made aware by both our taught course students and distance-learning students who had purchased *Cracking Case*™ that another large tuition provider was allocating tuition time to criticising our book. In particular, it appears that the other provider informed its students that using a separate background or context paragraph or section at the start of their report sections was contrary to the advice of ICAEW examiners and would result in all points made in such a section being ignored by the marker.

We have discussed this matter with ICAEW and we can confirm that this allegation is false: we confirmed in writing and at the 2015 Tutor Conference that there are no section headings which would result in a candidate losing marks in this way. We are extremely disappointed by the actions of the other provider and we have lodged a formal complaint with ICAEW.

This kind of behaviour is unfair and unprofessional. If you find that your provider is allocating tuition time to disparaging our work, we would be grateful if you would please inform us as soon as possible so that we can take appropriate action against unfair attempts to damage our reputation.

Appendix 4   Review of Key Learning Points from the 2017 ICAEW Study Manual

The ICAEW Case Study Learning Materials were significantly updated and rewritten for 2017 so we wrote an Appendix for the July 2017 and November 2017 editions of *Cracking Case™* to review some of the key points in the new materials. The 2018 update was extremely minor in nature and has not added anything of significance so we have retained below our review of the 2017 update for your information.

We strongly recommend that you read through the Study Manual in full: at only 227 pages, the Study Manual for Case Study is relatively short and does not have many exercises to perform – most content is simply direct advice from the examiners.

In this Appendix, we have summarised some of the most important points that struck us when reading through the heavily-updated 2017 version of the ICAEW materials. This Appendix is in no way intended as a replacement for the Study Manual but is rather our attempt to reinforce some lessons which we believe are absolutely fundamental to your chances of success in the Case Study examination. For speed, our points are included in note form only and we will not repeat any points which we feel are sufficiently covered already elsewhere in this book. **All page references in this Appendix are references to the ICAEW Study Manual and not to this book. In all cases, the page references for the 2017 and 2018 editions of the Study Manual are identical (in line with our statement above that there have not been any significant changes for 2018.)**

Chapter 1   Introduction to the Case Study learning materials

Additional research may be a factor in your answer but should not be allowed to dominate your response (page 9).

It is suggested that you would spend 2 hours drafting your report, 1 hour doing your reading and planning and 1 hour performing calculations and financial analysis. However, the suggested time allocation is just a suggestion as different students will work in different ways (page 10). (ACA Simplified comment: we would strongly suggest that you try to allow **more** than 2 hours for the physical writing of your report – see chapter 3 of *Cracking Case™*.)

The Exhibits in the Exam Paper are grouped together in Requirement order with little, if any, overlap so your answer to each Requirement can be planned separately and tackled in a discrete way (page 10). (ACA Simplified comment: we would agree with this statement most of the time but as noted elsewhere in this book, there has recently been an increase in the number of marks awarded in Boxes such as Boxes 2.2 and 3.2 for linkages back to the recent financial performance of the revenue stream involved in the proposed Requirement 2 and Requirement 3 projects. On this basis, it is recommended to complete Requirement 1 first. Please see chapters 9 and 10 for further discussion.)

Regarding writing style, you should avoid technical jargon and use simple language, be professional, be succinct, be relevant and be tactful (page 13).

Calculations will be required in each of the 3 exam Requirements (page 13).

We would finally observe that the examiners repeatedly refer to the need to understand where the business is in its "life-cycle" throughout this first chapter. Bear this in mind when you are reading the Advance Information.

Chapter 2   Financial statement analysis

You should not waste time questioning the basis of preparation of the management accounts i.e. the fact that they may not have been audited or drawn up under IFRS rules specifically – you would only obtain credit for such a remark if there is a specific indication in the Case Study on this issue such as a statement that the accounts are being challenged by the auditors (page 22).

We would strongly recommend that you look at the key points under the heading of profit or loss analysis on page 24 and page 25 of the Study Manual. As explained elsewhere in this book, the emphasis in the Case Study is on the P&L rather than the balance sheet so although there are some pieces of advice on analysis of the balance sheet on page 25 and analysis of the statement of cash flows on page 26 which are worth looking at, ensure you always prioritise the P&L.

You must know the financial story that the components of the main financial statements are telling – you must be able to explain that story in whatever way might be requested (page 26).

In all analysis you should ask **why** and **so what** – why have things changed (what are the reasons?) and what is the impact on the business? (page 27)

An updated version of the November 2013 Case Study, LT, is then presented at the end of chapter 2 as an example of how to complete Requirement 1. We recommend that you read through the tabular presentation starting on page 55 which shows how the analysis can be built up into stronger responses – however, be careful not to assume that writing more necessarily means you will score a better grade and be careful of over developing any single individual point under time pressure in the examination.

Ensure you focus only on the **specific** requirements of the examination paper and not the question you wish or had expected to have been set, nor one that tuition companies may have predicted would be set – you must take full account of the specific updated scenario information provided by the Exam Paper (page 61).

Chapter 3   Financial data analysis

Some relevant analytical tools for the Case Study include (page 69):

- financial forecasting
- financial appraisal reporting
- breakeven analysis
- product mix analysis

- project appraisal through payback and present value calculations
- investment valuation
- working capital analysis
- risk and decision-making
- financial strategies for developing the business
- sensitivity analysis

The financial data analysis in Requirement 2 will tend to focus on a current issue and imminent decision that will affect future operations (page 69).

You should always consider the provenance of the information supplied and the timeframe over which the forecast is being made (page 69).

Note that the Study Manual briefly reviews some of the key elements of breakeven analysis, investment valuation and sensitivity analysis in a section starting on page 70 – it is well worth reading through these pages given that these specific methodologies appear to have been singled out for explanation by the examiners.

In respect of professional scepticism, the examiners recommend that you consider the "7P's" (page 72):

- Preparer?
- Purpose?
- Precision?
- Predictions?
- Problems?
- Priority?
- Perspective?

Ensure you have read the Study Manual section starting on page 72 to understand what these terms mean.

An updated version of the July 2013 Case Study examination, Palate, is then provided at the end of the chapter as an example of financial analysis. Some useful exercises on breakeven analysis, sensitivity analysis, financial forecasting and SWOT analysis are presented on page 96. We would recommend that you complete these 4 exercises but, in our opinion, the breakeven analysis and sensitivity analysis would be the exercises to prioritise as these methods have been tested directly in some Case Study examinations.

Chapter 4   Commercial analysis: financial, operational and strategic analysis including business trust and ethical awareness

For the examiners, "commercial analysis" has 2 elements: financial, operational and strategic analysis on the one hand and then business trust and ethical awareness on the other hand (pages 115-116).

It is extremely unlikely that you will be specifically requested to produce a PESTLE, SWOT or Porter's Five Forces analysis in the examination but you may wish to use these techniques as part of your preparation (page 116). (ACA Simplified comment: we agree that these may be reasonable methods to help you learn the Case Study but note that we have never seen an examination paper which either directly asks for these models or requires answers that could only have been developed by using these models – in our opinion, the answers which are given credit are of a much more commonsense nature, based on practical understanding of how businesses operate, and **are in no way dependent on using specific business strategy models**. Therefore be careful of trying to force in a point which you think is particularly clever (if it is particularly clever then it may not be mentioned by many other candidates and so would not be likely to figure on the final markscheme) and also do not use up too much of your precious preparation time by working in depth on such models.

Candidates should always try to evaluate the relative importance of an issue and the potential impact of it on the business and its operations (page 121).

Candidates should use a structured approach to their analysis and discussion of ethical issues (page 124):

- gather the relevant facts and identify the problem
- identify the affected parties
- identify the ethical issues involved
- consider and evaluate alternative courses of action and associated consequences
- decide on a course of action

In our opinion, the IIR framework which we have proposed for your ethical analysis elsewhere in this book should cover these steps to the required depth, and also quickly.

There will be approximately 10% of the marks available for the discussion of ethical issues in your answer (page 127).

As indicated on the examination paper itself, ethical issues could involve any of the 4 broad types of problem:

- lack of professional independence or objectivity
- conflicts of interest among stakeholders
- doubtful accounting or commercial practice
- inappropriate pressure to achieve reported results

The chapter ends with updated versions of both the July 2014 Case Study, ZM, and the November 2014 Case Study, RS, as examples of how to attempt Requirement 3. We recommend that you look at these example sections.

The Appendix to chapter 4 again includes a tabular example of different quality answers – once more, remember it is not necessarily a case of simply writing more in order to achieve a higher grade (as might appear to be the case at first sight of the tabular presentation) – your points must also be relevant and look at different issues in order to build up the marks.

Candidates often seem to underestimate the importance of the Advance Information when tackling Requirement 3 and seem to think that they can answer it successfully just by referring to the exam material – this is not the case (page 204).

Chapter 5   Professional skills, the Executive Summary and exam techniques

As a general comment, this chapter in the Study Manual attempts to explain what is really meant by the relatively technical terms used as the 4 column headings in the markscheme (i.e. Assimilating & Using Information, Structuring Problems & Solutions, Applying Judgement and Conclusions & Recommendations). Whilst it is helpful to have this explanation, our approach is rather to focus on the specific Tasks on the markscheme (i.e. the 40 Boxes) rather than the 4 columns, on the basis that focusing on the specific Tasks that tend to be tested is more informative than looking at the rather general and open nature of the column headings only.

We would obviously recommend that you work through this chapter in the Study Manual but try not to lose sight of the fact that **targeting the Boxes should probably give you better guidance than targeting the column headings**. Only certain points will be awarded credit and therefore you definitely cannot afford to wander off into areas which may seem to be interesting and relevant if we look simply at the language in the column **heading** but which never actually attract specific marks in a Box.

Whilst you should definitely "plan to the 40 Boxes", we would definitely never recommend that you "plan to the 4 columns" and it is interesting to note that, despite this being a common technique that some tuition providers suggest, there is no place at all in the Study Manual where the examiners make **any suggestion whatsoever that 4 column planning sheet should, or must, be used**. Therefore, please do not listen to your tutor if they attempt to defend the 4 column planning sheet approach on the basis that "this is the method that the examiners recommend" – it is not.

According to the examiners, the Executive Summary is given a relatively high weighting of 15% of the total marks (page 222).

The main Executive Summary skills being assessed are to (page 222):

- summarise key results
- integrate appropriate numbers and text
- evaluate and apply judgement on the key points
- draw conclusions
- make recommendations

The examiners mention that a terms of reference (a section at the start of the report which explains what each section of the report will consider) is unlikely to be awarded any marks because it frequently just repeats information from the Exam Paper requests – therefore the examiners do not recommend that you include this section. However, you should include a disclaimer and/or limitation on scope (page 222) (ACA Simplified note: this is exactly in line with our advice elsewhere in this book – a terms of reference simply is not needed.)

The Executive Summary should not contain any material that has not already been discussed in greater detail in the body of the report – it is not the place to insert a sudden brainwave or idea (page 222).

Your Executive Summary should generally be 2 or 3 pages in length and around 10% of the total length of your script – it should be a stand-alone document (page 223).

The Executive Summary should not be simply an index of the report which informs the reader what will be discussed in each section – this prevents it being a stand-alone document as the reader would then have to go to those sections to understand the content (page 223).

The Executive Summary should encapsulate the main points from across the whole report, with key points taken from each part of the report (page 223).

Although the Executive Summary is written as your final piece of work in the examination, it should be placed in its appropriate place at the front of the report (page 224). (ACA Simplified note: as already discussed in chapter 7 and as noted below, we strongly disagree with the approach of separately writing all 3 sections of the Executive Summary as your "final piece of work" at the end of the examination. Instead, we strongly recommend that you write the Executive Summary section of a Requirement immediately after you have completed the main report section for that same Requirement. See chapter 7 for further discussion.)

It is recommended that you spend around 30 minutes on the Executive Summary overall, or approximately 10 minutes per each section of the report, on the basis that the Executive Summary is worth 15% of the total marks and should be allocated 15% of your total time (page 225). (ACA Simplified note: strictly, 15% of your time available is 15% x 4 x 60 minutes or 36 minutes so this suggests that the examiners do want the Executive Summary to be relatively short and that it can be completed quickly, in less time than the strict percentage would require.)

The approach of leaving the Executive Summary to the end of the examination will require careful time discipline – another option is to write the Executive Summary as you finish each section and this method is clearly preferable to running out of time without completing an Executive Summary at all so this may be an option to consider if you struggle with timing (page 225). (ACA Simplified note: we have suggested that writing the summary as you finish each section should be your default approach, regardless of whether you struggle with timing or not so we would not entirely agree with the examiners that you should only consider this method if you do not have "time discipline" ... **we would actually recommend this method to all students**.)

Appendix 5   Further ACA Simplified Case Study Resources

Live Mock Exam Pack

Our popular Mock Exam Pack includes 5 full mock examinations and model answers based on the live Advance Information. We are the only ICAEW Partner in Learning to provide 5 live mocks so our pack provides the maximum possible opportunity to familiarise yourself with the live Advance Information through practical, exam-style work.

We strongly believe that sitting full exam papers based on the live Case Study is much more time efficient than doing past papers – our mock pack allows you to practise your timing and technique 5 times whilst only reading 1 set of Advance Information, and a set of Advance Information which is more relevant to you than a past paper.

All mocks come with a full ICAEW-style marking grid so that you can assess your performance in all 40 markscheme Boxes. We also include a fully written out narrative answer for all mocks so that you can see how to translate the points in the 40 Boxes into appropriate sentences which respect our advice on the correct Case Study writing style, as set out in chapter 3 of this book.

Our July 2018 Mock Exam Pack retails at £210 plus VAT for original purchasers of this edition of *Cracking Case™* (£230 plus VAT for other students). Please note that no VAT is due if you are based outside the European Union.

Free samples of our past Mock Exam Packs are available from our dedicated Case Study website **www.acasimplifiedcase.com**.

Exam Room Pack

Our Exam Room Pack is designed to condense and simplify the live Advance Information. We will reduce the 40 to 50 pages of the Advance Information to around 18 to 20 pages of easy-to-read and punchy "slide"-style text. We will also work hard to identify the key themes within the live Case Study, reorganising points that are scattered throughout the Advance Information onto single theme-based pages so that you can quickly see all the relevant points on a particular issue – this will (1) save you time flicking through the Advance Information and (2) will also help you to spot patterns that you may not otherwise have noticed.

Our July 2018 Exam Room Pack retails at £70 plus VAT. Please note that no VAT is due if you are based outside the European Union.

A free sample of a past Exam Room Pack is available from our dedicated Case Study website **www.acasimplifiedcase.com**.

Cracking Case On-Demand™

We are very excited to be launching our *Cracking Case On-Demand™* video course for the July 2018 sitting.

Cracking Case On-Demand™ will contain the on-demand video resources that we have separately provided for the last few sittings but will also contain new content which we have designed to help students learn some of the most important lessons set out by this book.

Whilst we continue to believe that this *Cracking Case™* book provides an excellent opportunity to learn how to tackle Case Study, there are a few things that we think may be easier to explain using the technical possibilities provided by a video presentation format. We would also like to provide students with tutorials based on the live Advance Information (something which is not possible in a book format as we need to finalise the text of the book edition of *Cracking Case™* well before the live Advance Information has been released, for production reasons) – use of a video format will allow us to quickly and easily upload our latest thoughts on the live Case Study and we will explain how these ideas link into the core examination technique taught in this book.

Cracking Case On-Demand™ will include general technique training available before the live Advance Information has been released to allow you to make a start on your preparations.

After we have had time to absorb and digest the live Advance information, we will then upload various further resources to the course.

Videos within the **technique** element of *Cracking Case On-Demand™* include (amongst other content):

1. **Requirement 1, Requirement 2, Requirement 3 and Executive Summary – Key Lessons**: in this session, will take you through some of the most important learning points from the book edition of *Cracking Case™* to ensure that you have fully appreciated the fundamentals of how to pass these elements of the examination.

2. **Planning & Reminder Sheets – Key Lessons**: in this session, we will take you through our popular Planning & Reminder Sheets to ensure that you have fully understood the most important aspects of how to use these Sheets in your own examination.

3. **Commentary on student scripts**: in this session, we will review some example scripts from students who took our classroom course at previous sittings of the examination and we will comment on a line by line basis on what the student is doing well and badly – this will provide some real-life illustrative examples of our general advice on how to write up your own answers.

4. **Interpreting the Exam Paper wording**: in this session, we will review some recent past paper Exam Papers so that you can understand how to turn the question wording into the appropriate allocation of Boxes, thus helping you allocate your efforts and time effectively.

5. **Markscheme Masterclass**: in this session, we will review the official ICAEW markscheme "grids" for the last 4 past papers, looking for patterns in the types of point which have attracted

credit in the recent examinations. Given the relatively harsh way in which Case Study is marked (only points which are on the official markscheme "grid" can be given credit by the marker), this session will provide invaluable direction to your answers and will greatly increase the likelihood that the points you are making in your own script will actually achieve credit.

The above listing is provided simply for **indicative** purposes as we do expect to provide a number of other sessions as we develop the course further.

Once the live Advance Information has been released, we will aim to add the following sitting-specific **application** videos (as indicative examples) to the course:

1. **Advance Information Review**: in this session, which is expected to last around 4 hours, we will work through the live Advance Information for your Case Study business on a line by line and page by page basis to make sure you have noted and understood all the key points which we think could be tested in the real examination. Using our experience of writing mock exam packs for the last 12 sittings of the examination, and our experience of working with students via our classroom, distance-learning and marking and feedback tuition services, we will point out some important ways in which the examiners could use the live Advance Information on exam day.

2. **Requirement 1, Requirement 2 and Requirement 3 – Key Lessons from the Advance Information**: in this session, we will return to the live Advance Information again but this time looking specifically at points which are relevant to Requirement 1, then Requirement 2 and then finally Requirement 3. This will give you another perspective on the live Advance Information by pointing out issues which we think are more likely to be tested in each different part of the examination.

3. **Session-specific Tips and Tricks**: in this session, we will draw on our experience of teaching the live Advance Information to students by recording some key session-specific points. Such points are obviously very dependent on what the Advance Information contains but typically we will look at key points that students are getting wrong or not appreciating, any unusual aspects of the Advance Information and ways in which we think you could use the Advance Information to deal with specific parts of our examination technique. Once again, the content of this session very much depends on what the live Advance Information ultimately contains, and on what students seem to be doing well or badly based on our classroom sessions, but whatever the specific content of the session, hopefully it will further improve your confidence with the live Advance Information.

Students will be able to purchase individual sessions or the complete *Cracking Case On-Demand*™ course – students who purchase the complete course will automatically receive free and instant access to any additional content that we upload before the examination. (Unfortunately, purchase of individual sessions of the course does not entitle the purchaser to view any other sessions, including any new content that we upload.)

All our on-demand video content can be viewed an unlimited number of times during the relevant subscription period. You can view the content on any device with an internet connection (subject to your connection having a speed sufficient to stream video content).

Our *Cracking Case On-Demand*™ course can be purchased via our website using a credit or debit card – access is instant so you can start studying straight away!

For further information on all the above resources, see our Case Study-specific website at

www.acasimplifiedcase.com

273

Printed in Great Britain
by Amazon